MW01148952

Pieces of Tradition
An Analysis of Contemporary Tonal Music

Daniel Harrison

OXFORD
UNIVERSITY PRESS

UNIVERSITY PRESS

Oxford University Press is a department of the University of Oxford. It furthers
the University's objective of excellence in research, scholarship, and education
by publishing worldwide. Oxford is a registered trade mark of Oxford University
Press in the UK and certain other countries.

Published in the United States of America by Oxford University Press
198 Madison Avenue, New York, NY 10016, United States of America.

Library of congress cataloging in publication data
Names: Harrison, Daniel, 1959– author.
Title: Pieces of tradition : an analysis of contemporary tonal music / Daniel
Harrison.
Description: New York : Oxford University Press, 2016. | Series: Oxford
studies in music theory | Includes bibliographical references and index.
Identifiers: LCCN 2015038879 | ISBN 978-0-19-024446-0 (hardcover : alk. paper)
Subjects: LCSH: Music—21st century—Analysis, appreciation. | Music—20th
century—Analysis, appreciation.
Classification: LCC MT90 .H39 2016 | DDC 781.2/58—dc23
LC record available at http://lccn.loc.gov/2015038879

CONTENTS

Pieces of Tradition

CHAPTER One

Inheritance

Some time ago, two scholars squared off in print over comments one had made in a book review. Perhaps not expecting his contribution to elicit much more than passing acknowledgments for his scholarly service, the music historian Robert P. Morgan was clearly unsettled by the "heat and intensity" of William Thomson's response (all the more stunning since Thomson wasn't even the author of the reviewed work). While Thomson lathered excessively at times, his final blow did find a mark:

> Finally, it seems reasonable to ask, as we near the end of the twentieth century, if it is not time to find new metaphors to describe the state of the pitch hierarchy as it prevailed in art musics within the closing years of the nineteenth. Artifactual evidence at hand—music created by the least revered as well as by the most revered composers from 1890 to the present—contradicts the overworked metaphors of our received wisdom. Morgan is not alone in exploiting those tired phrases, the "dissolution of traditional tonality," "tonality's demise," and that magical moment when "tonality collapsed."[1] Perhaps what he and others mean by "traditional tonality" eludes me. But if in any way it refers to a hierarchical condition, with a single pitch class operating as a locus of perceptual ordering, then I am compelled to observe that these conventional images of death constitute just one more of our century's premature news flashes ("Twain Dies!" "Dewey Wins!"). Our world is unceasingly flooded with new and old, with pop, folk, communal, and art music that inescapably possesses tonality.[2]

Morgan responded, but weakly. Although making the all-important point that "tonality, *as a lingua franca* ... is quite dead"—I emphasize the crucial phrase here—he later ditched such nuance and essentially justified Thomson's critique:

> And if Prof. Thomson thinks that reports of Mark Twain's death were greatly exaggerated, he is mistaken. Once considered premature, they have long since proved to be accurate. Mark Twain did indeed die—he went out, along with traditional tonality, shortly after the turn of the twentieth century (1910). (Morgan 1991)

---

1. Thomson finds these images in the first five paragraphs of Morgan's review (1990) of Kramer (1988).
2. Thomson's pairing of Twain and tonality perhaps unintentionally alludes to Travis (1959, 281), where this illustration was used to secure the same point. Again, perhaps unintentionally, Hyer (1994) invokes Twain, and in much the same spirit as Thomson (2000, 746) "Tonality."

This claim leaves a number of post-1910 composers—what shall we say?—
"out." What about Vaughan Williams, Hindemith, Britten, Prokofiev, Copland,
Martinů, Poulenc, and a host of similar others whose music has palpable
connections to traditional tonality? Adding more from perhaps unexpected
sources—George Gershwin, Stevie Wonder, Andrew Lloyd Webber, Taylor
Swift—we might conclude that Thomson's complaint, though greased with vit-
riol, penetrates to some deeply held ideologies about the history of twentieth-
century music. Word choices like "collapse" and "demise" clearly reflect a
modernist triumphalism familiar from other contexts—namely, that the history of twentieth-century music is coextensive with the history of nontonal
compositional techniques, that the twelve-tone system was supposed to "domi-
nate German music for the next hundred years,"[3] and that "it can no longer
be argued, not even by his detractors, that this [twentieth] has been anything
other than Schoenberg's century" (Peles 1992, 35). A glance at Thomson's other
writings shows him delighting in hunting these and other creatures of naïve
historiology, flushing them out in print, and blasting away with his blunderbuss
(see Thomson 1991 and 1993–94).

If Thomson's point is conceded, questions nonetheless remain. For more than
a century, tonality has certainly ceased to be the only resource for pitch deployment in music, and Morgan is justifiably puzzled at Thomson's obtuseness about
this point. The writings of pivotal early-twentieth-century composers (Busoni,
Debussy, Schoenberg, Stravinsky, among others) are full of images and rhetoric reminiscent of earlier musical revolutions. New resources were clearly being
claimed in order to enact individual artistic programs, and the musical language of
all but the most conservative composers was affected—enriched, even—by these
resources.

Reconciling these issues, the present book assumes that tonality did not "die"
or "go out" in 1910, but was in fact so supplemented that in the hands of many
composers, it continued to be a fresh and artistically compelling means of musical organization. An exemplary case is the charming passage shown in Figure
1.1, the first period of Prokofiev's Sonata, op. 94, composed in 1943. A number of features are familiar from pre-1910 tonal practice, among which are a
perfect-fifth (P5) tonal frame around D and A, predominantly stepwise voice
leading, antecedent and consequent phrase structure, and triadic harmonies.
These all might contribute to the claim that the piece is "in D major"—a phrase
invariably appended to the customary title. Yet this is not the D major that Bach,
Beethoven, or Brahms would have composed. Neither is it a D major that would
be proffered as exemplary by leading harmony textbooks. That the great historical theorists of tonal music would find it a nonstarter perhaps goes without
saying. It is, therefore, a theoretically dubious D major. Yet I venture that no one
would claim that the passage has any other tonic than D, or that it would pass
as "atonal" in the context of what was considered progressive and prestigious
composition by the times.

---

3. H. H. Stuckenschmidt (1959, 82) reports that Schoenberg made this claim in a conversation with
Josef Rufer.

Figure 1.1 Sergei Prokofiev, Sonata for flute, op. 94, I, mm. 1–8

Despite the "obvious" tonality exhibited in the Prokofiev passage, it seems to disable a number of music theories designed to explain tonality. Those of the musicologists Heinrich Schenker (1868–1935) and Hugo Riemann (1849–1919), to take two quite different examples, had trouble enough with certain late-nineteenth-century music and clearly could not support twentieth-century innovations. Both theories were refitted by, among others, Felix Salzer (1952 (Schenker)) and Hermann Erpf (1927 [1969] (Riemann)), yet these versions have not held sustained interest, partly because of underlying problems in assumptions and formulation, but also because they have continued to be understood as degenerate variants of their respective sources instead of productive developments of them.

Among attempts to fashion music theories that take pieces like that in Figure 1.1 as mainstream instead of distributary, Paul Hindemith's, from the 1930s, is the most ambitious, and the present work relies to some extent on its considerable achievements. A preview of one of its most useful innovations—sorting the wide range of chords available to contemporary composers—gives an idea of how problems that hinder traditional theories can be approached if not surmounted.

The role of consonance and dissonance as a governing factor in Common-Practice tonal music is well known. As part of musical processes, the interplay of consonance and dissonance gives rise to procedures such as "resolution," the following of a dissonance with a satisfying consonance.[4] In contemporary tonal music, the traditional, strict membership assignments of intervals and chords into consonant and dissonant sets no longer apply, meaning that the added-sixth chord, for example, can function as a tonic consonance instead of a (traditional) dissonant seventh-chord inversion. Yet even after the loss of strict distinction between consonance and dissonance, harmonic resolution continued to be a resource for many composers. How might this rupture between procedure (resolution) and means (emancipated dissonance) be repaired theoretically? Both Hindemith and Ernst Krenek, among others, went about the task by analyzing chord-intervals according to a scale of more-or-less dissonant, and then constituting new groups of chord types based on that scaling analysis. Hindemith in particular then reimagined the succession of dissonances and consonances as "fluctuation" among chord groups. Resolution, in this scheme, is motion from a more to a less dissonant chord group.

This definition is, helpfully, "backwards compatible" with traditional compositional practices. That is, the resolution of, say, V^7–I instances a more-to-less chord change. As a result, this and other traditional procedures can be construed as style-specific enactments of a general principle about fluctuating harmonies. And further, contemporary tonal composers can not only avail themselves of such enactments but can also take advantage of "upgraded" ones unavailable to earlier composers, using a wider vocabulary of acceptable verticalities. The resolution heard at the end of Prokofiev's phrase in Figure 1.1, which comes into sharpest focus in the second half of m. 8, is explained entirely satisfactorily in terms of the more-to-less chord-group fluctuation that V^7–I belongs to, despite not resembling that progression in the least.

As the previous paragraph suggests, this relationship between tradition and innovation in contemporary tonal composition seems not much different from what has happened in the digital electronics industry. There, the traditional interests of the "installed customer base" are set against the hoped-for profits from innovative, "new and improved" products. During times of rapid technological change, the short lifespan of both hardware and software means that new architectures, devices, and storage media appear at a rapid clip, making yesterday's achievements obsolete. The market has to put a brake on technological consumption, since few existing customers can afford to upgrade each time new system items are introduced. Thus, producers make allowances to enable the continued operation of obsolete (euphemistically called "legacy") hard- or software within a newer technological environment. Should only some components of a larger system be upgraded, backwards compatibility allows the remaining equipment

4. The basis of this feature in medieval scholasticism is explored in Cohen (2001).

to continue, even if the upgrade can take advantage of newer technologies the remaining equipment does not support. When that equipment is upgraded in turn, the previous improvements can come into their own—though they will likely have become by then "legacy" features, requiring an eventual upgrade, continuing the cycle.

The leading interest of this book is in contemporary tonal music that maintains backwards compatibility with traditional as well as other tonal musics. A benefit of this approach is that it obviates fussy caviling about how and when "traditional tonality" died and "contemporary tonality" began, a preoccupation that requires theorizing about well-defined limits of either kind of tonality. (To speak properly of "extensions," one should be able precisely to identify what they are and where they begin.) Further, this approach also frees up tonal theory in general by decentering the procedures of Common-Practice harmony. These changes enhances our ability to understand the tonal compositional techniques and resources of individual styles and style periods, whether they be within the standard eighteenth- and nineteenth-century repertoire or not. We have already witnessed a significant uncoupling of classical and baroque styles (Harrison 1992), and romantic-era music is peeling off as well (Harrison 1997–98; 1994). These repertories have supplied the bulk of examples and excerpts in the common harmony and counterpoint texts. Having emphasized commonalities, theorists are now coming to a better appreciation (and explanation) of differences. In these circumstances—in which "Common Practice" is not an explanatory hegemon with respect to compositional style—it is easy to slip into inquiries concerning the practice of contemporary tonality, since it is just another stylistic expression and enactment of basic principles. Backwards compatibility thus makes a case for an overarching common practice of tonality in Western music—which is to say, a common value system about pitch relations before, during, and after the so-called Common-Practice era.[5] As one writer put it,

> Let us admit at once that "tonal organization" can exist—in one sense or another—among peoples of widely different times, places, and stages of culture, whether or not it be recognizable to us. This is a broad theoretical concept of tonality, which, combined with historical perspective, sees, in the course of the last three or four centuries, the rise and partial decline (or at least occasional rejection) of a single manifestation of tonality, i.e., the "functional" tonality of the eighteenth and nineteenth centuries. (Hibberd 1961, 15)

This admission is prefaced by noting a crucial and troublesome ambiguity in the employment of the term "tonality," which has direct bearing upon the present work: "At least part of the trouble seems to stem from the application of 'tonality' to a theoretico-historical concept on the one hand, and to a psychological sensation on the other" (15). We will examine both of these in turn. The first will occupy the remainder of this chapter, and the second will be the focus of chapter 2.

5. This case is also powerfully advanced in Tymoczko (2011, esp. 224–25).

The Common-Practice Ideal

> Musical theory is not a set of directions for composing music. It is rather the collected and systematized deductions gathered by observing the practice of composers over a long time, and it attempts to set forth what is or has been their common practice. (Piston 1941, 1)[6]

The first appearance of the phrase "Common Practice" was intended by Walter Piston as an innocent one, signifying only a basic empirical generalization. The sentence structure and rhythm make this clear; it is the first word of the phrase— "common"—that is the emphasized term, not the second. After directing attention to the dimension of harmony in music, Piston made a crucial turn:

> Historically, the period in which this common practice may be detected includes roughly the eighteenth and nineteenth centuries. During that time there is surprisingly little change in the harmonic materials used and in the manner of their use.

The historical category thus became bounded, and the "common practice" phrase took a definite, demonstrative pronoun, which also subtly shifted emphasis to the second word. No longer describing the results of some kind of corpus analysis, "common practice" instead denoted a specific corpus. This shift proved to be a momentous one. The phrase steadily outgrew its originally limited and pragmatic purposes to become, in the end, a conceptual category of theory instead of an observation about harmonic practice.[7]

We can spot the initial stages of this expansion in the use of the term to describe compositional style in general rather than the particular stylistic element of harmony.[8] Then comes colonization of style-historical discourse by means of the adjectival phrase "common-practice period" (inspiring at least one textbook title).[9] With this precedent established, the phrase can double back to its origin and fortify "common-practice harmony" (again, sanctioning the title of a textbook) (Reynolds 1985). Nearing maximum expansion, it appears as "common-practice tonality." Finally, reaching *terminus ad quem*, the adjectival cocoon cracks open and the phrase achieves perfection as a substantive concept: The Common Practice. It lives more or less comfortably as such in contemporary music theoretical discourse.[10]

---

6. Subsequent citations in the text are from this reference and following pages. Similar wording is found in Piston (1933, v).
7. In later chapters, this term is abbreviated as CP (see chap. 3)
8. See, for example, the critique of Piston's ideas in Sessions (1951, xii), where the author writes: "The idea of a *style* as a 'common practice' is essentially a generalization." Italics added.
9. Benjamin, Horvit, and Nelson (2003). The subtitle, *From the Common Practice Period through the Twentieth Century*, is new for the extensively revised 6th edition. Previous editions were titled *Techniques and Materials of Tonal Music: With an Introduction to Twentieth-Century Techniques*.
10. See Piekut (2004), for an example of the formidable shadow Common Practice as a substantive concept casts on discourse even today.

This weight-gain that "common practice" suffered over the years as a term of critical art dulled its salient contribution to musicological discourse, the surprising (to Piston, at least) stability in only one significant area of compositional concern, that of harmony. We can recover the sense of surprise by reminding ourselves of the momentous and widespread changes in music-making during the two-hundred-year span during which a common harmonic practice held sway, a span that encompasses the *sinfonia* and the symphony, *dramma per musica* and *das Gesamtkunstwerk*, the harpsichord and the iron-framed pianoforte, Bach and Brahms. In the face of such sweeping changes, that musicians apparently agreed upon a certain fixing of "harmonic materials used and in the manner of their use" is remarkable. It is a kind of treaty with the art, a voluntary restraint of trade.

The Social Dimension

Piston's words encourage us to recognize an idealized and abstract social order—a harmonious and international society of common practitioners. And just as civil society requires limitations on personal freedom for the sake of the common good, so does an artistic community adhere to common practices, ideologies, and dogmas. These can be spelled out in rulebooks and other foundational documents, and adherence may be proclaimed or more or less appropriately assigned, in which case the community can be identified by name as a group or "school"— The Mighty Handful, *Les Six*, the Second Viennese School, Downtown music, etc. These need not be clearly named, however, but instead taken for granted or otherwise uncritically assumed, as is the case with larger and less focused associations—membership in an ethnic culture, social class, profession, or other loose-knit demographic group. The rules here are mostly unwritten, and the practices are learned just as much by (unconscious) modeling and observation as by direct instruction.

Until the middle of the nineteenth century, professional music composition resembled a guild in its social organization. The basic precepts of the art were taught to children, alongside instruction in performance, accompaniment, improvisation, basic instrument repair and tuning, and the like. The charitable arm of established churches frequently supported this operation (e.g., conservatories for orphans).[11] After this apprenticeship, any growth in the art took place through transformative encounters with good exemplars—composed locally, brought from afar by itinerant musicians, or even sought after by becoming itinerant oneself. Exceptional talent could be recognized and rewarded with posts at court or a major ecclesiastical foundation, with financially successful performances, or with some other fame. To rise in this system took time, since much was learned in settings not overtly pedagogical. Those who became most adept and comfortable were often those "born into it"—a situation well-known even to contemporary musicians, many of whom

---

11. Robert O. Gjerdingen has made these observations over a number of years in several publications, most recently in Gjerdingen (2013).

are advantaged with early-childhood starts.[12] The guild of common practitioners was highly regulated but in mostly hidden or assumed ways.[13] A member in good standing played by the rules of counterpoint and harmony. Chords, their relationships, and their structural function were a simple given, and failure to observe the proprieties was a sign not of creative genius but of incompetence, if not merely lack of taste or talent. Expulsion and subsequent unemployment were likely results. And since there was no alternative, nonmembers were totally silenced in the historical record. In this way the community-enabling restraint of harmonic innovation was heavily enforced, and thus nearly ideologically opaque.

This condition enabled systemized analyses of musical products by theorists. (How much easier it is to examine something when it is at rest than when it is in motion!) The apparent perdurability of harmony led many to universalize it, producing an ideological opacity of a different kind. Rameau, Riemann, and Schenker, to name just three, produced bodies of work that are foundational to currently accepted ideas about tonal composition. Despite recent critiques that expose and historicize their ideology, many of their claims, on account of analytic utility, have acquired a perdurability of their own: viz., chord root, harmonic function, prolongation. The two-hundred-year restraint on harmonic practice allowed for precise measurements and evaluations by analysts, resulting in substantial and comprehensive claims about compositional procedure.

Riemann witnessed the first chafing at harmonic restraint, and Schenker experienced its loss. Both were famously upset about it. (Rameau, writing at the beginning of the era, had a much more optimistic outlook.) In this light, although Piston's "common practice" image appears relatively neutral—a clinical and "statistical" stance toward compositional procedure—it may also be tinged with regret; the idealized social order in which harmonic restraint was practiced, a unified and harmonious community of composers, was no more by 1941, the year Piston's *Harmony* appeared. Further, judging by the examples in that book, this community was also multiethnic and transnational (according to the standards of the time), and this could not have but played on sentiments in light of the disturbing world situation of 1941. Read this way, the end of the guild was not a neutral event but a regrettable loss of social cohesion.

The Community in Dispersion

The events surrounding this loss have been thoroughly explored, though perhaps too little critiqued. It is not hard to read the many late-nineteenth-century

12. That elementary training still involves heavy dosing with diatonic finger exercises, tonal folk music, and simple Common-Practice works means that kids beginning music study are given indelible experiences of Common-Practice structures: cadences, periods, sequences, figurations, etc.
13. Hall (1976, 74–101), identified these qualities as markers of "high-context" communication. He notes that high-context communications "are frequently used as arts forms. They act as a unifying, cohesive force, are long-lived, and are slow to change" (88). See Hall (chap. 5, 165–66), for further developments. For a discussion of how choice—specifically, compositional choice—operates in this kind of high-context culture, see Meyer (1989, 3–13).

examples of pseudo-Darwinian rhetoric calling for an evolution in musical practice as registering pressure upon harmony to adapt to new cultural and compositional circumstances, just as other areas of musical practice had. The opacity of the
given and stable harmonic practice was clearing up, and the remarkable restraint
was being recognized and resisted. Among contemporary documents testifying to
this consciousness, Busoni's *Sketch of a New Aesthetic for Music* is particularly clear
(Busoni 1907 [1962], esp. 88–95). Noting that standardization of equal temperament as both a practical and theoretical standard had led to enharmonic equivalence, Busoni lamented the flattening out of the resulting tonal space and critiqued
obsolete ideas that did not recognize this—the fiction, for example, that there were
twenty-four individual keys instead of two keys (major and minor) transposable
to twelve pitch-class levels. As a way out and to recover expressive variety in harmony, Busoni famously played with the viability of microtonal scales. These and
other features make the *Sketch* one of the early manifestos calling for changes in
harmonic practice. Others soon followed, culminating in what music historians
might cite as the first official revolutionary act: the op. 10 quartet of Schoenberg
and its post-Edenic "air of a different planet."

What happened to "common practice" after restraints were removed? It certainly lost the adjective, and became a mere "practice"; it was no longer normative,
and no longer lingua franca. It was a choice, not a given. As options on other choices
were exercised, interested composer-theorists explored their potentials, diluting
the energetic and progressive spirit of late-nineteenth-century *Harmonielehre*
and stunting thereby its further growth as a comprehensive music theory, with
growth in other areas of interest taking its place. For some, the common practice came quickly to be regarded as a historical entity, its potentials known and
assumed to be fully realized. In this reading, its enabling conditions—self-restraint
and agreeableness—could be reimagined as timidity and conformity, provok-
ing a reactionary disdain, if not the contempt of the snob for those still wearing
last year's fashions. The end of common-practice agreement was thus marked by
heated rhetoric, astonishing reactions, and radicalized new practices. It was as if
pressure had built up at a site that had been inactive for a century; release of energy
upon it, like an earthquake, both destroyed the illusion of fixity and dramatically
altered the surrounding landscape, as if a city of clay and stone had been made
rubble. In this way come the widely applied metaphors of destruction and death
that were, until recently, accepted uncritically: as Robert P. Morgan basically put
it, tonality "collapsed" and "died" around 1910.[14]

Yet much of common-practice harmony survived and flourished, in suitably
adapted forms, throughout the rest of the twentieth century and certainly even to a
significant degree in this one. To the extent that the city metaphor can be extended,
then, it is better to see it not as destroyed but as having its confining walls taken
down to expand the range of settlement. The common-practice community, like a
modernizing city, spread out into new neighborhoods, villages, and suburbs. The
cohesion resulting from urban density was thereby lost, but not all of its practices.
To be sure, some who had felt hemmed in by the walls—the most individualistic,

---

14. A more detailed critique of the "death of tonality" is found in Taruskin (2005, 4:358ff.).

antisocial, or eremitical—struck out boldly, went as far from the center as they thought possible and established themselves along the marches of musical art.[15] Thus arose the twentieth-century avant-garde, which acquired cultural celebrity accorded the explorer and experimenter as well as the *outré* and gadfly. Others less celebrated, however, stayed in the vicinity, found conditions congenial to their art in various new suburbs, and continued to work in more or less traditional ways and to maintain some of the traditional practices. The result would be familiar to students of human geography: the historical center depopulated while suburbs grew. In this case, the area within the former common-practice boundary was rezoned for conservatories and museums, as well as for nursing homes and cemeteries.

Despite the sprawl it suffered, the Common Practice still exerted a pull on the creative imaginations of inner- and outer-ring inhabitants, and even to some extent on those of the avant-garde exurbans. It was, and remains, the urban core that supports and services its suburbs.[16] The continuing presence of the common practice in the sight of young composers—whether looming either in the rearview mirror or, during training, directly in front in the form of assignments for theory class—forced them into some relationship with it, even if unacknowledged or unspoken. Those relationships could range from the worshipful to the disdainful, but neither ignorance of the common-practice traditions nor utter insouciance about its achievements was possible.

As a result, we can discern in contemporary tonal music compositional practices that did, in fact, remain common, if no longer universal. This reminds (or informs) us that even to speak of "common-practice harmony" is really to speak of an interlocked system of components that includes conventions of counterpoint and voice leading, rhythm, vertical sonority, and normative syntax.[17]

In the extramural settlements, a composer could take an especial interest in counterpoint and voice leading, for example, and let the resulting verticals be pure creatures of linear activity; or, alternatively, focus on sensuous attributes of tall verticals, and attenuate other components (especially counterpoint) accordingly. Or some other combination. There could be as many practices as there were composers.

This hyperinflation of choice can be described in terms of disintegration and fragmentation, favorites of postmodernist critique, but I find these words overloaded with tragic loss and destruction. I prefer to understand the immediate fate of common-practice harmony as the decoupling and subsequent independent treatment of its elements. It became articulated rather than broken, discretely packaged rather than bundled together. If the common-practice offering was prix fixe, the new menu was to be entirely à la carte.

15. See Whitesell (2004) for an analysis of the relevant discourse. Note especially the tropes of revolution, expansion, and liberation discussed on 108–10.
16. This argument is expanded considerably in Straus (1990, chap. 1).
17. Consider the "perfect authentic cadence," which involves *chord-root* motion $\hat{5}$ $\hat{1}$, stepwise *voice leading* in upper parts, normally proceeding from weak beat to strong in the flow of *meter*, and used to mark a unit of *form*.

The new situation—a community dispersed from a center into a region (with some using the new freedom of movement to emigrate entirely)—allows for many different kinds of palpably tonal musics to be composed. The uncertainty of theorists in the face of this variety was understandable. Piston, for one, believed that history would tell: "The experimental period of the early twentieth century will appear far less revolutionary when the lines of development from the practice of older composers become clearer by familiarity with the music." He concluded that "as yet, however, one cannot define a twentieth-century common practice." A half century has passed since these words were written. Is it too soon to test Piston's hypothesis? This book assumes not.

CHAPTER Two

Overtonality

The Phenomenology of Tonality

> Tonality is a thing which you can no more describe except by metaphors
> and comparisons than you can describe the taste of a peach, or the pre-
> cise difference between venison and mutton or beef that has been kept too
> long. (Tovey 1941, 47)

Because the compositional procedures of Common-Practice tonality are so well-
theorized, the central phenomenological problem Tovey identifies—our inad-
equacies in describing the "feel" of tonality—can easily be bypassed by proxy
descriptions that use technical language of music theory. That is, instead of "This
sounds and feels tonal," it is "This is tonal because of the harmonic vocabulary, the
voice-leading structure, etc." Under these circumstances, tonality is not so much
sensed as it is legally constituted from heard bits of musical structure. Some, such
as Brown and Dempster (1989), would go so far as to send the phenomenological problem packing and set up tonality as an axiomatic system instantiated in
individual pieces. Yet even they acknowledge that "the theory assumes some independent and perhaps intuitive criterion of tonality" (88). Such an assumption is
all the more necessary when law-like principles, more or less easily inferable from
a relatively stable and common practice, became harder to discern after myriad
choices in practice were available in the early twentieth century. Tovey's problem
multiplies: not only how does a peach taste, but how does one peach taste different
from another?

    Brown and Dempster's intuitive criteria seem best constructed from the stand-
point of what Hibberd (1961) long ago described as "tonality as psychological
sensation." Many agree that the basis of this sensation is the (re)cognition of an
ordering relation on a set of tones, of a hierarchy in which some tones take precedence over others.[1] More recent discussions of hierarchical relations in music
distinguish between "event hierarchies" and "tonal hierarchies," first defined in
Bharucha (1984, 421). As glossed by Fred Lerdahl (2001, 41), the former "represent hierarchical relationships inferred from a sequence of events" in a piece
of music. Accordingly, tone x at timepoint a may take hierarchical precedence

---

1. A few representative citations from widely different intellectual perspectives support the point: Agmon
(1990, 292); Berry (1976, 27); Krumhansl (1990b); Lévi-Strauss (1969, 17); Wile (1995).

over that same tone x at timepoint b (e.g., it may be consonant at a but dissonant at b, as in a suspension). Event hierarchies are thus context-dependent in a local sense, specific, say, to a given piece or passage (though obviously generalizable to similar contexts in other pieces or passages, meaning that suspensions in general exhibit similar event-hierarchical relations). Tonal hierarchies, on the other hand, deal with "relations that accrue to an entire tonal system beyond its instantiation in a particular piece. Such a hierarchy is atemporal in that it represents more or less permanent knowledge about the system rather than a response to a specific sequence of events." (These may also be thought of as context-dependent, but in the larger arena of artistic style and cultural practice.)

Lerdahl further suggests that the two types of hierarchy are developmentally interdependent: "Exposure to music is a prerequisite for internalizing a tonal hierarchy, yet a complex event hierarchy cannot be constructed without such a schema. They bootstrap each other into existence" (41). Lerdahl does not go into detail about variables involved in "exposure to music," but a few, at least, are pertinent. For instance, if compositional techniques and norms are stable, then presumably a large sample of music will conform, so there will be both many more exemplars supporting a given tonal hierarchy and more likelihood that even low-level, background exposures will reinforce it. In these conditions of heavy exposure to a large body of music, analytical music theory flourishes.

And what about minimal levels of exposure: How many individual musical artworks are needed to support a tonal hierarchy? This question motivates in part the careful categorization found in Wile (1995). Through techniques of "context-assertive centricity"—an event hierarchy that more or less consistently affects accent, recurrence, duration, register, and dynamics of pitches (and/or pitch classes) in the piece—a tonal hierarchy could be built from the most salient pitch (or pitch-class) in the event hierarchy (104ff.). Other pitch classes could be ordered according to their degree of salience. Yet is such a context-assertive hierarchy really a tonal hierarchy, in the sense Lerdahl described earlier? Has it, in other words, been translated into "more or less permanent knowledge about the system" or is it instead, and temporarily, "a response to a specific sequence of events" turned into analytic fiction? Only when we hear similar (if not same) event hierarchies applied, *mutatis mutandis*, in some other compositions does the "permanent knowledge" of tonal hierarchy becomes possible. That is, habitual exposure to greater numbers of separate yet event-hierarchically relatable artworks produces the conditions for tonal hierarchy.

Once surely established as a stable norm, a tonal hierarchy is eligible for rhetorical treatment—using event hierarchies that can on occasion only weakly reinforce the structures of tonal hierarchy. Schemes such as understatement, implication, ambiguation, and other devices make for a more subtle relationship between the two hierarchies, and composers can thereby remove brute-force salience from the musical surface. In terms of Common-Practice harmony, the (large) set of these kinds of devices ranges from accented nonharmonic tones on the very small scale to implied keys on the very large. It is a thoroughly rhetorical compositional technique, and therefore capable, as we well know, of extraordinary musical expressions.

A Pre-Musical Tonal Hierarchy

Is habituation the ultimate "source" of tonality in music? In other words, are tonal hierarchies entirely the products of postnatal cultural conditioning? I suggest not, because of extensive exposure humans have with a particular tonal hierarchy that is immutable, precultural, and without a necessary musical context: that of the overtone series. Considered as a pitch set, the overtone series is a totally ordered hierarchy, with the fundamental as the first element, highest in precedence. Other elements are located at fixed, receding distances, usually in receding amplitude as well.[2] Typically, complex harmonic sound waves (i.e., the kind with overtones) are treated for integration before being presented to consciousness, meaning that they produce—without any cognitive effort—the sensation of a single effect instead of striking us as a set of simultaneously sounding overtones. (With proper ear train-ing, one can learn to hear some individual overtones, and keyboard tuners do this as a matter of course. The visual analogy is noticing and attending to the individual dots in a halftone image.) This single, unified impression results from the Gestalt quality of pitch perception. As Albert S. Bregman (1990, 228) has put it, "the har-monic series hangs together to generate the percept of a single tone." Suggestively, this quality is also experienced in tonality-feeling, as when, for example, the tonic is understood as the first element in a tonal hierarchy in a way consonant with its being the fundamental element of an overtone series. Even more telling is a strong urge toward completion-by-implication common to both domains: just as listeners can report "hearing" a pitch equal to that of a fundamental tone even if the fundamental is not present in the acoustic signal, so too can listeners infer and identify a key or tonal center from various tonal cues (232ff.).

This common Gestalt quality in the cognition both of pitch itself and of hierar-chically organized pitches leads to a hypothesis that the source for the very idea of tonal hierarchy in music is in the basic experience of processing complex periodic sound waves. In William Thomson's (1991, 127) phrase, the overtone series is a "cognitive archetype,"

> . . . a well-defined audible shape [that] encroaches upon our cognitive acts. Its sin-gular unity-in-complexity is transferred by the listener as organizing schema to extended as well as to brief tonal statements; it becomes the microcosm whose pattern helps to shape the musical macrocosm.[3]

This brings us to a well-known site of conflict. The mutual attraction of tonal-ity and overtone series has tempted some to suggest that the series is—or by rights should be—the model of (a proper) tonal hierarchy in music. Such dogmas were obviously nonbinding upon the exurban emigrants from the Common-Practice

---

2. This is to say that while the overtone series can be modeled by the set of natural numbers {1, 2, 3, 4 . . . }, with a first element (1) and no last element, the real acoustical situation does not present an infinitude of overtones but some finite subset.

3. In a later gloss, Thomson adds: "That vaunted archetype does not give us absolutes; it yields a condition more on the order of what the philosopher John Searle (1992) calls a *tropism*, a "tending toward." See also Thomson (2006, 89); Bregman (1990, 494ff.) covers similar ground.

community, and to the extent that they were used to cast judgment upon such people, they provoked sharp reactions:

> Naturally, since I am not concerned with normative allegations, I cannot be concerned here with the invocation of the overtone series as a "natural" phenomenon, and that application of equivocation which then would label as "unnatural" (in the sense, it would appear, of morally perverse) music which is not "founded" on it. Now, what music, in what sense, ever has been founded on it? . . . What is, what can be, the status of the overtone series in a theory of the triadic, tonal pitch system? (Babbitt 1965 [1972], 18)

Milton Babbitt then considered and dismissed various possible answers to his rhetorical questions before giving up on "the overtone follies." The emotional heat of this and related responses by similarly prestigious thinkers to any "normative" claims advanced for the overtone series has *tout court* burned it out from the discourse of respectable music theory.

Yet if we separate the antagonists, driving off the field both dogmatic foundationalism and the sarcastic scoffing it provokes, significant connections between overtones and tonality remain and cause us to pursue the matter further. One is that a number of tonal hierarchies, both Western and non-Western, have a structure in which the subordinate pitch (class) most closely related to the tonic is a perfect fifth above, mirroring the hierarchical position of the third partial relative to the fundamental. Such congruencies, asserts Carol Krumhansl (1983, 41), "may have played a role in the initial evolution of the particular system of pitch relations contained within Western tonal music."[4] Jamshed Bharucha (1994) goes farther, speculating how this role may have played out in the formative stages of the Common-Practice tonal hierarchy:

> Since the time of Helmholtz, the notion that relationships in harmony can be explained by aspects of the structure of sound and processes in early audition has been a leading hypothesis and remains so today. It would be surprising if the conventions that have been established were chosen arbitrarily. Factors such as spectral overlap and the consonance and dissonance it engenders may have played a role in the early establishment of the conventions that today drive our perceptions. One can imagine musicians in ancient and medieval times experimenting with combinations of tones and finding certain combinations to be more consonant than others, based entirely on spectral overlap. The ensuing choices then became convention, and today we are so inundated with music that adheres to those conventions that our internalization of those conventions can compensate to some extent when spectral overlap fails. (230)

This process describes the workings of what Lerdahl (1988) would call an elementary "listening grammar" influenced by overtone-series structure. To the extent that such spectral relations are an unmediated element of the natural order, producing

4. See also Krumhansl (1990a, 253–66), for estimation of tonal hierarchy in North Indian music, in which the perfect fifth above the tonic (Pa) "is considered the second most stable in the system," after the tonic note (Sa).

musical utterances that work with these hierarchical relationships might be said to involve a "natural" grammar. These relationships are remarkably stable, fixed into position by psychoacoustical constraints and not susceptible to significant variations in convention, taste, and perhaps even culture. To be sure, they cannot be responsible for the entire structure of hierarchies, since "beyond the octave, the fifth, and perhaps the major third, it is difficult to make any useful connection between the overtone series and the universality of tonality" (Lerdahl and Jackendoff 1983, 292). But even within these bounds are important implications for the practice and theory of tonality. For one thing, the connection is likely responsible for our inadequate descriptions of the "feel" of tonality—for it feels a lot like pitch itself. Our ability to synthesize and ascribe a single virtual pitch from a large input of individual spectral components *and* identify a tonal hierarchy from certain kinds of complex event hierarchies are similar if not the same behaviors.[5] (Did Tovey unconsciously substitute "peach" for "pitch"?!) Further, they are habitual and constant—automatic, even—and our vocabulary runs away from the concrete and specific. Note, for example, that the various metaphors of presence used to describe it—center, focus, home, vanishing point[6]—are evanescences: ideas without physical form ("home" vs. "house") or abstract cognitive constructions enabled by Gestalt qualities (vanishing point, center). Is the best description simply that it is a pleasurable condition of aural attunement? But what of that condition? In the end, is it enough that we can (re)create the experience in musical composition, teach others how to do it, and theorize about the enabling conditions?

Tonality and Overtonality

Many early twentieth-century emigrants from the Common-Practice community seemed sensitive to charges of nihilism, of tearing down the tonal order, of creating tonal anarchy, of being revolutionary atonalists, and so forth. Responses ranged from proclaiming overthrow of the *ancien régime*, to the creation of a benign, libertarian condition for *émigrés*, and to the promulgation of various pretenders that claimed to continue the line.[7] Insofar as the term "tonality" was understood as synonymous with order, it could be appropriated to describe any new hierarchical system. This would require refuting claims of overtone-series underpinnings for tonality—along Babbitt's lines—as well as asserting the synonymy of tonality and order, along the following lines:

> Contemporary musical developments have made it evident that triadic structure does not necessarily generate a tone center, that nontriadic harmonic formations may be made to function as referential elements, and that the assumption of a twelve-tone complex does not preclude the existence of tone centers. (Perle 1962, 8)

5. The term "virtual pitch" is from Terhardt (1974), whose work (e.g., Terhardt 1984) along with Parncutt (1988) strongly supports this suggestion.
6. Cf. the list in Rowell (1983, 235). See also the collation of pertinent remarks by other theorists in Rings (2006, 1:63). The recognition of these as presence metaphors is found in Hyer (1994, 40).
7. See Whitesell (2004, 106–13), for the war of words over this matter.

A reasonable analytical response is: "[there is] no reason why a major or minor triad, a seventh chord, a fourth chord, a polychord, or any other conceivable combination of tones ... cannot become the tonic sonority of a tonal music" (Travis 1959, 263).[8]

If we grant a turn to a generalized sense of tonality-as-order, how then do we characterize the difference between a Common-Practice tonic and a "referential element" made up of some "conceivable combination of tones"? That is, between a pleasurable condition of effortless aural attunement, as I stated earlier, and the hard work of discerning tonal hierarchy from a context-assertive event hierarchy both unfamiliar and complex? The referentiality of some combination may not be felt in the same way if at all, and then perhaps only after considerable analytic work. A tonal hierarchy, if there be one, would not be in contact with a listening grammar.[9]

At this point in the chapter, I should like to back out of the turn to generalized tonality-as-order, lest this study be overwhelmed by interest in any and all conceivable combinations of tones. Returning to the junction, I advise that the choice is between those referential elements that can be said to function, act, or serve as, to substitute for, and represent a tonic, and those elements that feel and sound traditionally like tonics—that offer, in other words, a tonal hierarchy palpably congruent with the overtone-series hierarchy and, as a result, the same ineffable sensation of Gestaltist synthesis as pitch-hearing. I'll call this tonal-hierarchical condition "overtonality," and the various overtonal hierarchies, and the musical compositions based on them, will hereinafter be my exclusive interest. I define it in this way:

> *Overtonality is a property of any tonal hierarchy that relies on spectral overlap for its stability conditions. It thus freely imitates the tonal hierarchy modeled in the overtone series. Minimally, overtonality is expressed by two pitch-classes related by perfect fifth or its compound; the lower of the two is foremost over the entire hierarchy. Additional pitch classes can be incorporated at subsequent hierarchical levels.*

Overtonality is normally an ingredient of tonal hierarchies in music rather than such a hierarchy itself. It is the essential flavor in many familiar kinds of music. It is particularly strong in two, nearly pure, forms, and a third provides a revealing, contrasting "deviant case."

---

8. Cf. with the following statement in Krenek (1940, vii): "It is undoubtedly possible to establish a broader definition of tonality. One might call tonality any method of setting up recognizable relationships between musical elements."

9. Fred Lerdahl presses this case forcefully in Lerdahl (1988, 100): "This gap [between listening and compositional grammars] is a fundamental problem of contemporary music. It divorces method from intuition. Composers are faced with the unpleasant alternative of working with private codes or with no compositional grammar at all. Private codes remain idiosyncratic, competing against other private codes and creating no larger continuity—so that, for example, 30 years later the serial organization of [Boulez's] *Le Marteau* becomes irrelevant even to other composers."

Dronality

Instruments with (perfect-fifth) drones, repertories that feature these instruments, and imitations of drone effects by other instruments all produce deeply embedded, immovable, and solid tonic anchors.[10] Bagpipes, of course, are the leading Western-music example,[11] but the Indian classical tradition provides a more instructive illustration because the aesthetic and theoretical attention paid to the drone leads to insightful descriptions of what dronality feels like, such as:

> The drone, or *sruti*, marks the tonal center—the center of gravity—for the melody and its *raga*. Unobtrusive, calm, quiet, static, the drone is like the earth from which the melodies of the musicians fly, from which they start and to which they return. It is like a blank movie screen on which images, actions, and colors are projected; the screen in essence does nothing, but without it the movie would be lost, projecting into nothingness. (Reck 1992, 231)

In a similar vein, the following description of an ear-training exercise also directs attention toward the effect of dronality upon the body, the site of pitch perception itself, reinforcing the connection between tonal cognition and pitch perception:

> When you hear a perfect fifth in tune, it is pleasing enough. But when you *sing* it in tune, it glows, and you glow along with it. Sing a perfect fifth over a drone as in [this] example: Sing the syllable *pa*, with the vowel wide open, and with the steadiness of the sun at midday. . . . What is this shining in the tonal world? The exercise is to experience the harmonic feeling—howsoever it may be described or thought about—consciously, so that you not only have it but also know that you are having it. (Mathieu 1997, 26)

It is a telling feature of thoroughgoing dronality (in which a drone is present from beginning to end) that melodic activity has remarkable intonational freedom. The melodic components of Indian music, for example, are less individual pitches than "precise but fluid melodic shape[s] performed on and in precise vicinities of fixed, finely-tuned scale degrees" (Morris 2001). Ubiquitous ornamentation is also heard in Scottish highland bagpipe music, with its repertory of grace-note ornamentations: shakes, throws, grips, etc. In both cases, because conveying the sense

---

10. This observation is consonant with that of Lerdahl and Jackendoff (1983, 295): "The claim that all pitches of a piece are heard in relation to the tonic can be concretely demonstrated in the many musical traditions where the melodic line is accompanied by a drone, which is invariably pitched on the tonic and/or "dominant." The term "dronality" is borrowed and adapted from Mathieu (1997).
11. A surprising exception is the Scottish highland bagpipe, the most well-known type, which drones only in octaves; most other bagpipes drone in fifths. Yet the rich spectral development of the drones lead one easily to hear "fifthiness" in their sound. See further pertinent observations in Tagg (2014, 207–10).

of tonality is the job of the drone, the other pitch elements are free to convey other types of melos. The more the drone grounds the tonality, the freer the other pitch material is to fly acrobatically.

Dronality has had a significant place in Western art music, though between the lengthy tonic pedal-points of seventeenth- and early eighteenth-century organ music and their revival in late nineteenth-century orchestral music, dronality was more a feature of Ratnerian topic—for example, the *pastorale*—than a significant structure. Even so, whether structural or topical, the same division of labor between drone and melody found in Indian and other musics can be heard, with the texture dividing into lightly coupled dronal and melodic components.[12]

Outside of obvious manifestations of dronality—that is, those in which the dronal element is highlighted either topically or structurally and, as a result, chiefly characterizes the musical utterance—dronal procedures can be built into more complex tonal hierarchies as fundamental tonal buttressing. They are frequently so used, for example, in rock music, where the guitar "power chord"—root and fifth only, without a third—is an overtonal timbre/pitch effect that relies on dronality to reinforce the root.[13] With barre-chord technique, a succession of power chords gives the impression of a very harmonically rich bass-driven melody, not unlike a melodically active drone. If another repetitive, drone-like layer is placed underneath, something very much like the piece captioned in Figure 2.1 can easily result—typical of much blues-driven rock music and the "heavier" forms of pop.

This accumulative introduction starts with a four-measure drum and bass groove, with the bass pulsing and droning on D. At rehearsal A, a guitar drone-riff establishes the basic overtonal relationship D–A. This continues for the next eight measures—eight seconds. The lead guitar's entrance at reh. B introduces nonovertonal pitch material, a series of mildly distorted dronal power chords built on successive subdominants from the D tonic, that is: D–G–C–F. The figure is arranged plagally to discharge twice upon a D power chord before being expanded at reh. C into a more active, thrice-repeated cycle, after which the first verse begins. All the while, the pulsing D of the bass groove and the D–A riff in the guitar fix the tonality firmly by dronal means, allowing the power-chord licks to explore the plagal underside of the overtonality, as it were, without losing contact with the established tonal base.

Another family of pop-music examples could also be proffered involving appropriations of Indian dronal styles, lightly mediated through Ravi Shankar, by the Beatles and other "progressive" rock bands of the 1960s.[14] The ease with which Indian dronality was incorporated into (or imitated by) various rock songs points out the ease with which dronality can cross stylistic and ethnic borders duty-free.

12. The textural division is frequently recognized in harmonic analysis by "ignoring" a pedal point and dealing solely with the chords above it. In a complementary relationship (i.e., performance instead of analysis), many thoroughbass authorities advised accompanists to play pedal points *tasto solo*, even if provided with "unusual signatures and successions of towering figures" (Bach 1753 [1949], 319).
13. This same kind of reinforcement by fifth (identifiable by the use of parallel motion between chords) can be found in some sixteenth- and seventeenth-century harpsichord repertories. See, for example, strain #2 of Thomas Morley's "Nancie," *Fitzwilliam Virginal Book*, no. 12.
14. "Infra Riot," the first track of the "Soundtrack of our Lives" album from which Figure 2.1 is taken (*Behind the Music*, 2002), begins with an obvious appropriation of Shankar/Beatles-style dronality.

Figure 2.1 Lundberg/Bärjed, "Sister Surround", 0:00–0:35. (The Soundtrack of Our Lives, *Behind the Music* [Republic 012 156 261-2], 2002). Pitch quantized to 12-note equal temperament

"Bugleity"

The social function of the military bugle, as well as its physical construction, encourages distinct intonation of its available tones, which correspond to the second through sixth partials of C_3. This contrasts to practices with other nonkeyed, "natural" horns (e.g., the shofar), where manipulation of the bell and changes in embouchure permit a greater variety of tones. "Bugleity" is a pure yet severely limited overtonal hierarchy of five pitches corresponding to the lower regions of the overtone series: C_4, G_4, C_5, E_5, and G_5. Like dronality, it presents to consciousness a clear and solid psychological sensation of tonality, but it is also in some sense the opposite of dronality, in that *all* pitches are isomorphic to harmonic-series partials, not just a foundational two. As a result, though bugleity has restricted musical possibilities, its repertory of calls and signals does show ingenious deployment of its available resources for artistic (as well as semiotic) purpose.[15] The breakthrough effect of the high G_5 in "Taps," for example, is a distinctive touch that has allowed this ostensible call to extinguish lights in camp to become a poignant musical panegyric of military funeral rites in the United States.

In concert music, bugleity is frequently bracketed between more complex tonal hierarchies, as in fanfare effects. More remarkably, it can also be encased within such hierarchies. John Philip Sousa, for example, incorporated parts for regimental bugles in *The Thunderer* and repurposed the signal "With Steady Step" for the trio of *Semper Fidelis*.[16]

A well-known and interesting example of (a slightly denatured) bugleity is Aaron Copland's *Fanfare for the Common Man*, the opening call of which is shown in Figure 2.2(a); the associated tonal hierarchy is shown at (b).[17] Because of its overtone-series structure, bugleity can seem to posit an actual *pitch* rather than an abstract *pitch class* as fundamental/tonic (in this case: C_3). Higher-numbered partials/pitches are proportionally subordinate to this tonic, symbolized by the increasing "quickening" of the musical notes in (b) from breves/double whole-notes to minim/half-note. As in dronality, the actual fundamental pitch indicated by the partial/pitch relationships is absent,[18] so the second partial, an octave above the fundamental, is its agent and de facto tonic (in this case: C_4). This arrangement establishes a form of octave equivalence, even though it is a weak one, since pitches lower in the series feel increasingly weighted in the same way that lower partials do in complex pitches. (Cf. the relative weight effects of G_4 and G_5 in "Taps.") In Copland's *Fanfare*, this linear tonal hierarchy can be sensed by comparing the

15. I explored a similar, "high-constraint" pitch system in connection with clock chimes in "Tolling Time," *Music Theory Online* 6.4 (October 2000).

16. There are, of course, numerous examples of Common-Practice instrumental tunes that arpeggiate through a tonic triad, but these are so well encased within a tonal hierarchy larger than bugleity that little is to be gained by focusing on the more restrictive overtonality.

17. The opening is scored for B♭ trumpet, but the following discussion assumes concert pitch.

18. Backus (1977, 260–68), explains this lack of fundamental pitch in brass instruments, and also details the way in which their natural resonances are *not* in harmonic-series relationships—in other words, how the effects of mouthpiece and bell work to adjust their resonance modes into such relationships.

Figure 2.2 Copland, *Fanfare for the Common Man*, (a) iconic theme. (b) overtonality frame, with upper-octave duplicates as small notes. (c) Analytic adjustment of frame to show Subdominant element. (d) Synopsis. The slur is an "ornament" indicating a complete upper third "trill": F_5–A_5–F_5. Subdominant element

effects of the final C_4 with an "impostor," C_5. From a pitch-class perspective, the two are interchangeable, but C_4 has the stronger tonic effect.

Figure 2.2(c) shows the slightly denatured, as-composed tonal-hierarchical structure, which projects subdominant pitches for relief and contrast, giving a modicum of harmonic and melodic fluctuation to the passage. Upper-octave duplications are active as shown.

Figure 2.2(d) unfolds the structure in time and enables further analytic comment. First is a rising plagal octave species, $\hat{5}$–$\hat{8}$–$\hat{5}$, then a falling, subdominant-inflected interval cycle, what we might style $\hat{4}$–$\hat{1}$–$\hat{5}$. At the first ending direction reverses again while the $\hat{4}$–$\hat{1}$–$\hat{5}$ cycle remains, producing the arpeggiated close-position triads of mm. 4–5. The second ending dramatically strips away all the notes that don't belong to the series (i.e., the subdominant ones) as well as the upper-octave duplications, leaving a pure *Ursatz* descent, as it were, of prime-number partials 5, 3, 2 of C_3. The whole anacrustic effect of the passage is now clear, with upper-octave rising and falling through *both* dominants, discharging with pure hierarchical fidelity to the final C_4 as the agent for an absent yet puissant C_3 fundamental.[19] I leave it to the reader to try these ideas out with the following measures of the *Fanfare*, allowing that the polyphonic bugleity complicates matters, but in suggestive ways.

I call attention to dronality and bugleity as ways of experiencing elementary overtonal hierarchies. These two cases have been easily incorporated and freely

19. Further, the "maximally closed motion" within the hierarchical pitch space at the cadence—from the most inferior to the most superior element—is a typical signal of closure, as is discussed at length in Murphy (2004).

traded as topics, effects, or mannerisms in the higher reaches of art-music, but considering them by themselves should refresh our hearing of basic overtonality. The minimal but deeply set overtonal anchor of dronality allows for significant play with lots of other pitches, and it does not affect (any) hierarchical position among them, which may be determined (and composed) by other means. Bugleity, in contrast, has no free pitches outside the overtonal hierarchy. It is thus a more extensive overtonal structure but is also severely choice-limited, and thus invites interpolation/intervention of extrahierarchical pitches (the relative strength of which is controlled by local event contexts) to achieve its art-musical flexibility. The extent of the artistic range composers could explore between these cases should be clear.

Spectralism: A deviant case

"Spectralism" is a broad term for a positive compositional attitude toward "the physical properties of sound itself" and which makes "the dissection of sounds into collections of partials or overtones a major compositional or conceptual device" (Hasegawa 2009, 349).[20] From this general perspective, spectralism offers a highly instructive case of overtonality embedded in generally atonal soundscapes. Some of its techniques are directed toward building simultaneities that occupy the space between chord and timbre, such as in Gérard Grisey's much-discussed *Partiels* (a part of *Les espaces acoustiques*).[21] Here, a trombone's E_2, the opening sound of the work, is "reproduced" by an orchestral rendition of its spectral components, shown in condensed score in Figure 2.3. This rendition includes the extreme upper partials of the trombone note, which have to be rendered as fractional tones. Because of the less-than-perfect intonation of human players, the slight inharmonicity of the acoustic instruments upon which they play, and the substitution of their own complex timbres for the simple sinusoid of an overtone, the instrumental simultaneity struggles to achieve acoustic fusion.

But such fusion is beside the point, since the listening experience rather involves a kind of figure/ground oscillation between chord and pitch—an artistic compositional event affecting the core psychological sensation of overtonality. In short, "the distinctions between note, frequency, timbre, and harmony become fuzzy, or even irrelevant, and accumulated traditional experience finds itself impotent to organize the emerging sound world" (Pressnitzer and McAdams 2000, 33).[22]

---

20. More background and discussion is in Fineberg (2000a and b) (along with other articles in that issue), and—particularly focused on Grisey—in Féron (2011). A historical-cultural analysis is undertaken in Drott (2005).
21. Thanks to Eric Drott for introducing me to this work. In addition to the composer's own discussion in Grisey (1991), see additional commentary in Hasegawa (2009, 349–50), Fineberg (2000a, 116–18), and Pressnitzer and McAdams (2000, 39).
22. See the pertinent comments about fusion among complex tones in Bregman (1990, 488ff.).

Figure 2.3 Gérard Grisey, *Partiels*. Chord at reh. 2

Importing effects from the electronic studio, such as ring modulation, into the orchestral context, Grisey was able to modulate the spectral elements into and out of harmonic relationships, with the spectral components variously going their own way (and engendering a conventionally "dissonant," atonal sound) and recongregating into harmonic partial-tone relationships. The piece is a fascinating study of psychoacoustical awareness, for both composer and listener.

Similar techniques within a different overtonal sound world can be heard in Jonathan Harvey's *Mortuos Plango, Vivos Voco,* where the overtonality is derived not from the partial-tone structure of string and pipe but from the English church bell, which has some (lower) harmonic-series partials mixed with inharmonic partials (clang tones). Again, considerable pleasurable attention can be paid to the modulation of spectral components and to the occasional fusion effects that might happen by. The final two minutes of the work, consisting of a tolling bourdon bell whose spectral structure is electronically processed and touched up with sounds from a boy soprano, also has a certain dronal effect on account of the bell, though the considerable attention paid to manipulating its upper partials puts pitch cognition on holiday, allowing the listener to hear the multicolored spectrum instead of the "white" pitch.[23]

While the dependency of these and related spectralist techniques upon overtone structures is clear, their contribution to experienced overtonality is more complex. The interest in higher-numbered partials and the purposeful exploration of the same is of a piece with earlier, Schoenbergian doctrines, which claimed all possible overtones beyond the easily heard earlier numbers (see, for example, Schoenberg 1912 [1978], 318ff.) However, the works cited here have a consistent dronality that helps orient the upper partials to the fundamental, whereupon the

23. Harvey (1981) discloses the specific compositional techniques for this piece. Detailed analysis has been undertaken in Clarke (2006), with background about the development of the specific analytic techniques given in Clarke (2005), and generalization to other works in Clarke (2012).

pitches can be contrived to fuse fitfully or to be heard as "dissonant" elements in a complex chord, which ambiguity is where much of the charm in this music lies. Removing the drone (or a bass line) leaves difficult-to-affiliate, dissonant upper-partial chords that characterize certain kinds of classical atonal music and be-bop jazz.[24]

Theories for Overtonality

The cases just discussed are special, in that overtonality appears as the most significant feature of pitch organization, which, not surprisingly, is highly unusual as a result. In the cases discussed in the following section—which are music-theoretical rather than compositional—overtonality is an embedded foundation upon which other important pitch relations are built. These cases involve tonal hierarchies in which overtonality is highly influential instead of dominating, allowing more complex relational transactions than possible in the cases discussed earlier—transactions that can variously obey or moderate the overtonal sovereignty of the system. Three cases will be given brief discussions. The first two are tonal hierarchies informed by research into cognitive psychology, while the third is a hierarchy originally created for compositional and analytical purposes, structured quite differently from the other two in some essentials, but remarkably like them in others.

Carol Krumhansl's tonal hierarchy

Figure 2.4, representing findings of the cognitive psychologist Carol Krumhansl and colleagues, shows an idealized model of pitch-class relationships in a given major key "0."[25] The size and position of the pitch-class integers indicate their strength in the hierarchy, with larger and more central pitch classes being higher in precedence. (0 itself may be imagined as being the bounding circle.) The data supporting the figure come from interpretation of empirical studies, the details of which need not detain us here; the basics, however, can be easily conveyed: given a key-defining context (a simple scale or cadence), musically trained subjects were presented with a "probe tone" and asked to rate how well it "fit" in the given context. The better the fit, the stronger the rating.

The overtonal component of the model is found in the inner portion of the figure, where the innermost element is the overtonal fifth, 7. Given the major key

---

24. Väisälä (2002) offers a rigorous theoretical development of the possibilities.
25. The data supporting the figure are from Krumhansl (1990a, 30), which reproduces material from an earlier 1982 study. "A" and "B" refer to pitch-classes 10 and 11, respectively. Krumhansl does not offer a geometric representation of this data; Figure 2.5 is inspired by a geometric representation used to illustrate results from a later study, as discussed later.

Figure 2.4 Geometrical representation of tonal hierarchy, following Krumhansl 1990a, 30

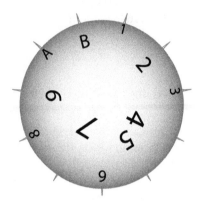

context, the next element in the hierarchy is the overtonal third, 4. Thereafter appear the remaining pitch classes in rank order. The complete ordering relation is ⟨0, 7, 4, 5, 9, 2, B, 6, 8, 3, A, 1⟩.

The probe-tone ratings supporting Figure 2.4 deal in one dimension only—the relationship of a single pitch class to the tonic 0. A later study, slightly modified in some details, replicated the procedure of the first but presented subjects with two tones in succession, with instructions to rate how well the second tone followed the first. This study thus explored pairwise relationships among all pitch classes in a given 0 tonic context, producing a more nuanced view of the hierarchy. The results of this study were visually summarized in a form like Figure 2.5, again oriented toward a given major key 0.[26] With the tonic 0 at the vertex, the remaining tones of the chromatic gamut are located at increasing distance both from the vertex and from each other. As in the earlier study, overtonality is strongly embedded according to the position of the overtonal fifth. The rank ordering of the remaining pitch classes differs somewhat from that in the earlier study, but the first overtonal elements are the same.[27]

The representation in Figure 2.5 has some shortcomings according to Krumhansl. Most importantly, temporal-order effects, which cause asymmetrical relationships among tones, cannot be portrayed in the spatial model. (That is, pitches *a* and *b* could be judged to be different distances from each other depending upon which sounded first.) In addition, the cone is somewhat too regular and smooth for the data it represents, which have been stressed in order to fit the shape. Additional simplification also likely results from the assumption of

26. This work culminated in Krumhansl (1990a) from which the example is drawn. The inauguration of the research project may be Krumhansl (1983). The adaptation here replaces the original note letter-names with pitch class numbers (with C = 0), which better reflects the enharmonic equivalence assumed in the research.

27. The rank order of the double probe-tone study is: ⟨0, 7, 4, 2, 5, 9, B, A, 3, 6, 8, 1⟩.

Figure 2.5 Geometrical representation of tonal hierarchy according to
Krumhansl 1990a, 128

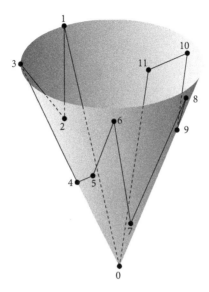

enharmonic equivalence, washing out differences between, say, G♯ and A♭ in their
relationship to both tonic and to other notes. (This is perhaps warranted given
the brevity of the key-defining context.) These issues, as well as Krumhansl's
commendable scholarly caution, lead her to note that the "conical representation is not a theoretical model, but instead a summary of psychological data"
(Krumhansl 1990b, 310).

Despite this useful distinction, Figure 2.5 can suggest or—in the case of Fred
Lerdahl's pitch-space theories—support a theoretical model. Such a model would
proffer a completely determined tonal hierarchy, reflecting the total-ordering
relation on the set of chromatic pitch classes observable in the data, in which 0
is the first and 1 is the last element.[28] This situation contrasts with that in the
cases discussed previously, which involved (1) partial ordering on the complete
set (dronality), (2) total ordering on an incomplete set (bugleity), and (3) passing attempts at total ordering on a nearly complete set (spectralism). In addition, the model would assert that precedence within the total-ordering relation
has the additional quality of interval—that is, *a* not only strictly precedes *b*, but
does so by a certain amount. Note that in the spatial representation of Figure 2.5,

28. The status of 1 as last element cannot easily be seen in the cone, but the numerical data shown in
    Krumhansl (1990a, 125) supports it. In addition, we should note another reading of tonal hierarchy
    that Krumhansl offers, one that measured pitch-class relationship to the tonic 0 alone by using a
    single probe tone after the key-defining context. Not requiring a multidimensional scaling solution,
    the data appear as number ratings in Krumhansl (1990a, 30).

Figure 2.6 Geometric representation of tonal hierarchy, adapted into segments

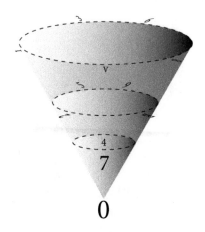

the least elements are not only far from the first element, 0, but also from each other. Thus, a kind of inverse-square law is suggested in which the greater elements are stronger in their hierarchical relationships than are the lesser elements.[29] A practical result of this would be the construction of tonal hierarchies for compositional use that rely on the stronger relationships of the greater elements to ground the overtonality, allowing the lesser elements with their weaker relationships to coalesce into a unordered set of remainders, as shown adapted in Figure 2.6.

A phenomenologically attractive feature of Figure 2.5, as well as its adaptation in Figure 2.6, is that it invokes the familiar three-dimensional space in which human beings move, in contrast to the flatter one-dimensional space of the line segment, upon which ordered elements ⟨0 . . . 1⟩ are mapped according to the total-ordering relation that defines the hierarchy. Further, the space depicted in Figure 2.5 has perceptual vectors associated with it. The vertex, for example, has the Gestalt quality of focal point or, alternately, a point of emanation. This evaluation connects easily to intuitions of tonic being a focal point from the perspective of the remaining pitch classes, and of tonic being some kind of source for these pitch classes.

We can imaginatively merge these features with the "sound and feel" of overtonality discussed some pages ago by reorienting the cone along the lines of Figure 2.7, where the tonic 0 is psychically absorbed into the subject and the remaining elements are perceived from this point as suggested in the lower part of the figure. Such "subjectifying" of the hierarchy enacts Gerhard Albersheim's perspective image of overtonal space, which he terms "harmonic hearing":

29. The connection between this inverse-square situation and the common metaphor of "gravity" applied to the tonic is suggestive.

Figure 2.7 Subject orientation of tonal-hierarchy cone

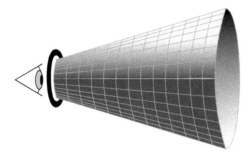

> Preharmonic [i.e., non overtonal] hearing compares to viewing a section of our earth surface from above, or making a topographical drawing of it. We note only the absolute locations and the distances between objects. Harmonic hearing, on the other hand, compares to the different views we will gain if we enter this area and successively look at it from several points within, or to perspective drawings of such sights. . . . In harmonic hearing the listener still perceives the individual tones of a triad in their "topographic" or absolute locations in tonal space, but he also hears them in their "perspective" or functional relationship to the root. (Albersheim 1960, 18)

Despite the attraction of Krumhansl's geometric model as an inspiration for a fully articulated overtonal hierarchy, her reservations about it reflect some real ontological trouble. A generous reading would be that it models an "average" hierarchy of a generalized "ambient tonality." Presumably, the subjects had—or were required to construct by the circumstances of the study—a homogenized sense of tonality supported by knowledge of musical utterances of quite divergent styles and tonal treatments—standard repertory, commercial and popular music, nursery and folk song, and whatever other musical flotsam had caught their attention. Ambient tonality is thus a kind of sonic emulsion in which J. S. Bach, Stevie Wonder, Igor Stravinsky, and Mother Goose are suspended, differences in their respective understanding and treatment of tonal materials notwithstanding. This homogenization reduces out characteristic tonal features of style, and thus loses some specificity. Although it seems of a piece with the broader view of Western tonality espoused in this study, its relationship with psychoacoustical or cognitive processing of the overtonal hierarchy remains obscure. Presumably, the latter underlies the former in some way, but beyond this it is difficult to proceed. It may be that it is difficult if not impossible to know more about ambient tonality outside of the experimental conditions that assumed it.[30]

---

30. A more critical reading of the issues involved is found in Butler (1989, 223–30), which focuses on the nature of subject response (e.g., what exactly did subjects think themselves doing when they were asked to judge the "fit" of probe tones?). Krumhansl responds in Krumhansl (1990a), following which Butler offers rejoinders.

Fred Lerdahl's pitch space

In his 2001 monograph, *Tonal Pitch Space,* Fred Lerdahl relies partly on Krumhansl's work to advance a sophisticated theory of tonal relations. A foundation of his approach is the basic diatonic tonal space, an instance of which, oriented toward a tonic chord in "0" major, is shown in Figure 2.8. Granting that a complete explication of its role in Lerdahl's theory is impossible here, we will focus on features relevant to overtonal hierarchy.

Unlike Krumhansl's total-ordering relation on individual pitch classes, Lerdahl's construction involves a total ordering of levels a through e, but elements within the levels are unordered. (As such, the conical representation of the structure is more like fig. 2.6 than fig. 2.5.)[31] Following the lead of Diana Deutsch and John Feroe (1981, 503–22), Lerdahl describes each level as an "alphabet" that is elaborated at the next level. Level a, the first element in the hierarchy, contains the root tonic pitch; level b partners the tonic with its overtonal fifth;[32] the local tonic triad appears at level c, followed by the major scale at d, and, finally, the background chromatic collection at e. The structure of Lerdahl's figure resembles that used to show metrical structure in an earlier study, Lerdahl and Jackendoff (1983), in that the height of the column is directly proportional to hierarchical position. Levels a, b, and c thus present totally ordered hierarchical relations: tonic, overtonal fifth, and—according to the local major-mode condition—the major (overtonal) third. At level d, four new pitch classes appear, $\{2, 5, 9, 11\}$, and these are unordered among themselves but hierarchically inferior to those presented in the first three levels. The same situation applies to level e with respect to pitch classes $\{1, 3, 6, 8, 10\}$.

Despite the apparent equality of pitch classes within each level, each has its own "reporting line" to the a-level tonic 0, and the number of intermediate "supervisors" through which a pitch class has to report can be counted; this number gives a reading of hierarchical position within the whole organization. It's important to work this through Figure 2.8 in order to understand the complex hierarchy Lerdahl has created, so an example is in order. Take pitch class 5, which first appears on level d. To reach a-level 0, five moves are required: (1) 5 laterally to 4; (2) 4 vertically to c-level 4; (3) 4 laterally to 0; (4) 0 vertically to b-level; and (5) vertically again to level a. Thus, to calculate a position of a pitch class within the hierarchy, find its topmost occurrence and count the minimal number of lateral moves needed to reach access to a higher column (choosing the direction toward the nearest local 0 if two such higher columns are equidistant), and count the number of moves up each column until 0 at level a is reached.

As might be expected, the pitch classes in levels a–c have unique values. Differences show up in level d, $\{2, 5, 9, 11\}$, where 2 and 11 report through four

---

31. Cf. Lerdahl's (2001, 50) own conical representation.
32. In a departure from Deutsch and Feroe, Lerdahl identifies the overtonal fifth at level b partly on the grounds that the fifth is "more stable" than the triadic third. Presumably, this claim relies on evidence similar to that which placed the overtonal fifth as the nearest neighbor to tonic in Krumhansl's representation.

Figure 2.8 Basic diatonic space, after Lerdahl 2001

level a:	o												o
level b:	o						7						o
level c:	o				4		7						o
level d:	o		2		4	5	7		9		11		o
level e:	o	1	2	3	4	5	6	7	8	9	10	11	o

intermediaries while 5 and 9 report through five, thus making 2 and 11 superior to 5 and 9. More pronounced differences are found in level *e*, {1, 3, 6, 8, 10}. Interestingly, Lerdahl preserves enharmonic distinctions here, so that 1 may report to 0 (= C) on the "flat side" as D♭, and then on up the column, resulting in a value of five; or 1 may report to 2 (= D) on the "sharp side" as C♯, and then up to level *d* and over to 0 in the first column, rising thereafter on up the column, resulting in a value of six. In this way, level *e* is partially ordered as follows: ⟨{D♭}, {C♯, D♯, E♭, F♯, A♭, A♯}, {G♭, G♯, B♭}⟩, with values of five, six, and seven for each unordered set in the ordering.[33]

Lerdahl's work beyond that presented so far—a vast development past the basic diatonic space—cannot be adequately summarized here, and fortunately, for the present purposes, it need not be. Yet one summary point should be made. By taking certain structural aspects of the basic space—the layered alphabet, the distribution of elements within each layer, certain hierarchical well-formedness criteria—Lerdahl is able to construct various other basic spaces that are not dia-tonic (although they all have the same level *e* chromatic background). He posits, for instance, spaces such as the triadic/octatonic and French-sixth/whole-tone, which, he maintains, support certain nineteenth-century repertories. Thus, the basic diatonic (and overtonal) space is not normative in Lerdahl's theory (that is, it shouldn't be considered preferable to other basic spaces he expounds). As a result of having an idealized set of tonal pitch spaces, Lerdahl offers a way to dis-criminate among and precipitate out elements of a problematic ambient tonality. Lerdahl's work with these various spaces may be the most significant contribution of his cognitive-psychological project to music theory.

Hindemith's Series 1

Figure 2.9 is a totally ordered tonal hierarchy based, like the hierarchies discussed earlier, on C as first element.[34] Unlike Krumhansl's hierarchy, the result of empiri-cal study of listening subjects, and unlike Lerdahl's hierarchy, a more abstract and

---

33. It is suggestive to note the equality in the reporting structure of *e*-level D♭ with *d*-level pitch classes 5 and 9 (i.e., F and A), all three of which report through five elements. This brevetting of the nom-inally chromatic Neapolitan degree to diatonic rank is not without precedent in harmonic theory. See, for example, Harrison (1994, 122–23).

34. The series 1 chart and the discussion surrounding it are found in Hindemith (1937 [1942], 1:32–50).

Figure 2.9 Series 1, from Hindemith 1942 [1937]

Children   Grandchildren

complex structure supported to some degree by empirical study, Hindemith's is an invented ordering, constructed by various manipulations of harmonic-series relationships largely for the purposes of composition pedagogy and analysis. The "children" of C are conceived with the help of Arthur von Oettingen—in particular, his phonic relationship, in which overtone x of some fundamental is considered as overtone y of some other fundamental.[35] Hindemith's particular algorithm used to generate the first elements of the series is to take x^{th} overtone of C and consider it as the $(x-1)^{th}$ overtone of some other fundamental, which then enters the series. Thus, for example, taking 64 Hz C as the parent of the system, we can see that 192 Hz G is the *third* overtone of 64 Hz C, but is the *second* overtone of 96 Hz G. And again, 256 Hz C is the *fourth* overtone of 64 Hz C, but is the *third* overtone of 85.3 Hz F. The "grandchildren" are conceived in like manner, but involve more complicated genetic engineering. The equivocal G♭/F♯ at the end is a hybrid, almost the bastard of the family. Even though this generational metaphor does not play much part in Hindemith's theory as a whole, it does show that the hierarchy is totally ordered on two strata: the pitches themselves, and that of the generations.[36]

Hindemith's method came under withering attack in well-known articles by Norman Cazden and Victor Landau, which chided it for being arbitrary (a numbers game with overtones) and inconsistent (E should appear before A, for one thing) (Cazden 1954; Landau 1960; Landau 1961). Scholarly opinion has considered these criticisms as definitive, closing the book on Hindemith's entire theoretical output as a result. But the Cazden, Landau, et al. critiques ignore or misunderstand the *rhetorical* purposes of the commentary, which was not to demonstrate scientifically that Series 1 is a natural phenomenon, but instead to do traditional *Musiktheorie* introductions before getting on to the business of writing a composition manual. In other words, the explanation for Series 1 is of a piece with the arithmetical manipulations of Zarlino in Part I of *Le Institutione harmoniche*, and accordingly should be given the same weight in Hindemith's theory as it is in Zarlino's—which is to say, not much. The "derivation" of Series 1 via the "overtone follies" thus should properly be seen as a "creation myth" couched in what was for a German musician of the

35. See Harrison (1994, 242–51), for an overview of Oettingen's ideas; references to relevant sources are found there as well. Some of Oettingen's ideas are discussed, without attribution, in Hindemith (1937 [1942], 1:76–7).

36. The "generational" annotations are not usually reproduced in discussions of Hindemith's series 1, but are suggestive in light of the present discussion of hierarchy. The lines separating the child, grandchild, and "bastard" tones are, however, present in the main chart inserted after Hindemith (1937 [1942], 1: 48).

mid-twentieth century the obligatory formal, even liturgical language of *Theorie*, the language of a mystical company of authors ranging back to Pythagoras.

A fresh look at Series 1 shows it to be an intuitively plausible ordering, not much different in overtonal essentials from Krumhansl's results. Figure 2.10 shows pitch classes in the left column and their order position in the respective tonal hierarchies of Krumhansl (from fig. 2.4) and Hindemith (Series 1). The rightmost column shows the positional-order difference between the two. The essential overtonal hierarchical relationship of 0 and 7 occupies the same position in both orderings: first and second respectively. Following this, pitch-classes {4, 5, 9} are variously mapped onto order-positions three, four, and five. Thereafter, greater variations in hierarchical position begin to show up, as evidenced by the greater values in the difference column.

Continuing the analysis of Series 1 while keeping its creation myth bracketed, we can explain these differences as arising from the compromises that Series 1 makes between pitch-class and regional hierarchies as well as between major and minor modes. For example, Hindemith's promotion of A (9) before E (4), in violation of his algorithm, is likely due to the greater importance of the relative minor over the mediant as a regional (i.e., key) center. In a similar vein, Hindemith, keeping the orthodox faith, hears echoes of diabolical power in the tritone, casting it out of the family and out at the end of the series. Krumhansl's subjects, however, making

Figure 2.10 Comparison of hierarchical ordering positions, Krumhansl and Hindemith, both normalized to C major context. Smaller numbers in the ordering columns indicate hierarchically superior pitch classes. Smaller numbers in difference column indicate greater agreement

pitch class	Krumhansl ordering	Hindemith ordering	Absolute difference in position
0	1	1	0
1	12	10	2
2	6	8	2
3	10	6	4
4	3	5	2
5	4	3	1
6	8	12	4
7	2	2	0
8	9	7	2
9	5	4	1
10	11	9	2
11	7	11	4

different kinds of judgments, heard the tritone as a more innocent entity. Finally, Series 1 conflates major and minor mode into a single hierarchy, promoting thereby E♭ (3) and A♭ (8) to follow E (4). In contrast, both Krumhansl and Lerdahl are careful to propose separate modal hierarchies. Those already discussed illustrated only the major mode, and the element that appears after the overtonal essentials in both of their orderings is 4, the major 3̂. Minor-mode contexts naturally offer 3 instead (the minor 3̂), along with higher ratings for the other two modal scale degrees, 6̂ and 7̂.

Minor and overtonality

The congruencies between the summary of psychological data that is Krumhansl's tonal hierarchy, the rigorously developed theoretical model that is Lerdahl's, and the more or less ad hoc compositional tool that is Hindemith's show clear agreement about overtonal essentials: the basic condition of the perfect-fifth relationship at the top of the hierarchy. Beyond that point, organizational options increase and do so in a systematic way. A later chapter will go into detail about these ramifications, but the first branch should be described here, especially because entrenched positions left over from nineteenth-century conflicts about it have seemed impregnable.

Any appeal to the overtone series as a referential structure has always had to account for the status of the minor triad as either the symmetrical inversion of the major, or as a less perfect acoustic formation but still an acceptable tonic sonority. Since the lower partial tones of a the harmonic series—the first six, say—so audibly analyze into a major triad, the existence (or acceptability) of minor cannot be accounted for if overtonal hierarchy is to be isomorphic with the harmonic series. Described this way, the doctrine of *harmonic dualism*, based on inversional symmetry, seems the more attractive of the two descriptions, since it fully covers key relationships in the Common Practice and, to some extent, in earlier seventeenth-century repertoires. It uses the harmonic series as a template for structural mirroring, and music theories based on it more or less rigorously pursue the systemic consequences of this initial maneuver (see Harrison 1994, chaps. 6 and 7).

While inversional-symmetry dualism has proven to be extremely stimulating and influential in music theory, it failed its original nineteenth-century mission of justifying the minor triad as co-equal with major. The point of contention was the final status of the template. First, what influence over composed music did it retain, and second, what similar object might the mirrored structure relate to? At the time, any answer to the first question acknowledging retained influence would prompt a search for something responding to the second. What resulted were products of syllogistic reasoning like "If the major chord models the first six overtones, then the minor chord models the first six undertones" or "If a P5 and M3 above some note together make a major chord, then a P5 and M3 *below* a note make a minor chord." These and related propositions, however, did not have the "determinate feel" of the overtone isomorphism with major—which is to say that they were abstractions, constructs, or heuristic "as ifs" at their most productive. If sensory access was demanded of them, however, they were mere illusions, vain hopes, or the dumb idols of philosophers.

One way out of this difficulty is to deny the overtone series any privilege in setting the boundaries of usable tonal systems. According to this view, while it may have had some role in propagating major triadic harmony, the isomorphism is inexact even here, since modeling stops after the first six overtones. Further speculation about the "higher numbers" and modeling the upper overtonal regions are the same kind of activity that provided major in the first place. Both major and minor are constructed, neither is necessarily "found in nature," and attempts to ground either somewhere "in the world" are misguided. Further, since an overtone-series template is an arbitrary one of many, other kinds could be imagined and swapped in to generate their own particular tonal hierarchies, giving rise to the kinds of abstracted "tonalities" alluded to in the previous chapter.[37] Indeed, the question of templating for tonal systems at all is perforce broached and perhaps begged. The position just outlined ends up, I believe, rubbing against the *palpable influence* that the overtone series has exerted on harmonic practice throughout Western music history. The voicing of chords, for example, defaults to overtone-series settings, with wide intervals in the bass, small ones in the treble.[38] Intonational practices based on spectral overlap, such as the "lock and ring" characteristic of barbershop harmony (as well as brass ensembles), attempt to realize the lower sections of the series as actual, audibly fused chords. And finally, spectralism cannot do without the overtone series. It is a considerable, not a negligible presence in Western music. Subtle and only gently normative, the overtone-series tonal hierarchy cannot but be largely responsible for the discovery, design, and development of its pitch structure.

Obviating all these difficulties is the other description of minor's provenance, most cogently presented by Helmholtz. Elsewhere, I have argued that it is reasonable, correct, and far less threatening to theoretical systematics than nineteenth-century dualists feared (Harrison 2005). Simply put, Helmholtz claimed that the minor triad must be less harmonious than the major on psychoacoustical grounds alone, and that further systematic developments from the minor triad will of course be less consistent with the overtonal model than those starting from major (see Helmholtz and Ellis 1954, 301). Even so, the minor triad is similar to the major in its gross anatomy for it to model its function as a consonant triad, capable of closing a composition as a tonic harmony.[39] (In this way, dualism helps rather than clinches the case.) That is, major and minor have been and continue to be equivalent in their *structural prerogatives* within broadly overtonal compositional styles. With respect to the overtone series, major fits perfectly in its lower reaches, while minor fits tolerably.

The difference between *perfect major* and *tolerable minor* is responsible for the structure of their respective Common-Practice systems. The former takes

---

37. Harvey's *Mortuos Plango, Vivos Voco*, discussed earlier, uses a template provided by inharmonic bell tones. See Bregman (1990, 234ff.) for detailed discussion of how a series like this, and perhaps also those produced by other *n*-dimensional systems (e.g., drum, block) can be integrated as pitch.

38. The reader might find it interesting to be reminded of common instrumentation practices *across a variety of styles* that reinforce overtonal voicing dispositions—the *coll 8vb* that the contrabasses add to the cellos and bassoons; left-hand octave passagework for piano; calling for 16' and even 32' stops on the organ.

39. The convention of the *Picardy third* shows that major could trump minor for an absolute final of a composition.

shape easily and maintains harmonic-series isomorphism through its first three elements. The latter splits off after the first two, requiring then infusions of major-system elements (e.g., the leading tone to tonic) in order to stabilize. And minor has other requirements that—as any student of Common-Practice composition can attest—make composing in it more technically difficult than in major.

In this account, the existence (i.e., tolerance) of minor depends upon artistic impulses that major cannot satisfy. These can be quickly and roughly apprehended by considering bugleity again. It is basically a major-only system, having no access to minor (let alone other pitches) without valves. The expressive opportunities that another, related tonal system offer can be comprehended at once by arranging a *minore* version of any standard military bugle call: quick tempo ones turn ominous, and the slow become mournful. Access to these affects is of long standing in Western music and fundamental to its expressive vocabulary.[40] Helmholtz's views about this are still pertinent:

> But I am by no means of [the] opinion that this character [i.e., the lesser consistency of minor compared to major] depreciates the minor system. The major mode is well suited for all frames of mind which are completely formed and clearly understood, for strong resolve, and for soft and gentle or even for sorrowing feelings, when the sorrow has passed into the condition of dreamy and yielding regret. But it is quite unsuited for indistinct, obscure, unformed frames of mind, or for the expression of the dismal, the dreary, the enigmatic, the mysterious, the rude, and whatever offends against artistic beauty;—and it is precisely for these that we require the minor mode, with its veiled harmoniousness, its changeable scale, its ready modulation, and less intelligible basis of construction. The major mode would be an unsuitable form for such purposes, and hence the minor mode has its own proper artistic justification as a separate system. (Helmholtz and Ellis 1954, 302)

All things considered, the tonic third in an overtonal hierarchy is best characterized as a bandwidth rather than a point—as a *range of acceptable realizations* between overtonal root and fifth. Put another way, distinctive overtonalities depend on deviations from the calculated points on a harmonic series within the tolerance for each point. The major third is the sweet spot at the upper end of the bandwidth, while the minor sets the lower bound. As Hindemith (1937 [1942]) put it, these two places mark the "high and low, the strong and weak, the light and dark, the bright and dull forms of the same sound" (78), suggestively illustrating the central point as in Figure 2.11. His representation enables an even more subtle understanding of the matter at hand that he does not mention: the actual tuning and tempering of pitches at these divisions involves another set of tolerances, ranging roughly between the Pythagorean and the just intonations of the respective thirds.

The insights of the previous discussion can nuance the isomorphism between overtonality and harmonic-series partial tones. Our cognitive template recognizes both the ideal locations of individual partials and tolerable realization of the same. As a result, partials can be modeled as line segments in pitch space rather than

---

40. Dmitri Tymoczko has demonstrations of random chord progressions in different macroharmonies, which give an idea of what bugle arrangements into environments like octatonic, whole-tone, etc. may be like. http://dmitri.tymoczko.com/whatmakesmusicsoundgood.html.

Figure 2.11 Representation of the variable placement of the third between the overtonal root and fifth, after Hindemith 1937, I:72. The range between the largest and smallest versions of the two identified intervals can be set by Pythagorean and just tunings

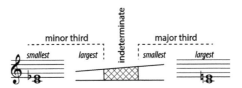

points, and their location can be described by the way that they split distances between other locations. All this has been explicitly enacted in the practice of temperament, which also discloses the usable length of the line segment (i.e., tolerance) for each interval: perfect unisons and octaves are less tolerant of tempered tuning than perfect fifths and fourths, the diatonic imperfect consonances accept more, and remaining pitches slot in accordingly.[41] But as suggested by Krumhansl's cone representation (supported by Lerdahl's unordering of the contents of levels *d* and *e*, and supported as well by Hindemith's generational distinctions), hierarchical influence is not evenly distributed over the organization but heavily concentrated on the first four partials. Since the remaining elements dispose themselves in increasingly less influential ways in the hierarchy, differences in their rank ordering are generally too fine to be worth having disputes over. This attitude conflicts with the dogmas of the high-church overtonalist, who, recognizing the fifth partial in the guise of major 3̂, would make normative claims for major as more overtonal. I prefer the broader view, sanctioned by the equal availability of major and minor modes in tonal composition, and consider such matters as adiaphora in the theory of overtonality.

Representing Overtonality in Musical Analysis

As we look back at this chapter's figures—from the scores and transcriptions to the conic sections and spaces—a few stand out as having illustrative, pedagogical, or analytic potential. I happily imagine 3-D animation on the conic sections (or on related geometric shapes, as Tymoczko would hasten to add), with points and lines "lighting up" according to the input of musical flow, perhaps correlated

---

41. In particular, fifths/fourths take 5¢ tempering, while the thirds/sixths are 22¢ wide. This observation can be extracted from data in Helmholtz and Ellis (1954, 453ff.), a table of intervals constructed by Ellis. The range of tempering for an interval is set between its Pythagorean and Just tunings (with equal-tempered pitches between them). A larger and individualized range of probability for each interval can be discerned there by incorporating as possible correct intonations "rare" or highly refined liminal cases, such as the "subminor" third between partials 6 and 7. See related observations in Bregman (1990, 239), among which is the finding that low partials can be mistuned as much as ±1.5% before pitch fusion is lost.

with dynamic level or the like; if the vertex moved according to the fundamental bass of a musical passage, then even more interesting geometric, dynamic, and graphical representations could be imagined.

Musicians with good aural imagination might prefer the score representations, such as Figure 2.2(b)–(d) (p. 22), which also have the virtue of being adaptable to other styles that use musical notation as the primary carrier of analytic judgment (e.g., Schenker, among many others). These are congruent with William Thomson's *Tonality Frame*, first introduced in 1966.[42] The frame is constructed from boundary tones, mediations, and reciting tones of a phrase (or a series of phrases, arrangements of sentences and periods, and the like). It's a report on generalized ambitus and tessitura for a given passage.

In Figure 2.2(b), the total ordering of the overtonal hierarchy is reflected by diminishment of note values. Square breve/double whole-note shows fundamental agency, round breve the overtonal fifth. Mensurally, these notes have equal value, and this helps keep their fundamental importance in mind. Note also that the smaller square breve shows a superoctave of the fundamental. Basically, the breve/double whole-note-shapes identify how the foremost pitch class is determined, and if the hierarchy is detailed enough to distinguish individual pitches within the class, then notehead size can encode that feature.

Insofar as they can be, might be, and ought to be discerned, subsequent hierarchical relationships can be keyed to subsequently quicker note values. In Figure 2.2(b), an upward stemmed minim/half-note shows the major-third partial, #5 in the overtone series. In general, the faster the note, the farther away, less "supervised," and freer to roam the pitch (class) is in the hierarchy. Indeterminate status can be shown with simple noteheads.

Figure 2.2(b) is a synchronic, static, "scale-ordered" macroharmonic representation of the bugleity background of Copland's composition. The graph at (c) extends it by showing Copland's artistic intervention: adding nonharmonic notes A_4 and F_4 from the subdominant side. The "underdominant" F gets the honor of a stemless note form, the semibreve/whole-note—shaped like the dominant yet lacking its stripes of sergeancy—and is decorated with an upper major third, signified by the upward stem on the black note A_4, similar in effect to the one on the 5th partial, half-note E_5. Superoctaves are again shown in smaller noteheads of appropriate values.

The representation at (d) is a diachronic, unfolding-view of the hierarchical frame, showing when each overtonal fastener is sounded and reinforced. (See caption for additional explanation.) As before, note values indicate hierarchical position instead of actual rhythm, making this view necessarily arrhythmic and, therefore, productively agnostic about the ways in which various styles of melodies can be supported by the structure. The ordering of framing elements in a melody typically outlines various structures of interval divisions—the way octaves are divided, in other words. Some of these are traditional, widespread, and even ancient, such as the *authentic/plagal* distinction of octave species, the distinction between harmonic and arithmetic divisions, and the like—basically, ideas about where a reciting, medial, or middle note is relative to a final and opening note.

---

42. For a concise introduction, see Thomson (2006). More extended discussion is in Thomson (1999).

Figure 2.12 Tonality Frame for "Sister Surround," in order of entrance. Dotted upstem on final D_3 shows major-mode bias of power-chord timbre

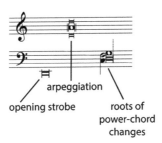

Figure 2.13 Hindemith Series 1 presented in a fully built note-value notation, details of which are offered in chapter 4. The dotted box encloses structural pcs analyzed in Copland's *Fanfare*, Figure 2.2(d)

Thomson originally used scale-degree numbers to describe divisional segments—as in the description of the plagal $\hat{5}$–$\hat{8}$–$\hat{5}$ division in the opening of the Copland piece. Later, he recommended pitch-class integers, with movable-0 according to tonic—thus: 7–0–7′, with the prime symbol marking it as a superoctave of the first one. In his writings, Thomson often created further reductions that bend Figure 2.2(d) back toward the style of (c), which also resemble Schenkerian graphs in their use of variously denominated noteheads connected by slurs. Unfortunately, some of these are hard to read, some unclear, and others dubious; Thomson's own notational practice is inconsistent and underannotated. Even so, the utility of schematic representations of tonality frames is easy to appreciate musically, and clearing up notation is not difficult.

Trying these ideas out on another excerpt discussed in this chapter results in Figure 2.12, an overtonality frame for "Sister Surround" (fig. 2.1). This example of dronality doesn't need much of a diachronic view. The bass guitar opens and locks on D_2. The rhythm guitar then articulates 0–7–0′ in the fourth octave, and then the lead guitar fills in the third octave with a plagal riff that completes the accumulation of a pentatonic macroharmony.

For an adaptation of the Copland hierarchy to Hindemith's Series 1, see Figure 2.13. The strong fit is not surprising, given how analysis of the passage implicitly took a "Series 1" point of view. The five notes from the Copland are bracketed, and the remaining notes are here sketched according to familiar ideas of note value, with stems indicating any modal affinities—up for major and down for minor. The mark of the bastard tritone is as shown.

CHAPTER Three

Geography

This chapter recapitulates themes from chapter 1, where Piston's "Common Practice" (hereafter, CP) signified a cohesive social order of proficient musicians. The challenge to this order, promulgated with increasing success just before the First World War by recognized and admired artists, was also described there as congruent with the challenge presented to the nineteenth-century European city by ancient or medieval city walls. Former gates had become mere openings through masonry, and large solid sections had to be dismantled to ease travel to extramural districts. Over time, some walls can disappear entirely, but their former site can be read from general geographic features—"historic" landmarked structures in the "old town," mixed development in suburbs at various distances from this center, and increasingly sparse and widely spaced homesteads in rural fringes.

Figure 3.1 maps the enlarged area of overtonal compositional practice with four compositional concerns placed as suburbs of a CP metropolitan area. As anyone who has lived in a city can appreciate, the nearer a suburb, the greater the need for the center to provide services and amenities; the farther, and the more those are done without or other sources substituted. For the figure at hand, the arrangement reflects similar relationships to the overtonal hierarchies structuring CP compositions.

- *Linearity* is where the CP begins: the emergence of chant, tune, melody, *cantus firmus*, *Zug*, and similar gestalts from successions of proximate pitches.
- *Meter* brings overtonal government to melodic lines by attaching them to metric hierarchies.
- *Harmonic Fluctuation* is regulation of metered polyphony to create tension/resolution effects.
- *Traditional Rhetoric* is the extension of long-standing and familiar expressive schemes beyond their originating contexts.

When all four of these compositional concerns are strongly exercised, the range of musical utterances narrows onto palpable derivatives of CP models; any further restriction leads to historical-style composition. That is, the more referential, conservative, and derivative a composition, the closer it is to the CP downtown. Reversing field and moving outward, releasing constraints one by one, we can appreciate how eschewing traditional rhetoric calls for a new and therefore

Figure 3.1 "Ring suburbs" representation of contemporary tonal compositional techniques

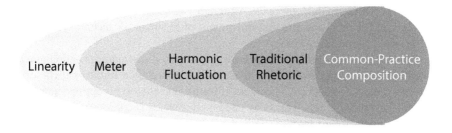

"modern" rhetoric, how indifference to harmonic fluctuation makes overtonal hierarchy harder to realize, and how suppression of meter leaves a soundscape solely of (potentially overtonal) *melos*. If even linearity is not in play, I wonder whether it is possible to compose an overtonal repertory at all beyond a few "demonstration" exercises.

The remainder of this chapter surveys these areas, moving outward from the innermost suburb. Where new analytic approaches seem warranted, some proposals are made and tried out. Musical examples have been chosen for their illustrative clarity, with interest also in suggestive comparisons and contrasts. A few passages of distinctive effect and noteworthiness are covered in graphic detail. Finally, a debriefing about the relationship of these suburbs to Dmitri Tymoczko's "Five Components of Tonality" (2011, 2) concludes the expedition.

Traditional Rhetoric

The CP core is defined and enclosed by its well-known conventions of dissonance treatment, particular types of which have characteristic names: suspension, appoggiatura, échappée, etc.[1] What Schoenberg famously described as the "emancipation of the dissonance" is the functional breaching of *limes*, with a telltale sign being toleration for "dissonant" tonics (a matter taken up in the next chapter). If this achievement was the predictable result of increasing dissonance-levels in nineteenth-century harmony, an equal-and-opposite reaction to this pressure can be discerned in pure-triad compositions that avoid even seventh-chord dissonance, and which also float their harmonies with barely discernible tonic tether. Much of Franz Liszt's late work displays both breakthrough pressure and its reaction; *Nuages Gris* and *Unstern!* (both 1881) are sledgehammer strokes, while *Introitus* (1884) and the Kyrie from the *Missa pro organo* (1879)

---

1. It's useful to remember that Piston's original conception of a "common practice" concerned harmonic techniques. Accordingly, they determine the boundary of the common-practice enclosure proposed here.

are the perfumed air of pure triad. Both techniques are emancipatory—one a dramatic breakout that ends up supporting atonal expressionism of, say, Schoenberg's op. 11 piano pieces (1909), and the other a kind of escape into mellifluidity discerned in works like Vaughan Williams's *Fantasia on a Theme by Thomas Tallis* (1913) and the first movement of Hovhaness's second symphony, "Mysterious Mountain" (1955).[2]

This innermost suburb permits both emancipated dissonances and emancipated harmonic progressions, but these are regulated by a traditional rhetoric that binds them to various CP models. If traditional rhetoric is applied so heavily that harmonic emancipation is effectively reversed, compositions like the first movement of Karl Jenkins's *Palladio* (1995) can result. Famously associated with an international advertising campaign for De Beers diamonds, this work is so thoroughly controlled by the composer's imposition of Vivaldi's expressive and generic rhetoric that in the ears of untrained listeners, it passes for an early eighteenth-century concerto grosso. (For the trained, awkward tutti/solo proportions, overuse of a simplistic ritornello theme, and occasional voice-leading and modulatory anachronisms give it away.) Traditional rhetoric can thus be a basic expressive code for an "any chord can follow any other chord" state, in which harmonic progressions may be underdetermined and arbitrary (perhaps charmingly so). By following conventions of CP expression, gesture, and style, such progressions reenact the CP interplay of compositional will and systemic protocols. Yet emancipated chords are actually driven by compositional will and choice alone. The protocols, like the monarchy in Canada, are acknowledged yet ultimately powerless.

Traditional rhetoric also has recognizable "figures of music" involving secondary parameters of dynamics, tempo, and timbre. The trope of "climax," for example, can be enacted by *crescendo, stringendo,* and *col* 8$^{va/b}$, working cooperatively, with length and intensity proportioned according to formal purpose. "Announcement," to take another example, may depend on *rit.* and a *fermata* while holding forth on active scale-degrees. (Prefacing effects may vary with application of *cresc./decresc., rit/accel.,* etc.) In this vein, Ferruccio Busoni's 1909 *Konzertmäßige Interpretation* of Schoenberg's op. 11, no. 2, is edifying, as it applies traditional rhetorical devices to an originally emancipated-unto-anarchic harmonic environment, creating thereby at least a suggestion of traditional tonality if not a fully realized tonal center. This curious work is an arrangement by which "the dissonances which Schoenberg had proclaimed with such conviction are beautified and—many people would say—trivialized" (Beaumont 1985, 40; see also Hamilton 2010 on Busoni). Figure 3.2 suggests a basis for this claim in the work's conclusion, showing Busoni's arrangement in the lower system aligned with Schoenberg's original on the upper.

In stretching Schoenberg's final two measures into six, Busoni intended to signal closure using devices typical of traditional concluding rhetoric—specifically, motivic fragmentation and written-out *rallentando*. About the former, a novel

---

2. Bernard (1998, 545), regards this work as a benchmark of this prolific composer from which later efforts "are actually *less* effective expressively."

yet already fragmented motivic technique is "traditionalized" by repetition (i.e., *anaphora*), as in m. 65, where Busoni takes Schoenberg's original pitch idea, increases its rhythmic activity, and repeats the gesture twice with down-octave transposition. (Note the hand-crossing that inverts some of Schoenberg's original pitch intervals.) Busoni's transformation creates a traditional, re-identifiable motive out of an aphoristic hint, making clear to "traditional ears" what must have been originally experienced as an obscurity.

These rhetorical additions beautify the original gestures, but they do not yet create a palpable tonal center. This only emerges in the next measure, where Busoni's interventions amplify the established signals of closure. (Perhaps aware of how touchy a subject this could be, he notated his additions using small, *ossia*-sized noteheads, as if to mark them optional.) As in the previous measure, the rhetorical idea is *anaphora*: the final chord succession is repeated, double-timed in its last presentation to impose a traditional piece-ending *rallentando*, accompanied by a repeated, stabilizing E♭ pedal point. From this emerges a Scriabinesque "tonic" chord over E♭, voiced in a right-hand configuration known in jazz circles as a "sharp 9" (and, later in this chapter, labeled i[6,5]). In other words, the imposition of traditional ending-rhetoric contrives to suggest a centered final chord. Apart from some registral differences and passing intervallic inversion, no notes of Schoenberg's atonal original have been altered, but Busoni's "beautification" creates a startlingly traditional, even familiar soundworld—yet depopulated of known consonances. From all this, we can derive a rule of thumb about analyzing expressive rhetoric: the more that ancient terms like *anaphora* aptly describe the expression at hand, the more influential a role traditional rhetoric plays in the compositional structure.

Traditional rhetoric is a crowded and diverse suburb, yet also déclassé and somewhat lowbrow. Although it houses well-regarded works of important art-music composers, it has a huge population of pieces satisfying commercial commitments—film, musical theater, recording industry, advertising, etc.—as well as functional music for social institutions such as the church and the secondary-school ensemble, where Jenkins's *Palladio Suite* is most at home. It is also a place easily disdained by those who think its residents have moved just beyond the city walls for certain suburban advantages but whose identities are nonetheless shaped by the center. In the same essay in which he coins "emancipation of the dissonance," Schoenberg condescends thusly to its inhabitants:

> Many modern composers believe they are writing tonally if they occasionally introduce a major or minor triad, or a cadence-like turn of phrase, into a series of harmonies that lack, and must lack, any terms of reference. Others hope the use of ostinati and pedal-points will do the same thing for them. Both are acting like believers who buy an indulgence. They betray their God, but remain on good terms with those who call themselves His attorneys. They use accidentals and key-signatures to fit the key that would like to hold sway . . . to cloak their secret sinful converse with dissonances. (Schoenberg and Stein 1984, 258–59, "Opinion or Insight.")

We will visit a site of "secret sinful converse" for Schoenberg (see fig. 3.18), but note for now that just beyond the inmost district of tract houses, strip malls, and

Figure 3.2 Upper system = S, Arnold Schoenberg, *Klavierstuck*, op. 11, no. 2.
Lower system = B, Ferruccio Busoni's *Konzertmässige Interpretation* of the same

other developments are more innovative and nontraditional structures. The transition is gradual, not abrupt, and thus differences are notional, like that between intramural neighborhoods, rather than well marked, like political boundaries. The infrastructure for both places is united by a compatible "master control" system for consonance and dissonance, which the next section elaborates.

Figure 3.2 (Continued)

Harmonic Fluctuation

Traditional expressive rhetoric requires careful attention to harmonic tension/
release effects, dissonance/consonance flow, cadence/closure devices, and other
harmonic activities, all of which are coordinated with secondary parameters
to create unified expressive gestures. Paul Hindemith viewed the harmonic

portion of these gestures as a matter of chord quality, and he called its purposeful manipulation *harmonic* (or chord-group) *fluctuation* (Hindemith 1937 [1942], I:115ff.).

This activity is highly regulated in CP composition by long-standing conventional treatments of dissonance and consonance, which limits the exercise of individual compositional will. As a result, motion of chord roots as well as deployment of harmonic schemas and formulas is of greater interest than direct observations of chord quality. In the progression i–VI–iv–ii°–V–i, for instance, the descending-third root motion linking into an authentic cadence receives far more analytic attention than the fact that no successive chords have the same quality.

Chord-quality fluctuation becomes increasingly important as a structuring device in the later nineteenth century and supremely so in the twentieth. The large palette of chromatic and dissonant chords used in the later nineteenth century enabled composers to uncouple chord quality from root-motion syntax, so that a chord-quality decision could be made independently at any change of chord root. (For triads, the effect produced by intentional play with quality is understood analytically as "secondary" or "double" mixture, in Aldwell and Schachter's [2003, 541] widely used terminology.[3]) Harmonic fluctuation is an ingredient rather than a product of traditional rhetoric and thus can be adapted to different expressive contexts and rhetorical devices. A leading example is rock music, which is capable of directed overtonal harmonic flow in contexts unimaginable to common-practitioners—involving, among other things, instrumentation, formal and harmonic formulas, and social function. (The influence of non-European—specifically, African and African American—overtonal practices is the warrant for "unimaginable.") Further, among the possible tonal systems rock music uses—organized by Walter Everett according to similarity to CP norms—those that rely on minor-pentatonic scales expressed with power chords (Everett's types 5 and 6) are unique to rock styles and therefore outside the technical as well as expressive norms of the CP enclosure (Everett 2004, para. 19–25). Everett cites a number of songs instancing these types, ranging from the light 1960s pop of The Monkees' "I'm Not Your Steppin' Stone" to the arty 1990s work of Portishead's "All Mine."

Rock and other forms of contemporary popular music aside for the moment, innovative expressive rhetorics have been used in works more easily understood to be within the Western Art Music inheritance. Consider the opening of Stravinsky's *Ave Maria* (1934; Latin version, 1949), shown in Figure 3.3. Despite the archtraditional text and genre, the soundworld of the piece lacks traditional rhetorical ornaments—indeed, the lack of such ornaments is a rhetorical

3. This decoupling is also recognized in neo-Riemannian theory by the "P" (parallel-mode) transformation, which shuttles major to minor and *vice versa*. The "transformational" quality discloses that the analysand is a consequence of compositional will rather than of systemic protocol. That is, neo-Riemannian theory "works" better in the kind of free-floating triadic environments of late Liszt than in normal protocol-driven ones of middle Mozart.

Figure 3.3 Stravinsky, Opening of Ave Maria (Latin version)

device in itself (i.e., systematic impassivity and understatement). The overall effect places harmonic fluctuation—the gentle tapering into E-minor chords at the end of mm. 2, 5, and 6—in an expressive atmosphere too thin for CP activity.

The passage in Figure 3.4 offers another good example of harmonic fluctuation expressed with more contemporary rhetoric. In fact, the passage is adduced as a textbook case of harmonic fluctuation, and the graphic underneath the score is intended to convey the degree of sonic tension in an intuitive way—the higher the line, the greater the tension.[4] Though a system of tension metrics lies behind the graph, knowledge of it is not necessary to grasp its basic ideas: (1) the fluctuation of tension is based on vertical interval combinations, and (2) fluctuation is assumed to be a structuring element in the passage. In the opening two measures, the graph conveys an undulation of tension that results from the toggling between chords belonging to set-classes 4-23[0257] and 4-20[0158]. As the melody enters in m. 3, tension generally rises to a high level before dropping back at the end of the phrase in m. 5, an effect comparable to that of a cadential release. The rest of the passage can be read along the same lines, positively correlating changes in general tension levels with seams in local structure. To be sure, the graph and the system behind it are not unquestionable in their details and operations—which is to say that the graph does not give an "objective" account of harmonic fluctuation, but only a theorized one. Yet the general picture it paints is not implausible, and the effort to capture this quality of the composition is neither misplaced nor beside the point of the compositional technique used here.

As noted previously, traditional and contemporary rhetorics of harmonic fluctuation are not separated by a clear border. It is easiest to understand the differences between them by citing limit cases—such as the deliberately archaic style-composition of Jenkins's *Palladio* against the modern art-rock of Portishead's "All Mine." In between are all manner of modern interpretations of traditional rhetoric,

4. The figure is reproduced from Ulehla (1966, Ex. 421 on 449), with extensive discussion on 448–50. The systematics of the graphing technique are discussed in the following paragraph and in her book on 423ff.

Figure 3.4 Norman Dello Joio, from Piano Sonata No. 3; analyzed by Ludmilla Ulehla

novel adaptations, evolved versions, ironic usages, skewed allusions, as well as genuinely new expressive manners appropriated from various specialized overtonal practices. The more traditional the rhetoric, the more appropriately that traditional analytic concepts can be invoked without qualification or hand-waving; the less traditional, the more such concepts have to be modified, extended, or even discarded in favor of new ones based on the structures at hand. A useful general guide for locating a compositional utterance depends upon the degree to which qualifiers such as "sort of," "quasi-," "-like," and or even simple scare quotes must (or should) be employed in order to acknowledge differences from traditional versions. In Figure 3.4, for instance, is the construction of mm. 3–9 "sort of" a period? A quasi-period? A period-like thing? The urge to identify the structure somehow with the period is easily identified: a basic idea in mm. 3–4 is repeated in mm. 6–7, and a contrasting idea can be discerned in m. 5, and (possibly) again in m. 8. Missing, of course, are the definite cadential structures that provide a sure articulation. As noted, a drop-off of harmonic tension is noted in m. 5, but does this create a cadence? A quasi-cadence? A functional equivalent of a cadence?

Analyzing Harmonic Fluctuation

Harmonic analysis of scale-degree progression is difficult to do convincingly with many nineteenth-century practices, with their large palette of chromatic and dissonant chords and long passages of floating tonality. The early-twentieth-century "emancipation of the dissonance" fully disables scale-degree analysis as an analytic lingua franca, since all traditionally required conventions of harmonic progression and dissonance treatment become optional—including the zero-use option (i.e., not be considered at all). Maximizing this option is a leading and persistent feature of certain compositional styles (e.g., atonal expressionism, "New Complexity"). Any less-than-maximal option, however, puts the composer on task for matters of harmonic control, flow, punctuation, closure, chord voicing, and the like. Given the powerful example set by the CP standard repertory, working this out with originality is difficult and, as we'll explore in chapter 5, psychologically fraught. Maintaining any traditional harmonic practices *except* those dealing with scale-degree and dissonance treatment is a hard matter; solutions are limited.

Despite a vast repertory that reflects a nonmaximal aesthetic, in which composers developed individualized, ad hoc, and occasionally explicit preference rules for the chord-quality flow and progression (not to mention "trial and error" approaches and experiments with atonality within otherwise tonal surroundings), defining a theory of harmonic fluctuation has proved elusive. Few attempts have been tried, and none generally adopted. This may mean that fluctuation is not a prime mover behind chord flows and motions, but it might also suggest that the contemporary concept has yet to be adequately theorized.

The Systems of Krenek and Hindemith

Though Paul Hindemith's theories of fluctuation and *chord group* are better known, the nearly contemporaneous sketch of interval and chord tension in

Krenek (1940) is simpler, suggestive, and gives a clearer view of the issues at hand.[5] That it is embedded in a primer on twelve-tone serialism marks it for special interest—one would think that serial composition is indifferent to fluctuation at best, and inimical to it at worst. Krenek's little book is as advertised: a study of contrapuntal texture, though daringly using classic, Viennese serialism as the *loci topici*. It's a work of *Satzslehre* (composition manual) rather than of speculative theory. Further, the problems he focuses on for the student composer—phrasing, gesture, expression—are not ones pure technique can address. Krenek thus wants composers to think about the absolute harmonic effects of various pitch-class set (pcset) combinations—including the extremes of intense chromatic and the sweet triadic.

Krenek sets up the basics of his system at the beginning of his chapter on two-part writing. Figure 3.5 reproduces his text. The highlights:

- He affirms traditional teaching about perfect unisons, octaves, and fifths as consonances, though given the post-emancipation context, all enharmonic spelling differences are ignored, as are differences between simple and compound intervals.
- His intervals are semitone-distances modulo the octave, as typically found in twelve-tone and atonal theory.
- The perfect fourth, "treated as" a dissonance in traditional two-part counterpoint, acquires here an ambiguous, context-dependent status. Ambiguity about the interval is familiar from traditional three-part writing (i.e., consonant between upper parts but dissonant with the bass), but Krenek finds it already in two parts, and moreover shifts the contextual grounds to the quality of preceding intervals in a sequence.[6] In this way, the appearance of tradition is maintained, while the substance is new.
- Also new is Krenek's classification of consonances and dissonances. The distinction between perfect and imperfect consonances is lost, but the formerly unitary category of dissonances is split into "mild" and "sharp" subsets, the former containing major seconds and minor sevenths (i.e., interval-class [ic]2), and the latter containing minor second and major sevenths (ic1).
- The tritone, traditionally a dissonance, is relegated to a special, "neutral" category.

Krenek's interval (dyad) classification scheme is the basis for sorting trichords; for comparison with the previous illustration, Figure 3.6 reproduces his text and examples, but for ease of commentary its substance is better represented schematically using pitch-class sets. The table below shows trichordal set-classes (and their

5. Michiel Schuijer also surveys Krenek's and Hindemith's schemes (Schuijer 2008, 138–44). Details omitted here are summarized and glossed there.
6. The effects Krenek adduces from his Exx. 27 and 28 may have as much to do with specific melodic line and absolute interval size (i.e., eleventh vs. fourth) as with the general properties of the intervals involved.

Figure 3.5 Ernst Krenek, *Studies in Counterpoint*, 7ff

3. The following intervals are regarded as consonances:

Ex. 24

4. Dissonances are distinguished by their degree of tension.

    a. Dissonances of lower tension ("mild" dissonances):

Ex. 25

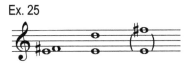

    b. Dissonances of higher tension ("sharp" dissonances):

Ex. 26

The degree of tension may be explained by vibration-ratios, combination-tones, or other acoustical phenomena; yet, the decision of what shall be considered a dissonance and how it should be handled is an arbitrary assumption inherent in a particular musical style, for it depends exclusively on aesthetic concepts.

5. Whether the interval of five semitones (perfect fourth) should be considered a consonance or a dissonance depends on the context. For instance, in the progression:

Ex. 27

the character of the fourth is rather consonant, because of the preceding intervals of higher tension, whereas in the following passage the fourth (represented by an eleventh) appears dissonant:

Ex. 28

6. The interval of six semitones (diminished fifth) is a neutral interval, divding the octave in two equal parts.

Figure 3.6 Ernst Krenek, *Studies in Counterpoint*, 19ff

According to the principles outlined in the paragraph dealing with the tension-degrees of intervals, we can make a survey of three-tone chords in regard to their tension-degrees. It is evident that these tension-degrees depend on what kinds of intervals are formed by the constitutent tones of the different chords.

Chords may consist of:
1. three consonances: (the third chord, for instance, has the consonances C–E, C–A♭, and E–A♭).
2. two consonances and one mild dissonance: (the second chord, for instance, has the consonances C–G and C–A, and the mild dissonance G–A).
3. one consonance and two mild dissonances: (the first chord has the consonance C–E and the mild dissonances C–D and D–E).
4. two consonances and one sharp dissonance:

5. one consonance, one mild dissonance, and one sharp dissonance:

6. one mild and two sharp dissonances:

Whether, in a three-tone chord, the intervals of five semitones...and six semitones...will assume the character of a consonance or of a dissonance depends on the third tone added. In the following table the chords containing the mentioned intervals are classified as "consonant", "mild", or "sharp", according to the influence exerted by the additional third tone.

Chords containing [five semitones]:

Chords containing [six semitones]:

The above clasification of chords does not involve any evaluation of their conformity to traditional ideas of "beauty" or "ugliness," or of their admissibility or usefulness in composition. From this catalogue of chords the student may learn nothing more than certain criteria by which to determine tension-degrees of chords in general. He should bear in mind that in practical composition the tension-degrees are subject to manifold variations, resulting from the position fo the intervals, dynamics, instrumentation, etc.

interval vectors) sorted into six *Krenek Groups* (K-groups, or simply K) corresponding to the numbered sections of Figure 3.6. Those in column A correspond to the chords shown in Krenek's Exx. 47–52, with the proviso that ic5 be represented by a seven-semitone interval or its compound:

Group	A	B
1 (cons.)	3-11[037] = ⟨001110⟩ 3-12[048] = ⟨000300⟩	3-10[036] = ⟨002001⟩
2	3-7[025] = ⟨011010⟩ 3-9[027] = ⟨010020⟩	3-8[026] = ⟨010101⟩
3	3-6[024] = ⟨020100⟩	
4	3-3[014] = ⟨101100⟩ 3-4[015] = ⟨100110⟩	
5 (mild)	3-2[013] = ⟨111000⟩	3-5[016] = ⟨100011⟩
6 (sharp)	3-1[012] = ⟨210000⟩	

Column B shows sets containing the "neutral" tritone (and, in 3-5[016], the contextually determined perfect fourth). These are further sorted into groups according to the presence of ics 1, 2, or 3/4 (i.e., sharp, mild, or consonant). Set class 3-10[036], for example, has neither ic1 nor 2, but does have ic3; it is, therefore, sorted into K1 by virtue of its consonance. 3-8[026] contains a mild dissonance, and thus is a K2 trichord; 3-5[016] is sharp and belongs to K5. Additionally, the stipulation that ic5 be expressed as seven semitones eventually falls away in Křenek's account, so that 3-11[037], for example, retains its group membership in first and second inversions. (The paragraph above Krenek's Ex. 53 describes this sorting rule.) In the end, Krenek's scheme makes fine, six-graded distinctions among trichords. Additional, finer-grained distinctions aren't undertaken, so the set/chords within each grade are unordered with respect to each other. One result: the diminished and augmented triads are of coequal rank with the traditionally supremely consonant major/minor triad.

Krenek does not treat four-part writing and its tetrachords, so the scheme does not continue past triads. It is not difficult to discover the serendipity of this limitation, since the number combinations of sharp and mild alone would dictate many more than six grades, creating fussy or overly subtle distinctions. Yet one could also see a different kind of effort, in which tetrachords expressing a characteristic trichord could "inherit" that trichord's grade. Thus [0347] would be a K4 chord because of its characteristic [014] subsets. But perhaps lower, on account of its perhaps equally characteristic 3-11[037] subsets. Since Krenek left no instructions, these and other extensions await testing.[7]

7. Bruner (1984) offers good empirical results to test the plausibility of Krenek's scheme.

Figure 3.7 Hindemith, Table of Chord Groups from *Craft of Musical Composition*

A Chords without Tritone

I Without seconds or sevenths

1 Root and bass tone are identical

2 Root lies above the bass tone

III Containing seconds or sevenths or both
1 Root and bass tone are identical

etc.

2 Root lies above the bass tone

etc.

V Indeterminate

Hindemith's system is most memorably represented as a table unfolded from the back cover of volume 1 of the *Craft of Musical Composition* (Hindemith 1937 [1942]). This table is transcribed in Figure 3.7. A quick (re)orientation is in order.

- Chords are divided according to the value of ic6 (tritone) in the chord's interval vector: no tritone = Group A; tritone(s) = Group B.
- The sequence of Roman numerals (NB not scale-degree signifiers!) zigzags downward between Groups A and B. In Hindemith's own analytic practice, the A/B designations were omitted, their information derivable from the odd/even distinction in the Roman-numeraled chord groups.
- The underlined descriptions connect this scheme to Krenek's: Note the sharp/mild distinction enacted here in the differences between groups II and IV.

Figure 3.7 (Continued)

B Chords containing Tritone

II <u>Without minor seconds or major sevenths</u>
<u>The tritone subordinate</u>

   a With minor seventh only (no major second)
      Root and bass tone are identical

   b Containing major seconds or minor sevenths or both

     1 Root and bass tone are identical

     2 Root lies above the bass tone

etc.

     3 Containing more than one tritone

etc.

IV <u>Containing minor seconds or major seconds or both</u>
<u>One or more tritones subordinate</u>

     1 Root and bass tone are identical

etc.

     2 Root lies above the bass tone

etc.

VI <u>Indeterminate. Tritone predominating</u>

- Groups V and VI depend on Hindemith's having imported considerations of chord-root location into this scheme—also signaled by the subgroups 1 and 2 for groups I–IV. Having indeterminate or questionable roots, the chords of groups V and VI have no 1/2 subgroups.

- Hindemith supplies model sonorities in musical notation. Easily overlooked is the subtle typography that indicates whether the model sonorities are the only ones available or whether there are more: a double bar for the former, and an *etc.* for the latter.

Hindemith's set of chords is much larger than Krenek's, revealing also how stretching to meet the demands of comprehensiveness makes for lumpier categories. The following table reproduces the earlier one and adds a column of Hindemith chord-group designations. The lack of sharp/mild distinction in the A-chords means that K6 3-1[012] and K2 3-7[025] are both A.III chords. Note, however, that K1 is made *less* lumpy in Hindemith's system, ostensibly on rootedness grounds. A wholly intended side effect is the isolation of the consonant triad 3-11[037] into its own group, A.I, with root position further distinguished by being the sole member of subgroup 1, the other two inversions lumped into subgroup 2. On the B side, the major-minor seventh chord is the sole inhabitant of II.a.

Group	A	B	Hindemith	
1 (cons.)	3-11[037] = ⟨001110⟩ 3-12[048] = ⟨000300⟩	3-10[036] = ⟨002001⟩	A.I,	B.VI
			A.V	
2	3-7[025] = ⟨011010⟩ 3-9[027] = ⟨010020⟩	3-8[026] = ⟨010101⟩	A.III	B.II
3	3-6[024] = ⟨020100⟩			
4	3-3[014] = ⟨101100⟩ 3-4[015] = ⟨100110⟩			
5 (mild)	3-2[013] = ⟨111000⟩	3-5[016] = ⟨100011⟩		B. IV
6 (sharp)	3-1[012] = ⟨210000⟩			

The table brings out the apparently *unsystematic* and asymmetrical membership categories of Hindemith's scheme. In group II, the "a/b" sorting is different from that in any other group, and a unique subgroup 3 (multiple tritones) is not used elsewhere. This is in addition to Group A's indifference to sharp/mild distinction—but which is the defining difference between groups B.II and B.IV. Wiegenfeld (1991) did the service of computing the total number of "Hindemith chords" (i.e., the complete set rather than a partial set with *etc.*). A pie chart, shown in Figure 3.8, shows the huge disparities in membership: a sliver for a few traditional triads and seventh chords, and a massive piece for all of the group IV chords.

Hindemith had some ideas about normative fluctuations—and actually more ideas about how to use chord-group fluctuation as a *diagnostic* for weak or insipid successions. In this respect, it is also tied into Krenek's program: using fluctuation as a pedagogical rather than an analytic tool. This is all the more apparent

Figure 3.8 Representation of chord distribution in Hindemith's system. Adapted from Wingenfeld 1991, 124–25

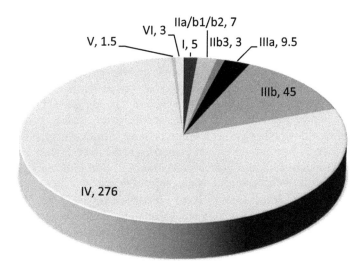

in Hindemith's well-known graphic analyses, found at the end of volume 1 of the *Craft*; his prosing of analytic results is meager, and no judgment calls are discussed, nor any fine points of practice. (His analysis of Schoenberg's op. 33a produced mostly group IV chords, for example, but this uniformity and lack of fluxion prompted no comment from him.)

Hindemith's chord groups have attracted periodic attention from composers and theorists. Luigi Nono used them in a spirit Krenek would have applauded—as a way of keeping track of harmonic effect in his serial music (Guerrero 2009)—and various tweaks of the groups have been proposed in Farrell (1971) and Wingenfeld (1991). These sympathetic readings contrast with the well-known critiques launched by Cazden (1954) and Landau (1961).[8]

More than Krenek's, Hindemith's harmonic-fluctuation scheme maintains contact with traditional scale-degree harmony, not only in its interest in chord-root location, but also in the asymmetry of the groups. The traditional authentic cadence is notated as IIa–Ia progression (as is its dual: the minor plagal with iv[add6]). Hindemith thus views harmonic fluctuation as a legacy feature; his updates and contemporary adaptations are generally backwards compatible, with landmarks from the common-practice system still used as guides, and the consonant triad 3-11[037] as the apex of perfection.[9]

8. Samplaski (2000, 74, 234) has a thorough summary of the "after-history" of Hindemith's theories.
9. The history of similar schemes after these two is a short one. Ulehla (1966), as we will see, developed a comprehensive and historically sensitive system based on complete chords (rather than on constituent intervals) and associated graphic representation to convey the "control of dissonance," but no publishing scholars adopted it. Persichetti (1961. 183) alludes to "texture tension" just once, with a suggestive diagram. Samplaski (2000) reviews some related efforts, notably that of Harris (1989, 77ff.) and Wolpert (1972, 84).

Ulehla's Style-based systems, and her tension graphs

Figure 3.4 introduced the basics Ludmilla Ulehla's tension graphs with her analysis of a passage from a Norman Dello Joio piano sonata. The urge to represent harmonic fluctuation in lines, shapes, and graphs is likely inspired by Hindemith's artwork, though Ulehla's use of musical staff is different and a pedagogical advantage to boot— that is, analysis can be done by hand on manuscript paper.[10] This urge likely points to a connection with other "continuous" secondary parameters in music, frequently indicated with artwork—the "hairpins" of *cresc.* and *dim.*, the dotted lines of a long *rall.*—which is to say that fluctuation is concerned with chord quality in context, as it occurs within a flow of other chords, lines, and events. Ulehla's own graphic practice was to draw step-functions—graphs of plateau and cliff—which mark changes as decisive and sudden rather than variably metamorphic, with smoother graphs having peaks and valleys. That nuanced refinement awaits.

Like Hindemith, Ulehla aspires to a comprehensive account of harmonic fluctuation; like Krenek, she is sensitive to how fluctuation is affected by stylistic rhetoric. Reconciling these interests, she proposes three styles of fluctuation. Figure 3.9 consolidates the key charts: fluctuation in the "classic" style (upper staff), the "impressionist" style (middle), and the "modern" (lower). The particulars of the degree assignments are not as rigorous as those in either Krenek's or Hindemith's systems, and they need not detain us here. So, too, for what counts as an "extension," and why some are named and others not. The confusion of degree functions (e.g., V^7, ii^7) and quality types (e.g., cluster, polychord) is likely not salutary for her overall scheme. Nevertheless, changes from "classic" to "impressionist" involve both merging and splitting of previous structures (making the scheme backwards compatible) as well as the deployment of new categories on various upper levels. The "modern" period relates likewise with its predecessor. Because she uses a standard staff to graph fluctuation, Ulehla has up to eleven possible slots to put chords (on, over, or underneath the five staff lines), but she doesn't strain to fill every opportunity, as in the upper part of the "modern" graph.

Ulehla's style-based scheme values backwards compatibility. The merge and splits of chord types from one period to the next—see the connecting lines between staves in Figure 3.4 for two examples—show previous distinctions lost and new ones made. This kind of process invites analysis of music showing marginal, blended, and transitional phases of such changes, as well as those perfectly exemplifying the proposed period-to-period differences. Compared to Krenek, Ulehla covers larger chords and more than a few of them, as well, but both agree about the causes of mild and sharp effects. The "carve out" for traditional practices, which Hindemith executed with chord group assignment, is in Ulehla enacted with idealized style types.

Toward more adequate measurements of harmonic fluctuation through chord voicing

Basics of both Krenek's and Hindemith's systems can be adequately described using interval class to cover definitions like Hindemith's Group B.IV, "containing

---

10. The same urge is acted on in Figure 3.9 of the present chapter. Persichetti (1961, 183) has similar artwork.

Figure 3.9 Keys to Ludmilla Ulehla's style-based tension graphs. Upper staff: the "Classical Period," adapted from her Ex.410a. Middle staff: the "Impressionistic Period," adapted from her Ex. 414a. Lower staff: "Modern Period" adapted from her Ex. 416a

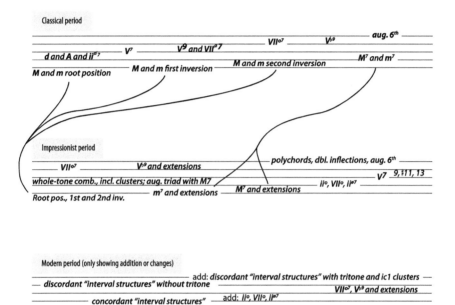

minor seconds or major sevenths or both," which is to say that B.IV contains chords with ic1. For this reason, it is easy to describe chords in terms of pitch-class sets (pcsets), as was done above. Though Ulehla's chords are defined more heterogeneously, and thus don't reduce to ic as easily, all three authors recognize that the actual effect of a chord resides in its realization through voicing—that is, from the disposition of pitches (rather than pitch classes) and their sounding with definite dynamics, timbre, etc. As Krenek (1940, 20) puts it, "in practical composition the tension-degrees are subject to manifold variations, resulting from the position of the intervals, dynamics, instrumentation, etc." (see also similar sentiments in Hindemith (1937 [1942], I:100.

While generally true, and something of a discouragement for further theorizing, the effects of voicing might be investigated, as existing rudimentary descriptions are ready at hand (open/close-position, *Lage*, doubling).[11] It is immediately apparent that strict mod12 interval-class concepts need to be nuanced by realizing them variously in real pitch intervals—that is, by distinguishing between a minor second, for example, and a major seventh (and, for that matter, a minor ninth and additional compounds).

11. Harrison (2014) covers the formalities involved in this enterprise as well as further pertinent considerations.

Figure 3.10 shows how this might be done, hypothesizing more or less distinct qualities for various voicings of ic1. The layout of the figure can helpfully be likened to that of a menu, with dishes characterized by the ic1 flavor arranged in rows (a) through (d), from the hottest and spiciest to the most lightly flavored. The orderings within rows are correct about extremities, with reasonably argued differences in taste about the middle. The middle of row (b) is very wide, while (c) and (d) are rather less so, with correspondingly wider extremities. In this way, putting distance between ic1-related pitches, as shown at (a), mitigates its pure sharpness to some degree at i[13], and to an appreciably greater degree at i[11].[12] Compounds of these intervals can reduce sharpness even further, though whether such large, unfilled intervals are heard chordally is open to question. An approach that considers them as stream-separated simultaneities—a relationship only of coincidence and not of harmonic mutuality—may be indicated. In general, octave separation of dissonating pitches reduces sharpness, with further and more dramatic reductions obtained through binding various consonances to them, filling the chord mass with buffers.

The filled-noteheads in row (b) show all potential consonant fills, those for sharper i[13] shown before duller i[11]. What counts for consonance is a note forming an "inside" ic3, 4, or 5 with the other notes of the unfilled interval; if it forms an ic6, a "B" marks the event, honoring the sense of Krenek and others that the presence of this interval in a chord must somehow be acknowledged or at least tracked. No additional "sharp" ic1s nor "mild" ic2s are permitted to disturb the consonant binder.

Row (c) shows more filling of the i[13] span with combinations of ics3, 4, and 5. These chords are analyzed into their successive pitch intervals as shown.[13] These all belong to a set of formal *chording intervals* that constitute traditional close-position chords, which is simply a space of i[3], i[4], or i[5] between any two pitches. While these (c) chords palpably moderate the effect of i[13], the first six also introduce "mild" ic2 dissonances, though voiced in the mildest form as i[10]. Moreover, the first four of those also have consecutive i[3]s in the chord stack. These can be understood as moderating fills of an i[6] gap. These are thus *potential* B-chords, in some voicing where the gap is exposed. This possibility is noted by italicizing the B. The last four chords are free of any of these complications.

Finally, chords for voicing ic1 as a filled i[11] are shown at (d). Little need be added after the previous comments, except to note that the final structure—a close-position MM7 chord—is claimed to be the voicing in which the effects of ic1 are the dullest. A session at the keyboard with all the others should confirm the presence of a sharp-to-dull gradient congruent with the one presented in the figure.

12. Ricci (2003) explains how i[13] is less mitigating than i[11] in jazz harmony, addressing directly the "avoid" status of the minor ninth and perfect eleventh over the bass note in standard accounts of chord voicing. His work connects to the "consecutive semitone constraint" developed by Tymoczko (1997) and applied in Zimmerman (2002).

13. The formalities of this notation were suggested in Chrisman (1977) and developed to the current point in Chapman (1981).

Figure 3.10 Voicings of ic1 in various chordal contexts, ordered from greatest to least "tension." (a) unfilled intervals; (b) i[13] and i[11] filled with one intermediating pitch from the set shown; (c) i[13] filled with multiple intermediating chord tones; (d) i[11] filled with multiple intermediating chord tones

(a)

(b)

(c)

(d)

For completeness's sake, Figure 3.11 offers a menu for ic2, the "mild" dissonance. Its flavor is most concentrated at (a), cut with an "inside" interval at (b), masked by other intervals at (c)—with only the final chord having a "pure" filled i[14]—and finally diluted to minimum strength at (d), the set of familiar minor seventh chords, with a single-fill 4th-chord relocated from its natural position at (b) on account of the chording-interval credentials, i[5,5], it shares with the others in (d).

The opening of Bernstein's *Chichester Psalms*, condensed and lightly annotated in Figure 3.12, shows one way to modulate the various flavors through the course of a phrase. An extra sharp hit on the opening chord, with an octave doubled i[1], gives way to progressively diluted mild chords before closing suddenly on a sharp i[11]. The second phrase, mm. 4–5, is strongly characterized by ic2, with an increased

Figure 3.11 Voicings of ic2 in various chordal contexts, ordered from greatest to least "tension." (a) unfilled intervals; (b) i[14] and i[10] filled with one intermediating pitch from the set shown; (c) i[14] filled with multiple intermediating chord tones; (d) i[10] filled with multiple intermediating chord tones

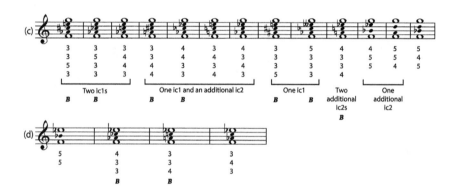

concentration of unfilled i[10]s at the end. The orchestral interlude here, rather than repeat, boosts tension further with i[2], punctuated by an unfilled extra sharp i[13]. The third and climactic phrase begins with another extra sharp hit on unfilled i[13] and i[11], followed by familiar dilutions of ic2 prefacing the concluding sharp i[11] on the downbeat of m. 8. The passage concludes with i[10]s, with a sharp i[11] (prepared by a noticeable i[2]) marking a syncopation into the long, phrase-ending chord.

For an instructive contrast, fluctuating through a wider range of sonority, Figure 3.13 analyzes the opening phrase of Germaine Tailleferre's violin sonata, noting, among other things, how ic1 and 2 are voiced as pitch intervals. The background here is much more relaxed than in the Bernstein excerpt, with a few well-placed sharp spikes punctuating a pervading mildness. The strategic handling of ic2 in the first two measures brings out a subtle undulation of tension, with a downbeated i[10] re-echoing at i[2] on the third beat, falling into profound i[26] and i[34] with C♯₂ in m. 2, with a final, barely registering pass through i[26] and i[22] on the third beat of that measure. This pattern repeats in mm. 3–4, much like a sentential basic idea, though an unexpected high concentration of i[2] breaks the symmetry at the end, closing off the presentation-phase of the phrase. Measures 5–7 contrast markedly, with eruptions of extra sharp i[13] and [1] over a new background of tritone-infused B chords. This transition exits to a non-chordal

Figure 3.12 Leonard Bernstein, *Chichester Psalms*, I. Instrumental reduction of mm. 1–10, with sharp and mild pitch intervals labeled between the staves. The bottom line shows bass-to-tenor interval, and the top line shows any additional sharp or mild interval. Stars mark chords with ic1

pentatonic melody in m. 8, which in the next measure acquires chords as well as extraneous pitches. In m. 10, a spike in tension and texture ("fifth thickening" in the bass staff) accompany a determined contrary-motion wedge, the goal of which is signaled by the sudden drop to soft, pure major-triad levels at the end of the measure—an effective use of cadential-fluctuation rhetoric to mark the quick, nearly breathless end of the first phrase, which subsequently tumbles into a lengthy transition section, the first few beats of which are shown in the figure.

Taking initial bearings from the two quite different compositions, by Bernstein and Tailleferre, sensitivity to chord voicing, registration, and density seems the best general approach, making special note of the distribution of sharp and mild features. The "menu templates" of Figures 3.10 and 3.11 suggest recognizing a few different flavor profiles for both, singly and in combination. The functional distinction between chords with ic6 and those without, so generative of CP procedures, may also be in play and can be monitored separately. All these can be brought to bear on a larger span of music, the fifth movement of Messiaen's *Quatuor pour la Fin du Temps*, which gives an idea of potentials for fluctuation schemes to interact with form. Figure 3.14 annotates a condensed score of the work. The octatonic macro-harmony of the work is well known and celebrated, with the derivation of pitches

Figure 3.13 Germaine Tailleferre, Sonata for violin and piano (1923), I, mm. 1–11

and chords seemingly explained therefrom (see Lester 1989, 165). The analysis in Figure 3.14 shows the strategic deployment of those chords according to tension value, highlighting usages of sharp and mild interval-classes as consecutive intervals in chords, as moderated by their pitch realization. All piano-interval chord measurements are shown (below the bottom staff); piano-with-cello intervals are shown selectively—generally, those that register mild and sharp values. A cursory look reveals that ic2 is realized in three progressively weaker concentrations, i[2] and unfilled i[10] and i[14]; ic1, on the other hand, is only realized as i[11]. The importance of i[6] as a contrastive agent is also evident, as is the intensive use of i[4] as part of a climactic scheme in mm. 23–26 (section C_2 in the figure).

The opening section, mm. 1–6, is analyzed in some detail, using chord labels for traditional CP-functional chords, and set-class labels for nontraditional. The general rise in tension from traditionally consonant E major triad to the atonally relevant all-interval tetrachord 4-z29[0137] is represented by positions of the chord labels as well as by the thickness of any borders labels might have. (Differences in shape, by contrast, have no bearing on tension, being influenced instead by any need to "point" the label to the event.) Chords labeled above the top staff can be realized as B-relations (and the downbeat chord of m. 5 is actually so, with an i[6] between cello and lower-staff piano). Those between the piano staves, having no ic6, thus have no B-realizations.

The downbeat of m. 4, i[9,8,10] is further analyzed to show how ic6 is voiced—as an i[18] filled slightly on the undertone side of middle as i[8,10] (smaller interval below larger one). Some other voicings of ic6 are shown similarly elsewhere in the figure. The entire pitch distribution is i[9,8,10], a near even trisection of the size-27 pitch space. For technical reasons that would distract instead of clarify at this point, I will forgo demonstration of the *inversional dispersal* relationship to some set of chording intervals—in this case i[3,2,4] in a size-9 space—which provides the means of recognizing and analyzing relationships among various spacings a chord might scale to. I will rely instead upon the well-founded intuition that i[9,8,10] is an "open voiced" form of i[3,2,4].

Further to this point, the piano part in this piece treats spacing as a coordinate of form. Only in m. 17, halfway through the piece, does an interval smaller than i[6] appear, and this event heralds new, comparatively thicker and tritone-rich chords that initiate a climactic run-up that slows temporarily at m. 22 (making an intrasectional seam, noted on the figure), but then regathers energy for discharge on m. 27. Note the consistent high pitch density to this point from the starting point in m. 17.

The outliers in the chord-density scheme are instructive to note. The end of section C_{-1} (in m. 21) redeploys a wide configuration from the end of A_{-2} in m. 12—itself a variant of an established ic2 and 6 association noted in m. 5. Here, it is boosted by an additional mild relationship with the cello. The event separates dense massings of i[6,3]s in the previous measures from the equally dense i[5,4]s of the upcoming one, reprising the role as an unfulfilled penultimate configuration it played at the conclusion of section A_{-2} (m. 12) and will play again at m. 30, and finally—restored to a fulfilling penultimate position—in m. 32.

Owing to the *subito piano* at m. 27 that suggests a dramatically sudden and completely draining discharge, the emergence of a new low-tension equilibrious state

Figure 3.14 Messiaen, "Louange à l'Éternité de Jésus," from *Quatuor pour la Fin du Temps*. Analytic transcription. Pitch intervals of piano part shown below bass staff. Sharp and mild intervals between piano and cello are shown between staves, along with select consonances. No border around a chord label means no ic1 or ic2 in the chord; a solid border indicates an ic2; a thick border, ic1

Figure 3.14 (Continued)

is reasonably heard as Messiaen's depiction of heavenly bliss.[14] The reattainment of dispersed spacing there is made more profound by an 8vb reinforcement for the lowest pitch. Rounding out these observations by way of returning to the detail of the opening section, I suggest the sudden drop-off in tension at m. 27 is of a piece with that in m. 6, where the B-chord i[7,9,2]—whose tension was also attained in stages— discharged *subito* to a pair of low-tension major triads, the first in comparatively tense, $^6_4$ position, and the second in relaxed and overtonally clear root position.

14. An compositional alternative for m. 27 that doesn't use the scheme includes continued close-positioned, tritone- and ic[2] chords (perhaps just one), dynamic peaking at, say, *ƒƒƒ*. Various continuations from thence can be imagined—no let up until a grand pause (*abruptio*), gradual unwinding in stages, etc.

The remaining annotations in Figure 3.14 highlight other features of the generalized fluctuation scheme, which executes a gradual tensioning to quick-release points, including the substitution of sharp for mild from section $A._1$ to $A._2$ (dotted arrow); the set-up of the ic2 and 6 association as an articulation function in the form (dotted box, with arrow to another voicing); a series of the same interval (solid underlines); and the "dotted-line relationships" of prominent sharp and mild intervals. Not all suggestive and interesting detail is included (chord labels, for example), nor are other harmonic-fluctuation events identified in the detail provided for mm. 1–6 (except for a suggestion about the final measures). The reader is invited to pursue these at leisure, and to consider further refinements and applications of harmonic fluctuation as a shaping force in contemporary tonal music.

Meter

Many of the preceding musical excerpts are characterized by metric plasticity and corresponding loss of an isochronic consistency at higher levels. Shifting meter is the outward sign, which, in the case of Messiaen, reduces nearly to a single level of pulsing sixteenth notes in the piano part. This kind of highly attenuated metricity is arguably pioneered in Wagner's famous *Tristan Prelude*, where it is far less noted than the work's harmonic achievements. Even after m. 17 in that piece, where the slow compound meter can be sensed gently rippling beneath the surface, a habitual weakening of downbeats with agogically accented second beats suggests that the meter is more useful for the performers as a coordinating device than it is for listeners as a felt experience. In other words, the time signature is more a script direction than a palpable quality of the setting.

The increasing plasticity of rhythm and meter in nineteenth-century composition is a version of the same pressure on the CP enclosure that led to the emancipation of the dissonance—in this case, leading to the overthrow of the "tyranny of the bar line," to cite Stravinsky's apposite phrase.[15] Henry Pleasants (1969, 65), developing lines of argument first laid out in his controversial *The Agony of Modern Music* (1955), described it thusly:

> The dramatic, reflective and recitative character of nineteenth-century Serious music exacted a price in rhythmic debility, and the cost is conspicuous in most contemporary Serious music, especially in the dodecaphonic, which often seems incapable of any movement or rhythmic buoyancy at all. The dynamic faculty of tempo changes, both sudden and gradual, and all the dramatic inflection inherent in various types of acceleration and retardation, while they served an "interpretive" or expressive purpose in European music, also contributed to the weakening of the beat as a phenomenon collectively anticipated and collectively experienced.

15. Thanks to Gretchen Horlacher, who suggested Correspondent (1921) as the source of this phrase.

In Pleasant's earlier book (1955), this argument is made, much more tendentiously, in a chapter titled "The Crisis of Rhythm" (122–36). Despite his somewhat over-wrought tone, blanket condemnations, and eagerness to play the vigorous reaction-ary, Pleasants accurately predicted in both books the cultural sidelining—in the United States, at least—of "Serious" classical music in favor of new forms of popular music. (His consistent capitalization of "Serious" is an ironic affectation.) In a cir-cumstance that Pleasants probably would have applauded, the chief organs of cul-tural criticism currently devote at least as much space to popular music as they do to classical. Certain forms of popular music are, in fact, the "Serious" music of our time. To understand Pleasants's prophetic critique in the most sympathetic light, one need only consider episodes in the history of the Pulitzer Prize in Music. Instructive cases are 1965, when Duke Ellington was denied the prize on the apparent grounds that his wasn't a serious music at all, and 1997, when Wynton Marsalis's prize was taken as something of an affront by some academic composers. In hindsight, Pleasants's reading of the art-music situation placed too much responsibility on the music itself, ignoring other cultural changes that, for example, changed audience behavior in the concert hall or that rejected the marketing of classical music as uplift.

One cause of this rhythmic "debility" was the relegation of dance-inspired music to the lower divisions of mere entertainment, which was nearly complete by the end of the nineteenth century, with only the waltz maintaining consistent contact with the premier, "serious" league.[16] Social dance forms and their topics—the foundations of important early CP genres such as the suite and the variation set—had comparatively little if any influence on the rhythmic structures of late CP composition. (Ballet is the important exception, but compared with opera, say, it did not influence techniques of music composition and was moreover associated by then with Russian taste in art.) As dance music went downmarket, it eventually gained enough distance to satirize rhythmically enervated "serious" music such as Wagner's; examples include the *Tristan* quotations in Debussy's well-known "Golliwogg's Cakewalk" (1908) and in Chabrier's quadrille *Souvenirs de Munich* (1886). In the end, dissonance was emancipated, bar line tyranny overthrown, and dance music relegated, all at roughly the same time in the early twentieth century, which made possible metrically free atonal styles that were essayed afterwards.[17]

Yet dance music—specifically, of the American popular variety—gained a foot-hold in Serious composition after World War I in the "Parisian Jazz" works of Darius Milhaud, Bohuslav Martinů, and others, the deconstructive readings of Hindemith's *Suite 1922* and Stravinsky's *Piano-Rag-Music*, and in the successful careers of "cross-over" composers such as George Gershwin and Kurt Weill. Just as increased pressure for emancipation of dissonance engendered the equal-and-opposite reaction of float-ing triads (i.e., the emancipation of the consonance), pressure for overthrow of the bar

16. Eastern European dance topics—essentially a form of near-abroad exotica for cultured Westerners—also had a place in Serious music repertory, as in, for example, Brahms's *Hungarian Dances* and Dvořák's *Slavonic Dances*.

17. Christopher Hasty has attempted to read meter in this music, most sensitively in his analysis of Webern's *Quartet*, op. 22, in Hasty (1997, 257ff.). He cautions, however, that "especially striking here is the lack of a clear pulse. Indeed the projective field is so volatile there might be some ques-tion whether this music is genuinely metrical."

line created an opening for composing with increased submission to it. Composers who were receptive to new dance rhythms created the main line of overtonal settlement beyond the common-practice enclosure that we are currently surveying, for the "re-metricization of serious music" crucially enables the application of traditional rhetoric and the concentration upon harmonic fluctuation in the closer-in districts; it is the food source of the ecosystem, the breadbasket of the region.

We explore it by focusing on compositional techniques that give meter great power to create or control overtonal hierarchy. These techniques, as Pleasants recognized, are practiced most thoroughly in popular music styles, and by the mid-1960s, rock music had become the leading example, often using deep and highly coordinated metrical hierarchies that, to classical musicians and others, seemed simplistic, repetitive, and oversexualized. In such structures, the accumulation of accents—from submetrical strong pulses all the way up to hypermetrical downbeats—creates a metrical hierarchy analogous to that of a tonal hierarchy, with the highest-level accent a kind of metrical "tonic." That is, the very large downbeat, which might occur infrequently during some musical span of a few minutes' length (i.e., the duration of most typical popular songs), can be a focal point of musical structure. While the analogy is, of course, inexact, it is strong enough to support a wholesale unloading of overtonal pitch relationships onto the metric grid such that harmonic fluctuation among chords of identical quality can be made to happen through metric and other means. For example, KC and the Sunshine Band's disco hit "Keep It Comin' Love" (1976) toggles between two chords, A♭M and B♭M, for the song's entire four-minute duration.[18] The chord pair is fitted within a four-measure groove that remains constant throughout. Two groove-units form eight-measure choruses, which alternate with eight-measure verses. Certain aspects of the lyrics—a refrain "don't stop it now" and a climactic, satisfied sigh at 2:08—tonicize the B♭M chord, making the A♭M chord a ♭VII anacrusis, a venerable harmonic formula in rock. Developing this metric relationship further, the song is organized iambically in a consistent way—even the first half (up to 2:02) seems to be an anacrusis for the second half, which contains only choruses and whose arrival is punctuated by that satisfied sigh.

A more revealing case of the power of meter to construct overtonal structure is Neil Diamond's "Cherry Cherry" (1966). Its formal structure is unusually complex for a pop song, as the timeline chart in Figure 3.15 reveals.[19] The song consistently builds on its four-measure units to create eight- and sixteen-measure sections. (On two occasions, marked with "2," the phrases are cut short by half, shortening the higher-order groupings accordingly. The rhetorical effect of this *ellipsis* is to create a "rush" into the chorus.) The timeline gives the impression that the song is a standard verse-chorus configuration, but the disposition of verses and chorus is actually quite nonstandard and is the basis of overtonal issue at hand. Like "Keep It Comin' Love," "Cherry Cherry" has a restricted chord vocabulary—in this case, just three chords, EM, AM, and DM, which are cycled in two different ways, with either

18. Both chords are consistently embellished with upper neighbors to the fifth and octave, to the point where it's possible to consider the chords as added-note structures.

19. This graphic was originally created by the Variations Audio Timeliner, developed at Indiana University. http://www.dlib.indiana.edu/projects/variations3/software.html.

Figure 3.15 Neil Diamond, "Cherry Cherry," form diagram

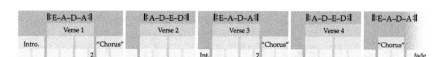

E or A as tonic. Figure 3.16 transcribes the eight-measure introduction, in which E is placed in the opening tonic slot of a familiar double-plagal riff, E–A–D–A.[20] This riff supports the odd-numbered verses as well as what passes for a chorus—an eight-measure unit with lyric invariance and focus on title-text. The twenty-five-second verse-chorus module is then followed by a contrasting verse of roughly the same length, based on a groove shown in Figure 3.17.[21] This groove, a permutation of the original, has A in the opening tonic slot—but no harmonic preparation, transition, or modulation, warned of this change.[22] It happens from the expectation of a hypermetric/formal event of some importance to follow the sixteen (minus 2) measures of verse and the eight measures of chorus, completion of which usually marks the end of a large cycle. At such a moment, norms and expectations built up by the previous cycle are easily reset, though usually back to original configuration (as, for example, in a first ending repeat or transitional bridge). Here, the reset is to a different configuration of the same three chords, and the "modulation" is thus achieved without any work needed from the harmonic dimension.

In danceable rock music like "Keep It Comin' Love" and "Cherry Cherry," the exceptionally deep and regular metrical hierarchy minimizes the felt differences among pulse, meter, and hypermeter. This kind of superstrong hierarchy is essentially a "metric dronality," and just as pitch dronality enables intonational freedom, metrical dronality enables exceptional rhythmic freedom in the form of consistent syncopation, accented backbeats, and—at the micropulse level—the ability to be "on top of" or "behind" the beat that characterizes the best jazz and rock drummers.[23] Coupled metric-overtonal dronalities is a feature of "heavier" styles of rock music, such as adduced in chapter 2. It is also, famously, a feature of certain minimalist works, as in Steve Reich's *Octet*, to be discussed in chapter 4. In both cases, harmonic fluctuation is strongly attenuated—in the Reich, practically to zero.

20. The verse riff of The Romantics' "What I Like About You" (1979) makes an excellent comparison—same chords, roughly the same tempo, and similar groove. A general framework for this kind of chord usage is provided in Biamonte (2010).

21. Some analysts would prefer to call this section a bridge, a catchall term for any module that isn't a verse, chorus, prechorus, or other standardized formal function. The size/duration of this section, the variant lyrics in each of its iterations, and the "hookiness" of the riff militate against that label. I suggest instead that the song has two different verse types.

22. Careful listeners can hear that the E–A–D–A cycle is changed to E–A–D–E at the last second in the chorus, thus providing a bit of tonicization into A at the beginning of the A–D–E–D cycle. This is more easily heard on the live album *Hot August Night* [1972] than it is on the original 1966 studio version. However, even the best Internet transcribers and tab-makers ignore the change as unimportant.

23. The landmark article that brought these issues to the attention of composers and arrangers is Stewart (1987).

Figure 3.16 Neil Diamond, "Cherry Cherry," Introduction

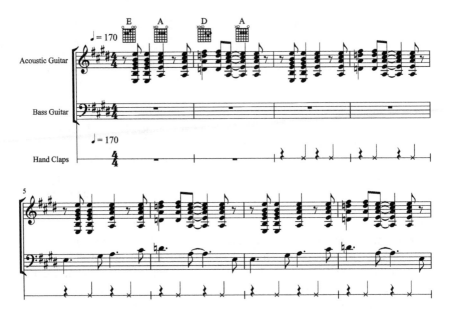

Figure 3.17 Neil Diamond, "Cherry Cherry," secondary verse groove

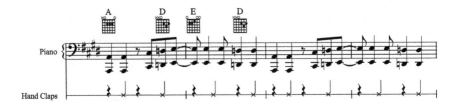

By now, it should be clear that what is meant by "meter" here is neither the basic, "has a time signature" sense nor a highly theorized or psychologized musical quality that sustains book-length exploration. "Meter is first and foremost grounded in the perception and production of a pulse or *tactus*" (London 2004, 17). And it is this periodic, isochronic pulsing, along with the possibilities for nesting above and below (that is, levels of periodicity) that is the basic condition of this outlying district and which is essential to the ecosystem of the inner rings of harmonic fluctuation and traditional rhetoric. Most theories of meter require more than one level, in order to perceive strong/weak beats,[24] and this condition is indeed normative in

---

24. "At minimum, a metrical pattern requires a tactus coordinated with one other level of organization," London (2004, 17). This stipulation leaves single-level pulsing in limbo—neither metrical nor (from a listener's perspective) ametrical. Pulsing is closer to meter than no pulsing whatsoever, so it is here incorporated as a metrical entity, albeit a special one.

most common-practice styles. Stripping down to one level, however, is a character-istic technique of contemporary tonal practice, where it communicates unfettered rhythmic vitality without deference to hierarchical control. The *locus classicus* is the "Dances of the Young Girls" in Stravinsky's *The Rite of Spring*, where "unpredictable" accents in a regular pulse stream produce a sense of ametricity in an environment of pulse. This effect has funded a variety of contemporary metrical practices—asymmetrical and irregular meter, shifting meter, polymeter, and the like.

These features were on display in musical excerpts analyzed in the previous section, by Bernstein, Tailleferre, and Messiaen (figs. 3.12–14), which showed harmonic fluctuation operating without much influence from metric hierar-chies. In contrast, the popular-music examples minimize fluctuation (chord-quality change) and create tonic accent largely from such metric hierarchies. Of the countless examples of middle cases, the passage shown in Figure 3.18, from Schoenberg's organ variations, op. 40, is particularly informative. It is highly chro-matic and constructed according to strict pitch transformations, yet it is shaped by a metric hierarchy unusually deep for Schoenberg. Along with the *Variations for Band*, op. 43, this earlier set for organ highlights compositional techniques that Schoenberg had earlier employed in works like the op. 9 *Chamber Symphony* and the op. 13 motet *Friede auf Erden*. The choice to revive these techniques forty years later, in light of his experiences with expressionist and serial techniques, is a curi-ous feature of these two works. That the theme given for the organ variations is a recitative gives a strong clue about the rhythmic freedom afforded the organ work, which is typical of his practice for twelve-tone keyboard compositions. It is also found in Schoenberg's source models for organ writing in Max Reger's works from the early 1900s. Harrison (2004) explores this connection in detail. In this context, variation 5 (mm. 56–66), which is excerpted in Figure 3.18, is a notable exception because of a refreshing excursion into a well-articulated and deep metric hierar-chy—yet also one that accommodates high aggregate turnover, unlike the penta-tonic rock systems considered earlier. The highly chromatic pitch environment notwithstanding, this metric hierarchy is the main reason a palpable overtonality emerges at this point in the composition.

Before considering an excerpt, we should get oriented to the metric environ-ment of the previous passage, which will help us appreciate how the overtonality is supported. The twelve measures prior to the excerpt are in a slow and metri-cally subtle $\frac{12}{8}$. Shortly before the beginning of the excerpt, subtlety is pushed into obscurity, culminating in a *molto rit.* in m. 55 that coincides with an "unhearable" time change to $\frac{4}{4}$. The complete metric unpredictability here works using rhetoric appropriate to "introducing the next idea." This idea is shown in Figure 3.18.

Coming off the previous metric atrophy, the opening of variation 5 snaps along with clear motoric rhythm at the sixteenth, marked in lowest level of the "dot notation" at the top of the figure.[25] Each measure of the excerpt is technically divided in half by a nearly strict inversion around the pitch D_4. (In fig. 3.18, extra whitespace in the middle of beat 2 makes it easy to identify this inversional "dou-ble counterpoint.") In keeping with the recitative theme—the first notes of which,

25. See Lerdahl and Jackendoff (1983, 68ff.).

Figure 3.18 Schoenberg, *Variations on a Recitative*, op. 40, mm. 56–59, with analytic overlay

D, A, G♯, can be spotted in the lower stave—the two halves are grouped by pickup beats: eighth-note anacruses to strong beats 1 and 3.

The shaded columns in the figure highlight recurring instances of low-tension major/minor triads on beats 2 and 4 of each measure. For the first two measures (56–57), they are G♯ minor and C♯/D♭ major, respectively, this difference being symbolized by different corner-shapes for the columns. In the next measure, relative-related triads are deployed on opposite beats, as shown in the figure. The enharmonic problems here suggest that we use pc integers for convenience, thus substituting for the C♭ at the end of m. 59, pcset {B,3,6} and pcset {8,B,3} for the G♯.[26] The last measure (59) places familiar but now "decorated" triads in new modes: the fourth-beated C♯ major {1,5,8} of the first two measures is here slotted into beat two and paralleled into minor {1,4,8}, with pc 5 now sounding like an unemancipated appoggiatura. Similarly, G♯ minor of the opening now finishes as major {8,0,3}, with pc B performing the same appoggiatura role at beat 4, according to the inversional scheme. It is a telling touch that this play with parallel relations at the end of the phrase harks back to the opening pickup of the passage, where a D-major chord turns minor on the second sixteenth.

Other passing triads, such as C major {0,4,7} on beat of m. 59, are heard elsewhere in different form in another measure *on the same beat*, such as the right hand {0,4,7} at the corresponding spot in m. 56. (The inversional scheme dictates that an A minor {9,0,4} appear in the corresponding beats 3 of these measures.) These triads pop out of the texture as consonant contrasts (resolutions!) to strong-beated dissonances. These dissonances are contrived as stepwise displacements of the triad notes which, as Ernst Kurth would hear, give them a certain kind of leading-tone energy that can be discharged onto the triad.[27] The chords formed by these insertions can be tuned to various levels of discharging dissonance. For example, at the beginning of m. 58, the {0,6,B} left-hand B-chord contains both a prominent ic6 and an ic1 softened as i[11]. The notes involved discharge onto the B♭ triad on beat 2. The right-hand A-chord figuration there is spread similarly but more mildly voiced, with neither ic[6] nor ic[1] but overtonally stronger ic[5]s along with a mild ic[2] softened as i[10]. These discharge onto B♭, too, but in the opposite direction from the left-hand. (All this is inverted in the second half of the measure.) Some inspection of the materials adjacent to the shaded columns in the figure will bring out other similarly structured "displacement-dissonance chords."[28]

Figure 3.19 schematizes the situation, with the pcs of the weak-beated consonances of mm. 56–58 arrayed on the outer circle and those of the strong-beated dissonances in the inner. Paths of semitone discharge, converging on pcs in the outer ring, are indicated. Some pcs in the inner ring can discharge in either direction; they're connected by gray lines through the center of the figure. The general

---

26. There are some interesting observations to be made about the choice of accidentals in this passage, but this footnote is too short to contain them.

27. Rothfarb (1988, chap. 8) summarizes the ideas involved. After Kurth, more original work along these lines is in Erpf (1927 [1969], 55–57).

28. This harmonic and voice-leading technique is discussed in Roeder (1989), and given a broader context in Schoenberg's practice in Lewin (1968).

Figure 3.19 Partition of pitch-class function in Schoenberg, op. 40, mm. 56 ff

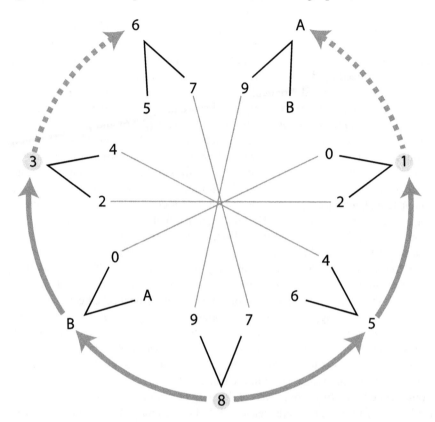

inversional situation is marked by arrows emanating from pc 8, the other end of an inversional axis involving pc 2 (realized in the passage as D_4). Any triad described on the outer circle can be approached by some semitonally displaced trichord built from inner-ring pcs. Options on offer include sets with mild characteristics, as in mm. 56–57 (though, in the latter measure, boosted slightly with a sharp passing event on the fourth sixteenth of beats 1 and 3) as well as sharper approaches from B-chorded 3-5[016] in m. 58.

The partition of pcs into familiar functional categories of consonant chords and variously dissonant other entities is basic to harmonic fluctuation. Schoenberg uses an additional, metrical partition to activate this scheme by consistently locating the chord types on a metrical grid—strong-beated appoggiatura chords discharging upon weak-beated consonances. The phrase following the excerpt in the figure gradually dissolves this partition partnership. Briefly put, it introduces faster rhythms to the sixteenth-note motor and releases the pitch-inversion constraint (m. 61). Starting in m. 64, it reintroduces the metric unpredictability that characterized the lead-in to variation 5. By m. 67, Variation 6, notated in a rhythmically and metrically free $^6_8$ typical of the rest of the work, takes over.

Linearity

For as pure and compelling an instance of overtonality to be found in a nontonal environment, consult Figure 3.20. If you have seen a movie in the last thirty years, you have undoubtedly heard this before the feature presentation in "THX certified" theaters.[29] The impression it makes is memorable: from a random beginning, with pitches in apparent Brownian motion, some kind of harmonic vibration is introduced into the flux, which then drives pitches onto powerfully overtonal nodes, determined precisely (in Hz) as a just-intonation timbre/chord hybrid (cf. Spectralism), detuned slightly in order to "shimmer" the sound.

What is this "harmonic vibration" imposed on inchoate, purposeless tones? It is easily experienced as tendency or (more urgently) drive toward overtonal hierarchy. As the drive kicks in, the emergence of purpose, direction, and coordination is easily felt. In the beginning: a dense, wiggly mass of thirty pitches confined within a 200 Hz bandwidth; at the end: a lighter yet immeasurably more stable unitary chord/timbre/pitch whose thirty elements are flung out over eight times the space. It is as close an instance of an ecstatic *fiat tonica!* as could be composed.

Consulting the moving image accompanying this soundtrack clip, we see a white sans serif text on a black background announcing a rare, once-in-thirty-five-years event: a new sound system for theaters. The wiggly mass is now coded with buzzing expectation. As linear direction emerges from the Brownian motion of tones, the capabilities of the THX system are unveiled as side-mounted speakers in the theater are turned on, revealing also a huge increase in wattage of the entire sound system as well as vastly improved speakers themselves—including, significantly, powerful subwoofers that could reach the 37.5 Hz bass final. The coordinated effects of moving image and sound here set up expectations for a similarly coordinated "big reveal" moment, the *telos* of the gesture. As the final chord is reached, the THX logo fades in, unexpectedly glowing blue and arted-up in other ways as well. All this is an extremely clear cue for affirmation, victory, achievement, and assertion. It is hard to think of making all this even stronger, so overdetermined is the effect from the tight linkage of all compositional techniques here, including multimedia ones as well.

There is some more to be said about the impression this advertisement made in its time. In the increasingly smaller movie theaters of 1980s America, having a system capable of delivering a well-provisioned 37.5 Hz signal could produce tingly, "touch" effects on the body, and so part of the THX system "reveal" was an exciting, combined "sight-sound-touch" movie-going experience that was as different from before as home-theater system is to a single-speaker TV. The overall effect was likely stunning to first-time audiences (especially older people who hadn't experienced the sound pressures of youth-oriented rock shows). Tellingly,

---

29. The clip can be heard at https://youtu.be/pOSPgmRKngY. [Nov. 2012] The score in the figure is what the composer, James A. Moorer, used to register the piece for copyright, but the originating document is actually a computer program.

Figure 3.20 James A. Moorer, "THX logo theme." Courtesy of James A. Moorer and THX Ltd.

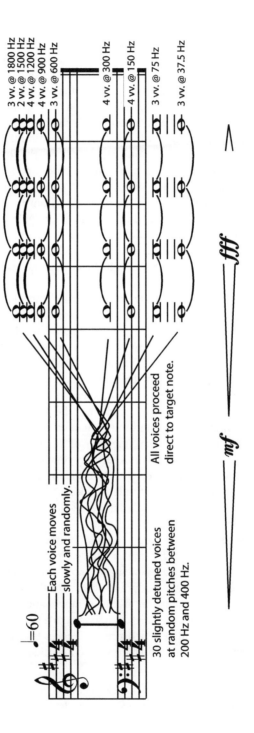

it got named *and trademarked* as the "Deep Note."[30] Further, as the penultimate number in the buildup to the feature presentation, the THX advertisement likely set up a tingly, wiggly vibration of expectation to hear these effects in the feature film itself—which, designed for the capabilities of the system, were spectacular: at the Los Angeles premiere, the feature was *Return of the Jedi*.

If the Deep Note has inarguable claims to tonic in this piece, these are suggested by activity in the composition, which is to say that the artwork has an event hierarchy that manages fully to illuminate the tonal hierarchy. This is common practice in traditional tonality, in which the tonic note is marked as hoped-for, and pleasantly and not too frequently satisfied at certain points in the piece, often preceded by the articulation signals of authentic cadence. Generalizing the practice, Wallace Berry (1976, 27) wrote, "the tonal system consists of a hierarchic ordering of [pitch class] factors, with the tonic (final, axis, center, etc.) the ultimate point of relationship which tonal successions are contrived to 'expect.'" By this measure, the THX theme is so compelling because it strives to maximize both elements. Disorganized and restless, definitely and undeniably out of equilibrium, the pitches of the opening are contrived to move directly into equilibrious, superstable relationships with the 37.5 Hz, "deep note" final. Listeners may have no reason to "expect" this final, especially given the confused opening state, but upon reaching it, should have no trouble recognizing a compulsion of the pitches toward it. All this is confirmed when the volume reaches what Moorer notated as *ff* but which moviegoers frequently experience as a ne plus ultra of decibel level.[31]

Figure 3.20 transcribes the THX logo using mostly conventional staff notation, with some text annotations given to specify procedures staff notation cannot represent (e.g. "Each voice moves slowly and randomly").[32] Although this direction is understandable and describes the activity adequately, Moorer supplements it with an unconventional staff-notation element that more perfectly conveys the action: line segments that begin as squiggles, then straighten out to vector onto their target notes. Thus materializes the metaphor of "line" that describes the grouping effect of close-ordered pitch succession. In the case of the THX logo, the pitch succession is created by a continuous function acting on real numbers, producing a glissade. (In geometry, such a function is actually represented by a line, so Moorer's visual supplement is particularly apt.) More common in music is "motion" to and from discrete pitch points, as on a scale, but it turns out that we are easily able to "connect the dots" mentally (thanks to Gestalt qualities of pitch cognition) and understand these successions as linear, too.[33]

The THX logo is an instance of nearly unalloyed *Linearity* contriving to make the root of a very simple overtonal system. More specifically, it takes a *curvilinear* form here, having short-term successions that create an impression of a shaped,

---

30. "Deep note" is THX Ltd.'s characterization of the final sonority. See http://www.thx.com/about-us/the-story-of-deep-note/.
31. One (illegal) transcriber of this theme put the dynamic level at *fffff* and added "fuck, yeah!" Details available upon request.
32. This score is based on one provided to me by the composer, to whom I'm indebted for the courtesy.
33. Zuckerkandl (1956, 75–148) offers an extended discussion of the matter.

directed line from place to place in pitch space. A typical melody or tune is cur-vilinear, as are other mostly conjunct pitch successions—including not least uni-directional scale segments (i.e., "straight lines," which are indeed curves in the geometric sense). The fundamental preference for curvilinearity in pre-twentieth-century Western musics is exemplified by the cantus firmus used in species counterpoint—a line made up of pitches connected mostly by conjunct motion in variously ascending and descending directions.

Not all musical lines are best described as curves. *Rectilinearity* describes a rarer but distinctive impression of melodic strata created by pitch successions of zero-to-minimal slope and narrow register. Extensive repetition of pitch or pitch-cells is a common expression of it, as are psalm recitation tones, extended pedal points, *concitato* figuration, and tremolo effects (including trills), to take a few examples from music history. Rectilinearity was until the twentieth century largely a special effect in Western music, a relief from default curvilinearity. As all these examples suggest, rectilinearity thrives at extremes of rhythmic activity. On one side, it is a leading feature of highly rhythmicized, groove-based styles, such as in many minimalist compositions, not to mention contemporary pop songs. On the other side, rectilinearity can also be presented in highly unrhythmicized environ-ments, in which the repetition of pitch is replaced by remarkably elongated sonor-ity, such as a pedal tone. Extreme cases are found in the organum sections of Notre Dame polyphony. Any further immobilization of a musical line leads to dronality.

A particularly clear and suggestive example of unrhythmicized rectilinearity is Messiaen's *Apparition de l'Église Éternelle* (1932). Figure 3.21 shows mm. 25–37, in which eighth notes last a little over a second each. Thus, the long notes at the end of the anapestic motive—those in mm. 26, 27, 29, 31, and especially 33–37— seem like immobile blocks of sound granite. (The chord of mm. 33–37 lasts for twenty seconds.) Although the visual impression of the figure suggests curvilin-earity, since the pitch-to-pitch motion is stepwise or minimally disjunct, the abso-lute effect of each chord—the sense that immobility is the rule and change the exception—removes the essential curvilinear quality of directed motion. Instead of moving lines, the pitch successions are a series of plateaus.[34]

A contrasting treatment is heard in the opening of Steve Reich's *Octet*, shown in Figure 4.18 (chap. 4, p. 125) and discussed in more detail there, which illustrates how metric influences create special expressions of rectilinearity. Because of the many gaps between adjacent pitches, linear continuity is heard from registral persistence, with pitches lighting individual rectilinear layers like strobe lights—a basic descrip-tion of compound [polyphonic] melody familiar from the CP. Reich's main idea after inventing this groove was to deploy it repetitively for several minutes before a cross-fade brings a bit of curvilinear flute tune into relief (reh. 3B in the score).

The importance of curvilinearity in particular to the expression of over-tonal hierarchy was suggested in a short study (Deutsch 1972), which dem-onstrated that something like Figure 3.22(a) is malformed and perhaps even

---

34. The extreme-case quality of linearity here may be one of the reasons this work was featured in a remarkable documentary film by Paul Festa, "Apparition of the Eternal Church," which recorded the intense reactions and responses of thirty-one people who listened to the work on headphones.

Figure 3.21 Messiaen, *Apparition de l'Église Éternelle*, mm. 25–37

incomprehensible as a tonal-music utterance while (b) is not, despite having the same pitch-class content and rhythm as (a).[35] Obviously, the registral explosion of "Yankee Doodle" destroys its melodic plasticity and hence any linear continuity. But the effect upon overtonality is no less significant: the transformation of a curvilinear melodic line into a set of disconnected, independent points raises high barriers to apprehending overtonal hierarchy. The reader's likely knowledge of examples far more complicated than this suggests how necessary and fundamental linearity is to setting up overtonality.[36]

---

35. No score appears in Deutsch (1972). The present figure has been constructed according to a description in the study.

36. The Deutsch (1972) illustration also suggests that octave equivalence works differently in the harmonic and melodic domains. Whereas in the former, it is so strongly suggested by overtonality that it hardly needs cognitive intervention; in the latter it requires more mental effort—viz., the exact amount it takes to hear "Yankee Doodle" in its dilapidated state at (a) once its instauration at (b) is known.

Inheriting a template from the CP, lines emerge when pitch adjacencies are generally no farther than two semitones apart—three semitones being the minimal "leap" interval.[37] If a line of any significant length is constructed, the emergent structure will be recognized as belonging to some kind of *scale*. The chromatic supplies lines of least overall slope. Steeper motions can be obtained from the venerable diatonic scale as well as from six other so-called *Pressing scales* of evident use in contemporary tonality, presented in order of increasing slope: octatonic, acoustic, harmonic major and minor, whole-tone, and hexatonic.[38] Complex curves can modulate among all the Pressing scales, taking advantage of local diatonicism (i.e., not consecutive semitones); they can also decrease into chromatic. For these reasons—the plasticity of compositional line that can shift into and out of characteristic scales—analytic work with scale concepts should be carried out with a certain circumspection, as illustrated in chapter 5.

Scale in the etymological sense of "ladder" is expressed in a curvilinear form. It can also be experienced as a Gestalt, or what Tymoczko (2011, 2) has termed *macroharmony*: "the total collection of notes heard over moderate spans of musical time." That is, the shorter the line segments and the more registrally dispersed they are in a given melody, the less any underlying pitch succession resembles a ladder; yet the whole collection could very well be represented as such. The difference can clearly be illustrated in Figure 3.22: (a) has a diatonic macroharmony, but (b) expresses an F-major scale. This scale Gestalt likely underwrites our ability to hear linear connection in scales that contain generic steps *larger* than two semitones, such as the harmonic major and minor Pressing scales; with the anhemitonic pentatonic being a reasonable upper bound. Beyond that, successions by leaps are better understood as arpeggiations rather than lines.

Expressions of Curvilinearity

For music-analytic purposes, we will identify three basic curvilinear character types, which differ in the degree to which they are disciplined by other techniques and structural interests. They are introduced briefly below, named after theorists associated with their general idea; analytic illustration follows immediately.

Kurth-lines (*K-lines*) are temporal and spatial pitch adjacencies without harmonic underpinning or lacking directed motion to or from any significant pitch. K-lines are simply unconstrained linear id. K-lines thus are not inherently or necessarily overtonal. The opening phase of the THX logo, the "wriggly mass," is an example, as well as many moments of contemporary music (e.g., Lutosławksi's *Three Poems of Henri Michaux*) where lines are realized *portamento, glissando,*

---

37. Tymoczko (2004, 222–33) demonstrates how these are well founded starting points; Zimmerman (2002) pointed to similar conclusions.
38. After musicologist Jeff Pressing, who first documented them. Tymoczko (2004) provides more background. Persichetti (1961, 44) identifies some scales that result if the "no consecutive semitone" constraint is relaxed.

Figure 3.22 "Yankee Doodle." (a) registrally "exploded" (b) "restored"

with siren effects, and the like. If an overtonal foundation is strong, however, K-lines can sound as superstructure—of which trills and other "ornaments" are the leading example in CP composition. To note that Figure 3.22(a) lacks K-lines is to comment on its incoherence as an overtonal utterance.

Hindemith-lines (*H-lines*) are step progressions:

> those tones which are placed at important positions in the two-dimensional structure of the melody: the highest tones, the lowest tones, and tones that stand out particularly because of their metric position or for other reasons. The primary law of melodic construction is that a smooth and convincing melodic outline is achieved only when these important points form a progression in seconds..(Hindemith 1937 [1942] I:193)

Figure 3.23 reproduces fig. 175 from Hindemith (194), showing with solid lines his analysis of H-lines in a made-up melody. (Since these lines can be as short as two notes, nothing prevented my dotted-line addition, which completed the incorporation of every note in the excerpt into some H-line.)

David Neumeyer (1986, 67) interprets H-lines as:

> Pitches in step-progressions do not require harmonic support: some members of a step-progression may be chord members, and some may be non-chord tones. The step-progression is not to be equated with Schenker's Zug (line) but is more nearly like Kurth's . . . Step-progressions do not outline a particular interval, contain a particular number of notes, or move just along diatonic paths; they do, however move in one direction only, barring embellishment and repetition. Any one pitch may belong to several patterns of step-progression or arpeggiation simultaneously.[39]

H-lines are thus K-lines with certain directional vector. Once the THX logo leaves its opening phase, randomly moving K-lines become vectored H-lines.

Just as K-lines are disciplined by direction to become H-lines, these in turn are disciplined by harmonic anchors to become *Schenker-lines* (*S-lines*). Like Schenkerian linear progressions, S-lines horizontalize an underlying tonality frame, with the beginning and end points of the line belonging to hierarchically

---

39. The neighbor figure F–G–F marked in the fifth octave, mm. 2–3, is an embellishment of the kind mentioned in the quotation.

Figure 3.23 Illustration of step-progression from Hindemith 1937 [1942],
I. fig. 175; dotted lines added

important pitches in the local overtonal hierarchy (or, in a smaller scale, to notes
of a local chord). Unlike linear progressions, each pitch in the line may or not be
supported by its own chord, and even if chordal support is apparent, it may be
more the product of independently moving lines, perhaps shaped with harmonic
fluctuation, than of deliberate harmonic planning.

K-, H-, and S-lines involve increasing attachment to an overtonal foundation,
with K-lines not necessarily expressing overtonality at all and S-lines doing traditional, common-practice work of chord prolongation. The musically sensible and
correct analysis of these lines in individual compositions can tell much about their
relationship to any overtonal hierarchy. The relationship between H- and S-lines in
particular should be a leading indicator if the number of H- and S-lines identified
within a musical passage correlates to the clarity of overtonal expression—the more,
the clearer.

The opening of Hindemith's Piano Sonata no. 1 illustrates this hypothesis.
Figure 3.24) reproduces mm. 1–10 of the first movement, with an analysis of its
linear structures at (b). The symbols are derived from generic Schenkerian analytic
practice; further definition follows:

- Areas centering on a particular pc are bounded by heavy barlines, with
  the focal pc (generally a local root of the overtonal tonic) indicated with
  a square breve. Four such areas are identified. Measures 1–2 focus on A;
  mm. 3–4 focus on B; mm. 5–9 focus on C♯, though gradually and with
  intermediate stages; m. 10 articulates D♯, interpreted as a local tonic.
- S-lines are marked out with heavy gray beams; the start- and end-points of
  the line—belonging to the horizontalized chord—have "knobs" to which
  the beams attach. Measures 1–2 offer the clearest instance.
- H-lines have thin gray beams, without knobs, as in mm. 5–10.
- Slurs analyze embellishments, such as arpeggiations of triads in mm. 3–
  4, and the 4-28[0369] sonority in mm. 5–7; neighbor note in m. 3; and
  chordal skip in m. 9.
- Dotted lines or slurs indicate a change of octave between two linear pitch
  components, such as in mm. 3–4.
- This passage makes use of voice-leading "accompaniments"—in this
  case, perfect fifths projected from a structural pitch. (See Harrison 1994,
  §3.4) The accompanimental projections are shown with small note heads,
  attached to the main pitch with a vertical tie, as in m. 1.

The analysis highlights the sentential nature of the passage. A statement in mm. 1–2, clearly horizontalizing an A-major tonic triad with S-lines, is followed by a response in mm. 3–4 that S-lines B minor. Thereafter is a period of fragmentation and sequential repetition that characterizes a continuation, all finished off by a cadence.

The statement and response portions have S-lines exclusively, with the response complicating matters somewhat in the upper voice by means of arpeggiation, octave transfer, and a pivot on D_5 as an apex of two interlocking S-lines. This slight clouding in the response of the absolute S-linear clarity of the statement is an effective transition to the continuation phase of mm. 5–6, in which not only do S-lines give way to less harmonically definite H-lines, but even these lines are obscured by registral overlapping that foregrounds the arpeggiation of A–C–E♭–F♯. The linear soundworld at this point—a signature octatonic tetrachord arpeggiated over H-line whole-steps (and thus suggestive of whole-tone scale)—contrasts markedly with the diatonic S-lines of mm. 1–2, which reinforces other differences of rhythm and melodic plasticity that distinguish the continuation from the presentation. Thus, contrast of macroharmony and line type accompany fragmentation and other mid-sentence rhetoric, and the definite overtonal attachment that supported the claim of "A-major to B-minor" in the presentation is inoperative in the continuation, at least at the beginning. Harmonic underpinning gradually reveals itself by horizontalizing a dominant-seventh chord over G♯ using two S-lines (bass staff, m 6–8). The lower line, starting on E♭ ≡ D♯, is "dotted" rather than solid because of skips, but the parenthesized notes are straightforwardly inferred from the consistent major-third accompaniments elsewhere, both in the particular line and elsewhere in the piece. (Cf. the descending major thirds in m. 9 and later at mm. 33 ff.) The upper line, F♯–B♯, is activated on the downbeat of m. 7 with the attainment of F♯$_5$, though its fourth-octave doubling is preceded by an H-line extending from C_5. Both S-lines here express octatonic-scale segments, continuing the octatonic atmosphere of the A–C–E♭–F♯ arpeggiation.

The passage moves toward cadence using three clearly defined surface H-lines, each one expressing a different source scale previously suggested in the passage. B_5–E_5 is a diatonic segment; A_4–D♯$_4$ is octatonic; and A_2–D♯$_3$ is whole tone. A slower moving H-line first resolves the dominant seventh at the motion from F♯$_5$ to E_5, and then converges upon a tripled D♯ to effect a change of local tonic.[40] As the analysis shows, H-lines can cross changes of tonal focus, while S-lines are confined to their respective focal areas. This is why the S-line E_5–A_5 in mm. 1–2 does not continue to B_5 in m. 3, a note that initiates a new S-line horizontalizing the B-minor triad.[41]

In sum, the linear structure highlights the sentence scheme of the passage, providing a useful bridge to considerations of formal rhetoric. Five straightforward S-lines unquestionably express an A-major tonic in mm. 1–2, not to mention the support from the rectilinear sustained A_3. S-line density and length decrease in the response, with light ornamentation pushing down the upper lines from the

40. That the closing tonic is a tritone away from that of the opening is to be read, according to Hindemith's metrics, as a claim of maximal tonal contrast.
41. Note that while the open-fifth cadential sonorities of m. 4 and m. 10 are ostensibly modally neutral, the S-lines in mm. 3–4 suggest a minor tint for the B sonority in m. 4, while the persistent major-third accompaniments above the A_4–D♯$_4$ S-line in mm. 9–10 suggest a major tint for the D♯ sonority there.

Figure 3.24 Hindemith, Piano Sonata no. 1, mm. 1–10 (a) score (b) linear analysis

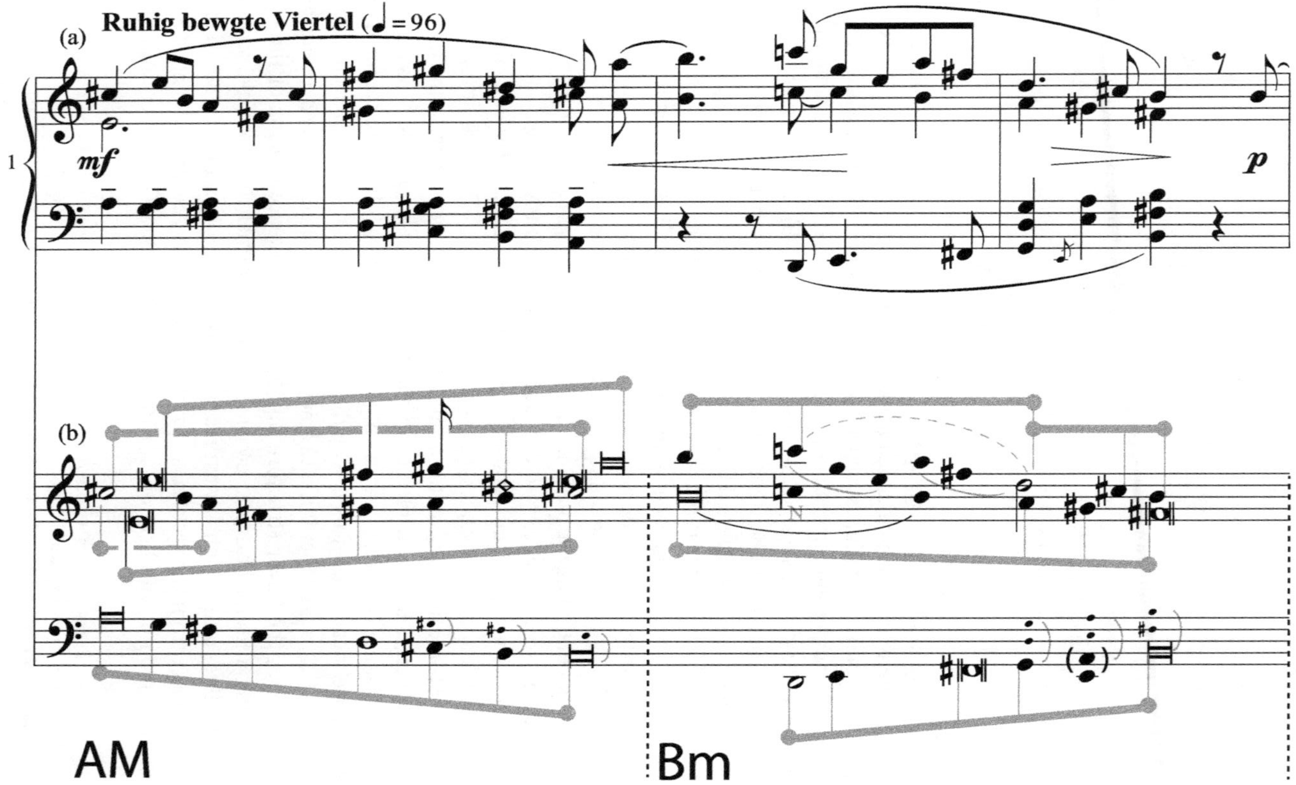

Figure 3.24 (Continued)

surface. In mm. 5–6, the replacement of S-lines by H-lines, which are themselves obscured by overlapping, is of a piece with the uncertain tonal center of those measures, the sense that they are "on the way." The reappearance of S-lines coincides with a sense of upcoming tonal discharge, which occurs *en passant* on C♯ minor in m. 9. The continuation of H-lines to D♯ assists in making it a one-off, unprolonged, and temporary tonal center of arrival.[42]

How are lines analyzed, especially where they are embellished or otherwise beneath the immediate surface? In the Hindemith passage at hand, many lines revealed themselves unproblematically as surface scale-segment adjacencies. Others were heard through interruptions of various kinds—single skips or neighbor notes, as in mm. 2 and 9—or the more complex triad-arpeggiations in m. 2. For these, we grant C_6 a place in line as a melodic peak that also initiates noteworthy local rhythmic activity (i.e., a string of five eighth notes) terminated with an agogic accent on D_5 on the downbeat of m. 4.

Warrants of this kind permit hearing lines through interruptions and embellishments. The H-lines of mm. 5–6, for example, are not surface phenomena for the most part, and they are heard through interrupting neighbor-notes and voice overlapping. It is the latter feature, in fact, which sends the linear analysis down its particular path and away from others, such as capturing more of the mostly semitone transposition of the surface figuration from m. 5 to m. 6. (This feature is only represented by the short bass H-line, D_3–E♭$_3$.) It turns out the "mostly" is a significant qualifier, for the odd E♭$_5$ puts the aforementioned A–C–E♭–F♯ arpeggiation into play. This calls for a closer look. Voice overlapping suggests itself immediately by another imperfect transposition in m. 5; the perfect-fifth projections from the outer voices on the downbeat are not preserved at the third-beat chord, although the 4-23[0257] set class is. Figure 3.24 interprets this as the first evidence of the overlapping that generates the arpeggiation, and the H-line analysis follows this implication. Thus, imperfect transpositions, both within the figures and between them, discourage a straightforward sequential reading.

For those interested in analyzing this way, another decision made about mm. 5–8 ought to be mentioned, this concerning line length and type. The H-line extending from C_5 to F♯$_4$ could be incorporated into the subsequent S-line, making an octave span from C_5 ($\equiv$ B♯) to B♯$_3$ in m. 8. This reads the dominant-seventh emerging quite subtly in m. 5 before becoming noticeable in m. 7. The hermeneutical overhead needed to sustain that claim seems unwarranted here, as it has to contend with the palpable loss of harmonic centeredness brought about by the sequential fragmentation. Even so, we could proffer that an H-line does indeed extend from C_5 to B♯$_3$, but acquires S-line properties at m. 7. This is to say that underneath every S-line is an H-line without a supervening quality of chord prolongation. The analytic claim in the passage at hand is that this quality appears at the boundary of mm. 6–7, which is marked by a changes in figuration, voicing, and doubling, and which is also a local registral and dynamic peak.

---

42. In this, they are helped by the phrase rhetoric, which signals closure by the completion of the sentence scheme, *diminuendo*, and harmonic fluctuation, wherein the 3-11[037] triad is second to the root-and-fifth overtonal i[7] in the local scheme. Cf. m. 4.

Chord Prolongation

What about structural levels? Aside from the simple distinction between surface and immediate subsurface assumed in the previous discussion, are there deeper middleground or even background structures to take into account? The short answer is no, because it is not clear how such structures would be identified. The ideas about linearity advanced here pointedly lack a priori background templates, such as found in Schenker, and for that reason they make the analysis of levels purely reductive rather than a dialectical, back-and-forth process of reconciling foreground and background through middlegrounds.[43] In this situation, reduction is in danger of creating artifacts of its own process, with questionable relations to the musical surface. Without a set of goals to be reached in a reductive process, there is no telling where to stop or where the intermediate stages are. A revealing illustration is the making of sauces. Cooks frequently have to reduce liquid to a sauce by boiling away water, which concentrates and deepens flavor. At some point, determined by art, the sauce is sufficiently reduced for use. It could, of course, take continued reduction, but anyone who has burned a pot through inattention, boiling away all the liquid so that only the solids and precipitates remain, knows that is no sauce at all. Any reductionist technique that could be constructed from ideas about overtonality and linearity would have to rely heavily on the art of the saucemaker—knowing by intuition where the deeper levels reside.

There is also a potentially pernicious problem of analyzing the musical surface with the intention of deriving a middleground from it—that is, of setting up individual notes as prolongable so that they may appear at the next deeper stage. David Neumeyer's analysis of mm. 1–2, shown in Figure 3.25, may be a very mild example of this. It is mostly congruent with my version—the octave line in the bass, ascending sixth in the alto, the small-scale descending third from the opening note. The telling difference is how the upper line is read. Neumeyer wishes to highlight a neighbor-note figure E–D♯–E, in which the first E is prolonged via a third progression. (This figure parallels other motivic neighbors in the piece, as Neumeyer points out.) To achieve this reading, the final A of m. 1 is suppressed and the third-progression devolves, in my terminology, from an S- to an H-line (the E–F♯–G♯ span does not horizontalize an underlying A major). In addition, no registral connection from the opening C♯$_5$ to D♯$_5$ in m. 2 is understood, which I believe to be an omission. My analysis was interested in reading linearity only, to the exclusion of motivic parallelisms, hidden or otherwise. Thus the final A$_5$, though felt as something of an anacrusis, is also felt to succeed G♯$_5$ as the registral highpoint.[44] Similarly, D♯ of m. 2 returns to the space previously occupied by C♯ at

43. The lack of explicit background templates—and, indeed, of definite structural levels—is the main problem of Felix Salzer's adaptation of Schenker's work for pre- and posttonal music in Salzer (1952). Neumeyer (1986, 49ff.) comments perceptively on this general issue.

44. B$_5$ also achieves this distinction, and it—as well as the following C$_6$—could be incorporated into H-line from the E$_5$ of m. 1. The strong harmonic component of the passage, however, is appropriately measured in the S-line analysis. Those who want to honor both qualities can draw an H-line connector from A$_5$ to B$_5$.

Figure 3.25 Analysis of Hindemith's Piano Sonata I, mm. 1–2 from Neumeyer 1986, 202

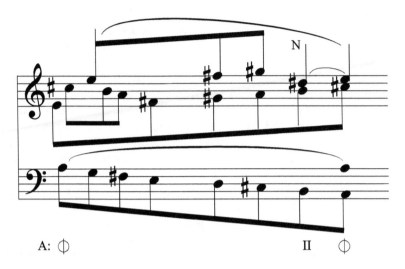

both the beginning and end of m. 1. In my reading, it is a passing rather than the neighbor note suggested by a separate motivic analysis of the movement.

The issue of prolongation as a license to construct reductionist middle-grounds is separate from the question of whether very large-scale lines can be heard and profitably analyzed, and the difference centers on claims of "presence" that underwrite the notion of prolongation. In Neumeyer's analysis, for example, the opening E_5 persists in some sense through the third-progression, which functions as an extension of E. Plausible reduction relies on prolongational analysis because the analytic act is largely to remove the extensions, branchings, and diminutions that accrue to notes on the next deeper level, which is to say that the analysis of any given level is done with a deeper one in mind. In contrast, incorporating nonadjacent pitches into H- or S-lines relies upon recency effects (if the nonadjacencies result from short-term interruption) or upon treatments that mark pitches for attention in a particular way, typically metric and registral. Put simply, given two nonadjacent notes on the musical surface, x and y, a prolongational approach essentially makes x and y adjacencies at some deeper structural level; a claim of large-scale connection, however, may rely on markedness of some kind without ever assuming any deeper levels. For example, noting that the bass H-line in mm. 9–10, A–B–C♯–D♯, encapsulates the large-scale degree progression of the passage (i.e., A in mm. 1–2, B in mm. 3–4, C♯ and D♯ in mm. 9–10) does not commit us to claiming that B (or C♯) is somehow prolongationally present through the fragments of mm. 5–6; instead, it notes an ordered series of salient pitch objects.

A pertinent illustration of these issues is in Figure 3.26. Locally, the passage starts in D major and then, by means of falling-fifth bass motion, modulates to C in mm. 3–6, with a half cadence at m. 4. It then returns to D at the conclusion. In this way, it could be analyzed as the Hindemith passage was in its opening phase,

Figure 3.26 Melodic analysis of Prokofiev, Sonata for flute and piano, op. 94, I, mm. 1–8

where the local changes of tonic within mm. 1–4 were acknowledged. In this case, however, a different formal scheme influences analysis—namely, a period instead of a sentence. The analysis above the melody takes place on that level, overriding the local and interior change of tonal focus in order to bring out and affirm D as the tonic of the entire period. Thus, G_5 of m. 5, which at the surface is heard to parallel the A_5 of m. 1 as $\hat{5}$ of the local key, is placed within the tonal hierarchy of D and notated as its $\hat{4}$. Two S-lines extend to D at the surface, and a larger S-line marks the step motion from A to G, made noticeable by the thematic parallel. As in the Hindemith analysis, solid knobs pin notes to the chord being horizontalized. The hollow knobs on G indicate that while it is not part of the horizontalized chord, it is nonetheless a high-ranking member of the overtonal hierarchy in force here.

Postscript: Tymoczko's Five Features of Tonality

Having taken a high-altitude survey of the CP conurbation, we consider here another set of tonality-features recently hypothesized by Dmitri Tymoczko (2011), focusing on congruences between his "five components of tonality" and the four overtonal suburbs as just surveyed. While differences between the two lists are just as telling—about respective interests, orientations, and other commitments—the concurrences are mutually reinforcing for both purposes, as the following section describes.

The features that Tymoczko identifies "are present in a wide range of genres, Western and non-Western, past and present, and that they jointly contribute to a sense of tonality" (2). In his words, they are:

1. *Conjunct melodic motion.* Melodies tend to move by short distances from note to note.
2. *Acoustic consonance.* Consonant harmonies are preferred to dissonant harmonies, and tend to be used at points of musical stability.
3. *Harmonic consistency.* The harmonies in a passage of music, whatever they may be, tend to be structurally similar to one another.

4. *Limited macroharmony*. I use the term "macroharmony" to refer to the total collection of notes heard over moderate spans of musical time. Tonal music tends to use relatively small macroharmonies, often involving 5 to 8 notes.

5. *Centricity*. Over moderate spans of musical time, one note is heard as being more prominent than the others, appearing more frequently and serving as a goal of musical motion.

Tymoczko's set of components is ideally illustrated in a website adjunct to his book, titled "What makes music sound good?"[45] There, he applies these singly and jointly, and in various strengths, to a "laboratory condition" of sonic random-ness. Starting from a series of arbitrary trichords played on a piano, he imposes conjunct melodic motion of upon each chord member ("efficient voice leading"), harmonic consistency, and then both simultaneously. These constraints bend the impression of randomness toward emergent tonality—or at least a sense that the resulting sounds approach norms of tonal music. Further restrictions, involving acoustic consonance and limited macroharmony, direct the results even more toward familiar-sounding music. Finishing off with a dash of rhythmic variety (randomized long/short values—thereby setting up a single-level metric hierar-chy), he finds it "remarkable how musical the final result sounds. Using just a few simple constraints, we've turned randomness into something recognizably musi-cal. It wouldn't win any composition prizes, but it is satisfying (and indeed, 'tonal') in some elemental way" (Tymoczko 2011, 8–10).

Tymoczko's five components are impressively good in making a basic tonal music ex nihilo. It is not clear whether they are ordered in some way—that is, whether conjunct melodic motion is somehow more "basic" than or "prior" to acoustic consonance. The constraints are indeed imposed in a particularly convinc-ing order on the website: voice leading (= conjunct melodic motion), harmonic consistency, and limited macroharmony can be played with independently, while acoustic consonance is dialed in for certain contexts (familiar triads substituting for stack of fourths at step 6. Judging from this, as well as from the progression of chapters in the book, conjunct melodic motion appears to have priority, mac-roharmony and centricity are treated together in a later chapter,[46] and acoustic consonance as well as harmonic consistency falls out from these as something of fortunate happenstance.

If Tymoczko's project with these components is to "build" pathways and operations of tonality—a tonality characterized as "psychological sensation" in chapter 1's discussion of the term—my project is to "separate" inherited and com-mon compositional techniques of fin-de-siècle Western art music into smaller, discrete packages. It is an analysis of a particular tonal repertory's historical condi-tions, rather than a synthesis of tonality from parts. This difference in approach explains where the greatest divergences between the two are. But both agree at a fundamental, metaphorical level: Tymoczko's conceiving of the components

---

45. http://music.princeton.edu/~dmitri/whatmakesmusicsoundgood.html. Also see Tymoczko (2011, 8–10), and Figure 1.2.1. (The website audio clips, while different from those notated in the figure, proceed in the same order.)

46. Though "scale, macroharmony, and centricity are independent," per the title of §1.3.2, 15.

as "vectors" spanning "a region that could be called 'tonality space'" is much the same as imagining geographic features that attract composer/settlers and promote development, with both images prompted by the urge to accommodate "the richness of contemporary musical practice" (Tymoczko 2011, 190).

The map of the two spaces align at an outer edge. *Conjunct Melodic Motion* is *Linearity* geometrized. Tymoczko examines this feature with respect to chords first, then to scales. His interest runs toward voice-leading properties between chords (i.e., toward a multiple-lined polyphony), and toward the grooved channels provided by scales into which conjunct lines can flow. Because of these essentially harmonic and collectional (ultimately, macroharmonic) interests, he leaves on the table matters concerning monophony, melody, and the "long lines" created by chord horizontalizations that Schenker, for one, was interested in. Because these operate in CP composition, they were available to contemporary tonal composers, with S-lines a "legacy feature," H-lines a result of newer kinds of directed motion, and K-lines (as well as extended rectilinear writing) an accommodation to a variety of special effects, experiments, or forays out of overtonal hierarchy.

Acoustic Consonance has no suburban counterpart, but is a basic feature of the CP tradition and thus resides in the center as *Overtonality*. It may be that what Tymoczko describes as a "broadly attractive soundworld" (26) is precisely an overtonal one, though the possibility that a full-featured tonal music based on, say, a diminished rather than perfect fifth could be determinedly realized should not be discounted. The leading property of overtonality is *centricity*. Or rather, a certain kind of centricity, detailed in chapter 2, is what overtonality describes. Tymoczko broaches the question, "where does centricity come from?" (177), and he answers by posing a binary:

> Internal explanations assert that the structure of a group of notes is sufficient to pick one out as a tonal center, without any effort on the composer's part. External explanations focus on what composers do, asserting that composers make notes more prominent (or stable) by playing them more frequently , accenting them rhythmically or dynamically, placing them in registrally salient positions, and so on. Rather than being a property of collections considered abstractly, centricity is a property of collections as they are used in actual music. (177)

Given this introduction, internal explanations are ultimately dismissed, since "internal contributions to centricity are relatively weak and can be easily overridden." (180)

Overtonal centricity suggests, however, that while they are weak enough to be overridden (though with effort), internal contributions—already dictating basic geometric structures—can be more easily reinforced, loaded, and further "Deep Noted" into psychoacoustical granite. And, of course, a number of "externalized internalist" mixtures can be imagined and composed.

Even so, chapter 2 "Overtonality" was careful to distinguish overtonal centricity from externally driven ones, described there as context-assertive. It also quitclaimed interests in "any conceivable collection of notes" that can "function" as a center for some context-assertive centricity—structures that, for Tymoczko, would likely put inordinate pressure on acoustic consonance and, therefore, on the efficient voice leading and harmonic consistency components; if these three fail, tonality is presumably lost (10). Chapter 2 concluded with a declared interest in the practice of overtone-series hierarchies, deeply embedded in the CP, and by now thoroughly globalized and duty-free. And, again, chapter 2 goes farther than Tymoczko, perhaps, in claiming that centricity encompasses not only both chord rootedness and tonicity (169), but even pitch synthesis from partials. In the end, the differences here are not substantive with respect to the possible expressions of centricity; my focus is rather on the historical and cultural grooving of those expressions by internalist factors, and on the resulting range of musical composition.

Harmonic consistency was referenced earlier in this chapter in connection with *chording intervals*, the restriction of the harmonic palette to transpositional combinations of i[3–5], and thus pertains to *harmonic fluctuation*. These intervals were proposed as a heuristic for defining chord as something separate from cluster or some other simultaneity of pitches. While it enabled some suggestive analytic methods, the theoretical issues involved are complex—the ontology of chords, their conditions of existence, and the voicing transformations that disperse chord tones into pitch space—and are best treated in a separate project.[47] But the need actually to constitute the thing that harmonic consistency refers to should be clear.

Limited macroharmony could take more nuance than it gets in Tymoczko's presentation. Except for small pieces (e.g., many numbers from Bartók's *Mikrokosmos* used in elementary instruction), macroharmony generally *fluctuates* among various collections and often between various states during the course of a medium-sized or large work. At any one time—a phrase, passage, possibly a section, in extreme cases a movement (like the Messiaen examples cited earlier in this chapter)—macroharmony may be indeed limited to a less-than-twelve condition (e.g., pentatonic, octatonic), yet it may also aspire to an always-twelve condition (chromatic), which could be described as an *unlimited* macroharmony. Most contemporary tonal compositions, and even most CP compositions, generally inflate to chromatic macroharmony over medium to long stretches of music, larger than most measurements of pitch class circulation Tymoczko makes. So limited macroharmony is mostly a local feature of tonality, and unlimited (chromatic) macroharmony over the same spans may be strongly shaped by overtonal influences, as the passage from Schoenberg's organ variations demonstrates. Macroharmony is better appreciated as a *compositional* feature through fluctuation and growth over time than it is through its discrete collections at any given time.

Meter is not a feature of Tymoczko's (2011) list, though he acknowledges having to neglect it and other "important issues" (10) in the press of other business. Meter and *Traditional Rhetoric* are perhaps best understood as context-assertive features of design and compositional shape. They are not components of tonality, but conveyances. Historically, however, they come packaged with the CP inheritance, and their role in actual pieces of music is unquestionable. Again, handling cultural legacy is not in Tymoczko's purview, so this lack of isography between the two maps is a natural result. Ultimately, all such differences flow from the critical nouns in each book title: *Geometry* (Tymoczko) and *Tradition* (Harrison). And all congruences stem from the CP tradition having a tonality that is well-modeled geometrically.

---

47. Harrison (2014) makes a start in this direction.

CHAPTER $\mathbb{F}$our

Harmony

Tonic Dissonance

A fundamental of CP music, in both practice and theory, is that only a conso-nant triad can stand as a tonic chord of a key. Thus, C major and C minor—but not C diminished, C augmented, or C "any conceivable collection of tones." For Jean-Philippe Rameau, the fountainhead of modern theories of CP tonality, consonance and tonic were fused into equivalence: a tonic chord required con-sonance, so consonance must then indicate a tonic chord. Commenting about the final authentic cadence of a composition, he noted that if the dominant chord were also fundamentally consonant, "the mind, not desiring anything more after such a chord, would be uncertain upon which of the two sounds [V or I] to rest. Dissonance [for the V] seems needed here in order that its harshness should make the listener desire the rest which follows" (Rameau 1722 [1971], 62). All this is to say that Rameau considered the dominant, in its true and characteristic form, to be a dissonant seventh chord, and even those appearing in composed music *as triads* were understood theoretically to repre-sent underlying dissonant tetrads.

In this state of affairs, we can dimly see a Gordian knot stranded of composi-tional practice, ideology, and psychoacoustics. Difficult to disentangle and demys-tify, this knot is responsible for some of the complex phenomenology of tonality discussed in chapter 2—of perceiving tonal hierarchy among overtonally related pitches, which in turn gives rise to the indescribable, taste-of-a-peach feeling of being "in" a key. These matters are of longstanding interest to musicians, and ancient verities like the "perfection" of the triad, the association of dissonance with tension and consonance with relaxation, and other philosophical investigations of music are easily identified.

While we may no longer advance "triads as incomplete seventh chords" doc-trines in our harmony classes, we nonetheless speak about "tonic" and "key" in ways that are completely consonant with these received ideas. In fact, from species counterpoint to Schenkerian analysis—the gamut of technical knowledge gener-ally taught concerning tonal music—the tonic-consonance symmetry observed by Rameau is an unquestioned given. Yet questions began to be posed in music literature a century after Rameau, starting perhaps with Chopin's Mazurka, op. 17 no. 4 (1833), the opening of which is shown in Figure 4.1 along with analysis of chord structure (using thoroughbass) and harmonic function (italic letters). The

Figure 4.1 Chopin, Mazurka op. 17 no. 4, mm. 1–14. Harmonic analysis uses thoroughbass and Riemannian function letters. T = a minor; l = Leittonwechsel; r = relative; lr = Leittonwechsel of the relative; rl = relative of the Leittonwechsel

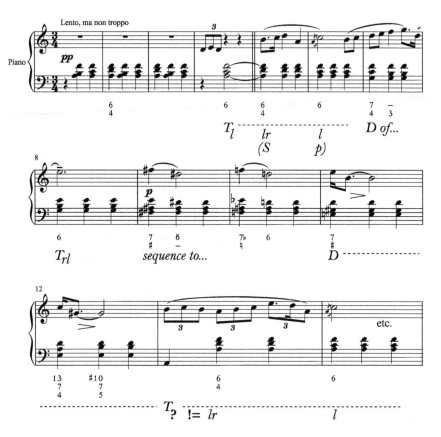

piece concludes with a reprise of mm. 1–4, which dies upon a famously open-ended first-inversion F-major triad. Presuming the key of A-minor, F sounds like an unresolved appoggiatura to E, with A and C as the root and third of an A-minor triad. Analytically, this intuition is expressed with T function whose consonance has been disturbed by a *leittonwechselnde* (leading-tone-changing) appoggiatura. Chopin clearly relishes play with tonic chord in this piece, for he adds yet another disturbance to it in m. 5, where the T*l* entity is briefly transformed into T*lr*. Even the tonicized relative major in m. 8 is disturbed by another *leittonwechselnde* appoggiatura. Measures 9–10 are striking in their own right, though clearly passing to a two-measure dominant pedal in m. 11. A satisfactory authentic cadence—which would resolve all of the pent-up *appoggiature* of the phrase previous—starts to be offered on the downbeat of m. 13, but it is denied on the second beat, where the supporting tonic chord has been transformed by *lr* by the time the top voice reaches Î, looping the progression back to m. 5.

This piece is an essay in special effect, where the point is not to incorporate dissonance into a tonic chord (and Chopin's chords being *Scheinkonsonanzen*, the dissonances were being sounded as Rameau's "incomplete tetrads") but to heavily underscore the (consonant) tonic triad as a site of longing, desire, consummation, perfection, etc. by permanently displacing one (and occasionally two) of its members. Somewhat later in the nineteenth century, possibilities with tonic tetrads were explored, especially in popular and semiclassical repertories. These chords—a few of which are referenced in Figure 4.2—have the same phenomenological attributes as (untransformed) consonant-triad tonics, but are dissonant by traditional CP standards.

The existence of these chords implies a compositional discovery about chordal statics made during the latter part of the nineteenth century: consonance could be relativized without damaging the supporting overtonal system. This development was a likely result from well-known nineteenth-century additions and dilations of chordal dissonance. That is, the increase in sharply dissonant non-tonic chords gave an opportunity for tonic chords to suffer mild dissonance without failing their function, as long as they sounded backstopped by some "root and fifth" overtonality. And, as discussed in the last chapter, both sharp and mild characteristics can be adjusted delicately and according to taste—suggesting to the music analyst that *harmonic fluctuation* might be considered for insight into structure.

What creates the dispositive tonicness of the circled chords in Figure 4.2? Two of the excerpts instance a familiar, meaningful unit of chord grammar, T–D⁷, D⁷–T.[1] The two chord types used in the scheme are composed in *antimetabole*, as two phrases built from the same "words" but in reverse order. Here, T is first subject and the D⁷ predicate; the dissonant seventh marks D as imperfect, concluding a phrase but not a clause, implying another unit yet to come. In the second phrase, T has no dissonance and can thereby conclude the compound unit. Yet its conclusive function is overdetermined. From a chordal-dynamics point of view, it is strongly predicated by the antimetabole construction, where a punctuated "pivot point" suggests the rest to follow and sets up the concluding period for a strong accent (e.g., "Fail to plan? Plan to fail."). In this way, the wild major-seventh chord sounds perfectly appropriate as the phrase-concluding chord of Figure 4.2(a), even withstanding a change in the otherwise strict five-semitone transpositional relationship between antecedent and consequent. The same grammatical archetype is composed out in Figure 4.2(b), with D expressed here by a ninth rather than a seventh chord. Note that the strict two-semitone transpositional relationship between antecedent and consequent is *preserved* by the dissonant tonic chord in this case. In these two cases, end position is a strong indicator of tonic and is indifferent to both absolute, triadic consonance and the products of motivic activity (i.e., the different transpositional structure of the melodies). They project systemic equilibrium at beginning and end points of structural time spans, with tension applied in

---

1. Riemannian function designators are used here to provide the minimum amount of specificity needed to convey the essence of the structure. T represents a tonic chord, and D⁷ represents a dominant seventh.

Figure 4.2 Excerpts from (a) "I'm just wild about Harry," Eubie Blake; (2) Waltz #1, from *The Skaters*, Emil Waldteufel; (3) "Mackie Messer," Kurt Weill

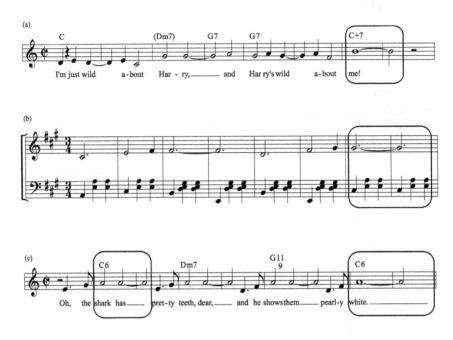

the middle. Further, a conventional rhetorical figure (i.e., antimetabole) sets up an event hierarchy that predicates static equilibrium to the end point, a predication strong enough to be unaffected by an unconventional end chord.[2]

Figure 4.2(c) instances another grammatical scheme: T–S–D–T, a bilateral exploration of functional relations working out a *Start–Depart–Return–Arrival* paradigm. While the concluding Cadd6 chord benefits from the same perfecting circumstances as in excerpts (a) and (b), conventional equilibrium at the beginning affects the opening chord, also a C$^{\text{add6}}$, endowing it with tonic function. This allows the chord's added sixth, A, to slip in easily and—over the course of the phrase—become the reciting tone of the tune. Harmonic activity (i.e., the T–S–D–T process) seems to take place underneath and without much notice from the A-obsessed tune, which only responds autonomically with a whole-step lowering

---

2. A limit case: John Philip Sousa's *Liberty Bell* march was appropriated for the opening credits of *Monty Python's Flying Circus*, a British television comedy that aired in the early 1970s. Apparently used nondiegetically underneath scenes of surrealistic animations, the march proceeded through its first strain to the point of its final cadence—highly predicated by the preceding music, as is typical for the genre. At the point of cadential resolution, the final chord was replaced by the (diegetic?) sound of flatulence to accompany the image of a giant foot squashing a cartoon chimera. Obviously not overtonal, and perhaps better analyzed as a kind of deceptive cadence, the final "chord" nonetheless points unambiguously to a tonic—albeit, one that has been squashed—and seems thereby to acquire significant tonic attributes, among which are (highly ironicized) predicated finality and structural closure.

of the motive's pickup notes in the second half of the phrase. Newly sensitized to the conventions of tonic beginnings, we return to excerpt (a) to note how little fuss ensues about the vocal D_4, a free-standing ninth against the tonic C-chord accompaniment. Does it perhaps "resolve" to C at the end of m. 2? Further, if D is assimilated into the tonic chord, does that render the acoustically consonant E in m. 2 a "dissonant" escape tone?

Figure 4.3 presents a more substantial situation involving concluding-tonic rhetoric. Excerpted from the closing measures of Maurice Duruflé's *Requiem*, op. 9 (1947), the passage is based on a cantus firmus, *In Paradisum*, that appears in the top staff. This antiphon is in F♯ mixolydian, with a key signature of five sharps; that this signature is the same as that of B major will prove to be significant in the following discussion. Underlaying the chant are a pedal on F♯ and a haze of chords (mostly conventional seventh- and ninth-chords) that, after reaching a nadir in reh. 101 + 2, gradually ascend until the uppermost note reaches F♯$_5$ at reh. 102 + 2. Here, the haze and the pedal clear away, revealing a simple B-minor triad—the first consonant triad heard in the movement.

It is not immediately certain what kind of tonal cue this triad gives. A *diminuendo* having started two measures before and the chant having reached its final, a conclusion seems imminent. But upon what tonic? It is not impossible or even unexpected that the piece should end on the B-major chord shown at the asterisked measure of the figure. The key signature and position-finding data suggest as much, and the F♯ pedal heard since the beginning of the excerpt can be heard as creating a lengthy dominant area preceding the final tonic arrival. Duruflé, however, famously concludes on an F♯ dominant-seventh chord, upon which he subsequently heaps a major ninth. Attempting to reconcile "key-signature hearing" with this fact, we might interpret the final chord as an unresolved dominant, perhaps yearning for some resolution in the afterlife. But key-signature hearing seems to miss the point here. The concluding F♯ sonority asks to be heard as the tonic section of a plagal cadence, with the B-minor triad acting as subdominant—an appropriate *Kirchenschluß* given both the sacred genre of the work and the mode of the cantus-firmus chant. And the powerful devices of concluding rhetoric are irresistibly at work here. As the *molto rit.* comes to bear during the cadential motion (joining the *diminuendo* begun some measures before), apprehension of conclusion changes from "imminent" to "in-process." Dynamics, tempo, and chord voicing all converge upon F♯; all then penetrate and bury themselves in this target, for the (*sempre*) *diminuendo* and *ritardando* (*très long*) effects continue past the initial arrival, and the major ninth appears afterwards as well. The chord then simply fades away, not in unrequited yearning for a B-major tonic but apparently in the eternal peace of an F♯ tonic—albeit one that contains a tritone that is mildly cut by a minor seventh and major ninth.[3]

---

3. Perhaps unsurprisingly, were the asterisked B-major chord sounded *after* the F♯ chord—as the tonic resolution of a "dominant ninth"—the effect would be decidedly pedestrian, even if the *ritardando* and *diminuendo* were stripped out of the passage in an attempt to prevent F♯ from setting up.

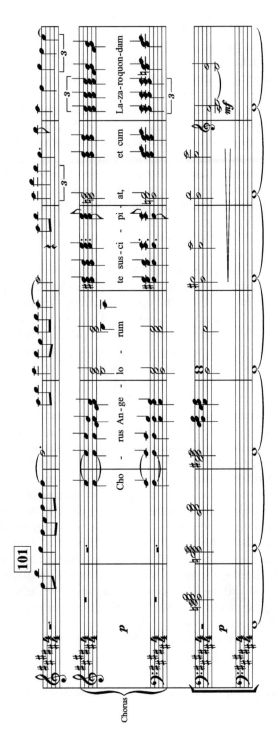

Figure 4.3 Maurice Duruflé, *Requiem*, op. 9. Conclusion of "In Paradisum," reduced

Figure 4.3 (Continued)

Overtonal Chords

The tonic effects heard in the preceding examples are, as chapter 1 announced, the distinguishing mark of a post-CP contemporary tonal music. They sound the essentials of overtonal hierarchy (root and fifth) and attach one, two, or more subordinate pitch classes ("pcs") that set mood/mode in various ways. Their basis in the consonant triad is as clear as the triad's in the overtonal root and fifth frame. Indeed, the subordinate pcs are arranged in ways that don't interfere with stability of the root, enacting a kind of transitive relation from pitch to overtonal root to chord root.[4]

Some pause on this last-named is warranted, since the chord root is a central concept in the analysis of CP harmony, identified as scale degrees of a local key using symbols like Roman numerals. When these symbols are understood to analyze syntactic content—when, in other words, they are related to some theoretically normative succession of roots—they attain a new level of theoretical sophistication that overshadows the mere identification of those roots. In analysis of CP music, at least, this overshadowing means that the sense of what a chord root sounds like in the mind's ear—of its phenomenal basis—can be largely effaced and replaced by knowledge of a class of chord roots (e.g., I, II, III, etc.) and their characteristic strings, patterns, and conventions. In the chromatic music of the later nineteenth century, however, where chords may progress in novel ways, chord-root symbols are often at a loss to explain chord behavior, and other symbols, such as the various chord-function labels derived from Hugo Riemann, have greater utility.

In contemporary tonal music, not only do novel chords progress in more novel ways, but the sense of key itself is often under pressure or in doubt—meaning that no sure assignment of root-as-scale-degree can be made at all. It is thus best analytic practice to follow Gottfried Weber's original scheme of 1817 and explicitly identify the root as a lettered pitch-class. This is precisely the opening move of jazz harmony theories, and it is, in essence, a return to the fundamental bass of Rameau, but it is also endorsed by a number of theorists interested in post-CP tonality, Hindemith chief among them.[5] As was the case with analyzing linearity from the last chapter, the analysis of chord root thus can benefit from multiple tiers of specificity:

a) Pitch-class root, available from any individual chord;
b) Function, when interpreting the chord above the root "in key" isn't necessary, is a matter of indifference, or the key is ambiguous;
c) Roman numerals, when common progressions are involved, especially in the well-known authentic cadential approaches to final tonics (e.g., II–V–I).

---

4. Tymoczko (2011, 169ff.) discusses this "closely related phenomena" of what he terms *rootedness* and *tonicity*.
5. See, for example, Ulehla (1966, 302ff., esp. 313); and Persichetti (1961, 183) whose exposition owes much to Hindemith's example.

Ultimately, supporting the "conceptual" pc root is a "sensible" pitch root, notated on a staff as a fundamental-bass note. What a pitch root may lack in theoretical generality it makes up for in phenomenological presence. Researchers in music cognition have established the viability of such "fundamental-bass" roots in chords as psychoacoustic phenomena. Ernst Terhardt (1984) writes:

> The fact that a pitch can be perceived although there does not exist any spectral component at the frequency corresponding to that pitch provides the key to understanding the whole harmony phenomenon, that is, tonal affinity, compatibility, and fundamental-note relations, as was pointed out on several occasions earlier. The conscious perception of fundamental notes of musical chords was experimentally verified, so that the reduction of harmony to the psychoacoustics of virtual-pitch perception basically does not require further hypothesis or theory. (287–88)

He provides an example:

> When a major triad, composed of the harmonic complex tones G_5, B_5, and D_6, is perceived, the fundamentals of the constituent tones will be treated by the "pattern recognizer" as the fourth, fifth, and sixth harmonics of a (nonexistent) G_3, and a virtual pitch corresponding to G_3 will be produced. This virtual pitch will be relatively faint because the spectral pattern of the actual stimulus (the chord) departs considerably from that produced by a single harmonic complex tone. Nevertheless, the major triad will be perceived not merely as an ensemble of three tones but will additionally possess a certain "label," namely the *fundamental note* G_3. (291)[6]

For traditional theoretical purposes, this conception of chord root is specific to an unusual degree, as Richard Parncutt (1988, 67; italics original) points out:

> The conventional theory of the roots of musical chords is generally understood to be octave-generalized. In such theory, the root of a chord is regarded as a *pitch class*, that is, a pitch whose octave register is not specified. Similarly, the root may be thought to be a function of a *chord class* (a simultaneity of pitch classes) and so to be independent of voicing (inversion, spacing, and doubling).

Even so, for the remainder of this chapter, chord roots will be referred to, as appropriate, either as pcs or, if voicing or arrangement is to be noted, as a deep tone which is essentially equivalent to Terhardt described earlier.

Pitch-Space Voicing, Spread, and Bandwidths

Traditional harmonic theory recognizes only weakly (if at all) that a chord is not simply another name for simultaneously sounding notes but a musical object that emerges from certain placement of pitches on the spectrum. We hear a *chord* if

---

6. Terhardt's work is discussed, along with that of others, in Thomson (1999, 99–103). This is within a wide-ranging chapter titled "Tonality as Global Root." See also Thomson (1993).

$\{A_3, C\sharp_4, E_4\}$ sound together, but an indistinct, incipient rumble with $\{A_0, C\sharp_1, E_1\}$, and an uncertain timbre with $\{A_6, C\sharp_7, E_7\}$. What we hear with $\{A_0, C\sharp_4, E_7\}$ is something else entirely—a coincidence of isolated sounds—not exactly a chord. The defining feature of chords is an emergent and supervening *harmonia*, a "belonging togetherness" of individuals that can be definitely named, for example, an A-major triad. As Victor Zuckerkandl (1956, 301) perceived, "the chord is the fruit not of the simultaneous existence of tones but of their mutual relation."

Functional Pitch Space

In general, emergence happens roughly within the *chord space* C_3–C_6, with some variation for timbre. For most purposes, taking middle C_4 as the middle of a normal distribution for CP chords is a good heuristic. Below C_3 and down to C_0 (the 32′ C on the organ) is a sparsely populated zone reserved for bass pitches, which in some textures (e.g., orchestral) have suboctave doublings. This *root space* is also the site of virtual-pitch activation for close-positioned chords in the fourth and fifth octaves. It frequently contains bass tones supporting "inverted" chords, and for large chords in particular, any suitably strong bass can take root, as examples to follow will show.

Above chord space, from C_6 to $C_{>9}$ (higher than the high C of the piccolo, or shorter than a ¾″ organ pipe) is *overtone space*, with an acoustically simple population having little additional room for audible upper-partial development. Pitches in this area are usually superoctave doublings of activity occurring an octave or two below, and thus are products of orchestration, arrangement, and registration. Rarely does overtone space contain the majority if not all of a chord's pitches, and then for special effect, illustration, or other marked signal. Indeed, simultaneities based in overtone space can fail to come off as chords at all. In Richard Strauss's *Also Sprach Zarathustra*, for example, the lowest notes of the final B-major chord, D♯–F♯–B, still barely in (fifth-octave) chord space, seem like ringing afterechoes of previously sounded chord-space structures. Pitch simultaneities built in root space generally end up sounding too "muddy" and indistinct to be heard as chords, as at the conclusion of Schumann's "Paganini" etude in *Carnaval* (chord: $F_{1,3}$ and $A\flat_{1,3}$). Even chords constructed at the lower border of chord space invite critical and analytic comment, as the famous opening measures of Beethoven's "Waldstein" sonata remind us (chord: $C_{2,3}$ and G_2 and E_3).

The partition of pitch space into functional zones is not an explicit doctrine of harmonic theory, largely because its precepts are taught—via either strict counterpoint or thoroughbass—entirely with structures centered in the low-middle of chord space. The constraints of vocal ranges for the former and the influential "intablulation" of those ranges in simple accompaniments for the latter means that significant work with root- or overtone-space pitches takes place with the instrumentation of pitch ideas, not their invention. The larger the tone-color palette, the more the entire pitch spectrum can be set ringing with super- and suboctave couplings from chord-space structures. But even in elementary part-writing and three-over-one thoroughbass style, the allowances for greater volume between the lowest two voices (i.e., up to two octaves, vs. a one-octave span for upper voices) shows awareness of spatial functions, with the result that root space is the site of a reinforced bass *line* instead of chord.

It's useful to reconsider Figure 4.3 in light of the preceding discussion, since the final F♯ chord perfectly exemplifies the voicing requirements for rooted chords: (a) root space is occupied by F♯$_1$ and (b) chordal mass is concentrated between F♯$_3$ and F♯$_5$, with an area of greatest density occurring in the fourth octave: E–F♯–G♯–A♯. Although other forces are at work in this passage to secure tonic for F♯ as we have learned, they would have a much harder task doing so were the final chord (or the final series of chords) transposed, say, down an octave, thereby invading root space with chord tones. The resulting opacity and psychoacoustical roughness would weaken the formation of a tonic impression, perhaps to the point of implausibility.[7]

For comparison, reviewing Figure 3.20 is instructive. This massive entity is grounded by pitches D$_{1,2,3,4,5,6}$, overtonally reinforced with A$_{5,6}$, and only finished off as a major triad with F♯$_6$, encroaching on the lower limit of overtone space—and then only lightly, with just two voices (rather than the 3–4 deployed on the other overtonal nodes). In effect, as the trademark notes, it's more a pitch than a major chord: D$_6$, F♯$_6$, and A$_6$ (if not A$_5$ and D$_5$) lock in as *overtones* of D$_4$, itself resting upon a triple-suboctave foundation reaching down to the depths of D$_1$.

The Proximity Conditions for Chord Emergence. Within chord space, what are the distance relations between pitches for emergence to occur? Simultaneously sounding pitches less than i[3] in distance produce increasingly disruptive beating and dissonance effects, starting with "mild" at i[2] and increasing to "sharp" at i[1]. Thus, we observe that distance closer than i[3] tends toward *cluster* rather than *chord*. This becomes evident if these intervals are "stacked," where a diminished-seventh chord coheres no matter how tall, while clusters build up at every addition of i[2] or i[1], eventually reaching mild whole-tone and sharp chromatic scales, respectively. Moving away from i[3], we can continue to hear chord emergence at i[4], which stacks as an augmented triad. Combining any two from i[3] and i[4] results in close-positioned triads—diminished, minor, major, augmented. Combining three produces familiar seventh chords. Ninth, eleventh, and the rest of the "tertian" chords can then fill up available pitch space.

It is important to recognize that chord emergence continues at i[5], since this opens the way toward contemporary chords beyond those built by simple "third stacking." Adding i[5] to the mix creates not only more consonant triad formations with i[3] and i[4], but also the fourth-chord i[5,5], which Schoenberg (1912 [1978], 399), for one, found to be the first harmonic resource outside the CP enclosure. Taken together, i[3], i[4], and i[5] are what the previous chapter referred to as the *chording intervals*. Here, they can also be recognized as defining *proximity relations* on chord emergence—which is to say that any stack of chording intervals in pitch space, of whatever size and order, merges into chord. A chord can tolerate

---

7. On the other hand, note that the chord can stand being transposed up by one octave, but probably not by two.

a cluster or two, of either mild or sharp kind, as long as chording intervals predominate in the stack and the clusters are tolerably if not maximally separated.

Testing for emergence at i[6], we discover the matter at hand shifts from one of proximity to one of *dispersion*—from how close pitches can be for chord to emerge to how far apart before pitches don't cohere into chord.[8] This shift is prompted by a change in size category: unlike the chording intervals, i[6] can be filled with another pitch without creating a cluster, viz., i[6] filled as i[3,3]. All this is to say that for i[≥ 6], any i[x] can be filled with some combination of chording intervals. Any interval of this size defines a *volume*—a simultaneity that can be brought into fusion with intermediating pitches.

Increasing distance to i[7], the prime mover of overtonality, we know from CP procedures what the infill possibilities are: a combination of i[4] and i[3]—a consonant major or minor triad. Should i[7] be stacked, the start of a "fifth chord," the resulting triad exceeds the compass of an octave (i.e., i[7,7], size 14). Enlarging the stack, the resulting chord fills all of chord space at the pentachord i[7,7,7,7,7], size 35 (= −1 from three octaves), and—given leeway to extend into root space because of i[7]'s spacious volume rather than proximate nearness—a size-49 septachord can be satisfactorily constructed, though this "special effect," like all very large chords, is difficult to arrange, independently voice lead, and transpose given the pitch limits in effect.

At i[8] and even more so at i[9], the pitches involved are in relation, but chord emergence depends upon consistent use of such volumes, which require large amounts of chord space (e.g., i[9,8,9], size 26). Alternatively, chord emergence can result from combinations of proximate intervals with volumes (e.g., i[9,5,3], size 17).[9] If volumes are distributed at the edges of chords, as in i[9,5,3], pitch *isolates* can be distinguished from chord *mass*—the upper three pitches are proximate, i[5,3], and the lowest (the bass of i[9]) stands somewhat apart. The larger the volume, and the more the rest of the pitches are massed, the greater the isolation. If volumes are distributed in the middle of chords and the masses at edges, conditions are set for *polychords*, about which more below.

Pitches involved in i[10] and i[11] are simultaneous and coincidental, but their respective mild and sharp qualities work against emergent fusion. Again, stacking mitigates the difficulty, though the resulting volumes are special effects, and the pitches can be heard without much difficulty as isolates—thus formally denying chord emergence. Beyond this distance, it becomes difficult to hear *chord* at all.

Articulated Overtonal Tonics

With these important features of chord now characterized—the emergence from a massing of chording intervals (and the dispersion of these intervals to mark out

---

8. Cf. Bregman (1990, 228): "All other things being equal, it appears likely that the further apart in frequency two simultaneous components are, the less likely they are to fuse."

9. Details about these combinations, measured according to spacing prototypes described in Morris (1987, 54ff.) have been offered in Harrison (2014).

volumes) as well as overall location in functional pitch space—we can resume inspection of tonicity in contemporary tonal music better equipped to analyze both structure and effect.

Colored Triads

Figure 4.4 shows the opening two phrases of Bartók's Bagatelle, op. 6, no. 4. The first, mm. 1–2, is composed entirely of root-position triads and has a D-minor tonic. The second phrase repeats the outer-voice counterpoint of the first but thickens the texture in two ways. First, the bass-clef open fifths of the first phrase are filled with thirds. This also has the effect of pushing the pitch root down into the zeroth octave, giving the chord mass greater perceived depth as well as thickness. Second, sevenths are placed in the individual chord stacks, one in each hand. Since the second phrase is heard solely as a textural variant of the first, this thickening of texture does not affect the sense of D-minor tonic, even though that tonic is expressed in the second phrase as a minor seventh chord and not a triad. To be sure, the bass-clef chords slightly cloud the sense of tonic since root space is invaded with chord tones, especially in m. 3. But the concluding tonic chord clears out the third above its bass, allowing D_2 to be heard distinctly as a pitch-class representative of the root and thereby fully re-securing the D-minor tonic.

The ease with which the tonic can be described as D minor even though the second phrase uses a seventh chord instead of a traditional triad points out the inadequacy of the term "seventh chord" here. For the evidence of the passage suggests that the sevenths are not organically part of the chord but supplementary or added tones. In this sense, one of the naming conventions for seventh chords accurately reflects the nature of the chordal association. Calling the tonic chord a "minor minor-seventh" shows it to contain, first, a minor triad and, second, an appended minor seventh.[10] In this way, the chord is still heard primarily as a triad, and the appended note produces what has traditionally if uncritically been called a "coloristic" effect—something that pertains to neither structure nor function, but rather operates somewhere *within* or *upon* the structure as a creature of timbre (see further Antokoletz 1984, 27–30).

Colored tonics such as these depend upon what Neil Minturn (1997, 61) has termed *tonal interpreters*, "a harmonic triad, a diatonic scale segment, or a functional bass segment or progression whenever such . . . is heard to organize pitches around it into a locally tonal scheme." In other words, tonal interpreters are creatures of dynamics because of their power of organizing, which can result only from context and placement. In the Bartók example, these are easy to recognize. From small scale to large, we note the preponderance of outer-voice octaves in the first,

10. There is some confusion about the hyphenation in this chord labeling system. Some (e.g., Aldwell and Schachter [2003]) would hyphenate between the two "minor" terms: "minor-minor seventh chord." While the underlying understanding of the chord is still a triad with a seventh, this hyphenation scheme seems to emphasize the unification of these elements into a single entity: a seventh chord. Hyphenating minor and seventh, in contrast, pulls the triad and added interval apart, emphasizing thereby the supplementary nature of the added note.

Figure 4.4 Bela Bartók, Bagatelle, op. 6.4, mm. 1–4

second, fifth, and eighth chords, all of which emphasize the overtonally important notes D and A. (The same applies, *mutatis mutandis*, to the chords of the second phrase.) Moreover, D opens and closes each phrase, occupying thereby a traditional tonic spot. Further, both outer-voice lines present diatonic scale segments anchored on D. The passage as a whole is thus heard to be constructed of pitches from the D-minor natural scale. And finally, to return to our initial observation, the first, triadically based phrase vouchsafes all these overtonal features to the second, which repeats its essential counterpoint and scale content. In sum, the first phrase is, as an entity, the tonal interpreter for the second.

Colored triads are characterized by *coloring agents* of various hues and intensities. Those in the second phrase of the Bartók excerpt are generally mild; the tonic chord belongs to set class 4-26[0358], which has one ic2 and no sharp ic1 in an otherwise consonant emulsion of chording intervals. The effects of a sharp coloring agent are apparent in the opening of "Ondine" from Ravel's *Gaspard de la nuit* (fig. 4.5), which colors a C♯-major triad with an A♮ agent, creating set class 4-19[0148].[11] Minturn encounters 4-19 colored triads often in Prokofiev's music, and his discussion of the third movement of the fourth Piano Sonata is pertinent here:

> The pitch-class set 4-19[0148] appears in two segmentations, which are characteristic of this work as well as many others. The first segmentation presents 4-19 as a form of 3-11[037], that is, as either a major or a minor triad, plus one more note attached chromatically to an element of the triad. The second segmentation presents 4-19 as an augmented triad (3-12[048]), plus one more note attached chromatically to an element of that augmented triad. (Minturn 1997, 61)[12]

Minturn then proceeds carefully to analyze the interaction of these two forms of 4-19—only the first of which can function traditionally as a colored tonic triad since the second is a colored augmented triad.

At the end of the movement, which Minturn does not discuss, two coloring agents are applied to the final, tonic chord. As the functional analysis in Figure 4.6 shows, the dynamics involved are clearly the same as in the authentic cadence, in which the concluding sonority is strongly predicated by preceding events, allowing

11. Of course, the score notation leads one to analyze the A♮ as a melodic upper neighbor to G♯. In performance, however, the rapidity of thirty-second-note attack and the use of pedal create a famous archetype of the shimmering colored tonic.
12. Note that 4-19 can only be created from *one particular* chromatic attachment from the 3-11 subset, whereas it can be created from *any* chromatic attachment from the 3-12 subset.

Figure 4.5 Maurice Ravel, *Gaspard de la nuit*, "Ondine," m. 1ff

Figure 4.6 Sergei Prokofiev, Sonata no. 4, mvt. 3, ending

the static structure of the tonic chord to bear greater dissonance. The chord indeed has two coloring agents (indicated by arrows), both sharp and thus particularly intense. The "left-hand" agent is attached in the fourth octave to the major third of the chord, producing 4-17[0347], another characteristic Prokofiev set according to Minturn (209). The "right-hand" agent, B_6, is attached to the pitch-class root well into overtone space and safely away from the C_1 root sounded at the beginning of the measure. The result is that the coloring effect of the left-hand $D\sharp_4$ predominates over that of the right-hand B_6, a particularly effective design here.

Polychords

The disposition of notes in the tonic chord of Figure 4.6 is likely a factor in its ability to bear two coloring agents. The right- and left-hand portions of the chord are separated by an octave, with the right-hand part close to the border of overtone space. It is not difficult to hear the chord as having two distinct sites of activity, one in the fourth octave and the other in the sixth, with the empty fifth forming a buffer zone between them. This suggests that the (singular) tonic chord at the end of the Prokofiev example could also be called the (plural) tonic chords. For the passage at hand, this description does not offer much advantage. In the passage shown in Figure 4.7, however, the utility of such a description is clearer. Here, what might appear to be multiple coloring agents of a single chord actually affiliate to form a separate triad, creating a polychord. The resulting overtonal effect is bitonal (see Harrison 1997).

Figure 4.7 Darius Milhaud, *Saudades do Brasil*, "Corvocado," mm. 19–30

The buffer zone here is only partly registral in nature; although the first beat of the opening measure contains a palpable gap between right-hand and left-hand parts, this is closed by the end of the measure, and this is maintained until the right-hand part ascends in the latter half of m. 3. Even so, the opening and concluding gaps of the right-hand melodic "U" shape are important markers of tonal separation. The alternation of rhythmic activity also helps separate the two parts; the right-hand part has first-beat attention, while the left-hand gets second-beat. This feature is especially important in the first two measures of each phrase (mm. 1–2, 5–6), since the focus on right-hand activity allows a sense of chordal arpeggiation to solidify, preventing individual members of the right-hand line from affiliating with the left. This effect is strong enough to prevent the right-hand F#$_4$ on the second beat of m. 1, for example, from being incorporated into a B-minor sonority offered by the left hand.[13] All in all, then, the conditions are present to offer the ear a left-hand part in G major

---

13. The half-note G$_2$, of course, is still nominally the pitch-class root of the left-hand part throughout the measure; yet its decay by that point, coupled with the insistently attacked D$_3$–B$_3$ dyad, gives opportunity to hear at least an attempt to form a B-minor chord.

and a right-hand part in D major (mm. 1–4), with the right-hand part pushing upwards to E♭ major in mm. 5–8.

The functional analysis beneath the score shows a continual undulation between T and D that operates, separately, in both parts through m. 7. (Thereafter, the right-hand part begins a process of merging into the G major of the left-hand, which is completed in m. 11.) Because of this alignment, a generalized sense of tonic and dominant can easily be felt—with the tonic "chord" consisting of a dissonant fusion of G-major and D-major triads. The scare quotes remind us that the relevant term may instead be the more neutral "simultaneity"; certainly, either description is superior to the structurally equivalent claim that the tonic chord is a $G^{9,\sharp7}$. This last might also be the equivalent of claiming the tonic to be a G-major triad with two coloring agents, A (=9th) and F♯ (= $\sharp7^{th}$). Both claim an underlying "G-ness" to the tonic that Milhaud seems uninterested in affirming.

Chords with Root Representatives

Another type of overtonal tonic comprises many individual techniques and exemplars. They have in common what Leonard Meyer might have called a "secondary-parameter" root, or Hindemith a "root representative." This is a marked bass note of some kind—planted in root space, loud, deep, or long—that usurps the office of root by salience alone. Strictly speaking, a root representative is *not* a traditional chord root, but a bass note that can characterize and support a chord.

The environments that support this kind of chord-tone usurpation vary, although many involve isolation of the bass in some way. One common root-representative structure has intervallic tracery or patterning in the chord stack. Such a chord inflates a stack of generic or specific intervals (e.g., thirds, fourths, fifths), building mass in chord space while frequently offering the lowest note of the stack (or, more convincingly, a root-space suboctave doubling of that note) as a root representative. A clear illustration is afforded in Figure 4.8, the opening of Ravel's *Daphnis et Chloé*. The overtonal tonic here is built up from the initial A_1 as root, subsequently reinforced by A_2 in m. 2. From there, the chord stack inflates by i[7] through $G\sharp_5$, all the while giving the impression that some kind of "A chord" is being built. Because of its placement at the opening of the piece, the chord is proposed as a tonic. If the chord stack were to go on indefinitely from here up to the limits of hearing and fill up with all manner of tones, the sense of A as root would not likely be shaken thereby as long as A remained the bass note. However, were the bass to change to, say, a D_2, with the A_2 coming in as written in m. 2 and the rest of the chord unchanged, D would then unquestionably take over as root during the inflation phase of the chord.[14]

14. See Ulehla (1966, 383): "Any combination of intervals can be mounted upon a low perfect fifth. It can be likened to an anchor gripping the sands of tonality. The lowest tone, by having the support of the immediate perfect fifth receives a root strength than cannot be shaken by any amount of upper dissonance."

This last point is illustrated in Figure 4.9, the opening of a ballad from a 1990s Broadway musical that sets up a pop-ballad groove typical of the genre. Although the tonic chord appears initially as a colored triad (E major with added ninth, shown at the end of the excerpt), the action of the bass over the course of the introduction encourages a hearing of the coloration as immobilized chord-space upperwork. E, B, and F♯ sound constantly in the treble (accompanied by G♯ at the beginning of the phrases, mm. 1 and 5), while the bass alternates between E and A in its gradual move downward toward root space, changing the chord root representative each time and therefore the harmonic function (E as T and A as S). The bass is strong enough to direct harmonic function so that the Bs that appear at the end of m. 4 and 7 communicate a brief D that authentically energizes the return to the E tonic chord in the following measures. The power of the bass to direct harmony in an overtonal setting was also encountered in Figure 4.2(c)—*Mackie Messer*—with its tune that focused on a single reciting note with harmonic activity taking place underneath it.

Figure 4.8 Ravel, *Daphnis et Chloé*, opening

Figure 4.9 Stephen Flaherty, "Human Heart," from *Once on this Island*, introduction

E(add9)

Integrated Overtonal Tonics

The first three types of "dissonant" overtonal tonics—colored triads, polychords, and chords with root representatives—all involve a distinction between structure and ornament. In the first type, a traditional major or minor triad is the structural basis, to which extra-triadic coloring agents are applied. In the second, the extra-triadic elements are themselves affiliated into triads of their own, and issues of primacy and subordination are thereby put into play. In the third, the structural element is the root representative, and the ornaments are those pitches in the chord-space superstructure offered as chord tones. All three of these, as Figure 4.10 suggests, take a dichotomous form of "element + supplement," for which reason they were labeled generally as *articulated* chords.

The analysis of tonicity in articulated chords can afford to put structural weight on the traditional triadic or rooting element as the essential structure, since this maneuver frequently does not pose interpretive difficulties. (In a polychord, however, because the two parts are roughly equal, the analytic assignment of element and supplement is difficult and may be beside the point as well. As a result, bitonality offers special and interesting compositional opportunities.) In addition, these types are more central tendencies than fully isolatable categories. In practice, more than one may be at work and influencing perception of tonic. This is especially the case with colored triads and root representatives, as we have seen not only in the excerpts from the ballads *Mackie Messer* and *Human Heart* but also in the final cadence of the Prokofiev Sonata (fig. 4.6), in which the concluding sonority was analyzed as a colored triad—yet surely the movements of the "big" bass notes there also make clear the basic harmonic functions at work.

Another type of overtonal tonic offers the same sense of unity through harmonious proportion that marks the major and minor consonant triads, and it thus stands somewhat apart in a separate category of analysis. The arrangement of chord tones in an *integrated* overtonal tonic is such that it is difficult and maybe even undesirable to pick out one or more as superfluous to the structure.

The next two examples show simple dynamic situations drawn from jazz practice that generate integrated major-seventh tonics. The basis for the first (fig. 4.11a) is a standard II^7–V^7–I cadential motion (voiced so that the resolution of the II^7 is taken over by the upper voice). In terms Ernst Kurth would endorse (see Rothfarb 1988), the energy of the progression can be boosted by means of a *leading-tone insertion* into the first chord, F♯, which displaces the elements of the voice-leading line, shifting them onto following chords by one "place"—in other words, taking version [1] into [2]. The resulting chords all have their dissonance settings raised because of this displacement. The final chord, however, despite being a major major-seventh chord, is well-predicated by the progression and its voice leading, so that it seems organically part of the structure instead of a supplement to a particular verticality.[15] The integration of the sonority comes about from the dynamic

15. Cf. the II–V–I cadence with concluding major seventh shown in McGowan (2005, 171).

Figure 4.10 Schematic of articulated overtonal tonics. (a) colored triad,
(b) polychord, (c) chord with root representative

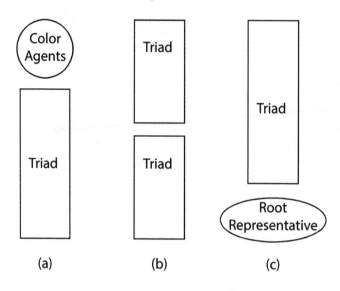

Figure 4.11 (a1) II–V–I cadence; (a2) the same, with F♯ leading-tone insertion
in first chord. (b1) Plagal cadence with minor IV; (b2) the same, with subposed
A♭ bass

process of voice leading interacting with that of the cadence. (It is instructive to
compare this example with the Waldteufel waltz, shown in fig. 4.2[b], in which the
concluding major-seventh chord also succeeded a dominant ninth.) The second
example (fig. 4.11b) shows another cadential situation, this time plagal. A typical
chromatic passing tone boosts the plagal effect, but the half-diminished sonority
also invites interpretation as the upper structure of a ninth chord. Subposing the

root of that chord, which happens at [2], makes B♭ a dissonant ninth. Allowing convention to play out here, the progression into the final chord pulls B♭ down by step, creating a tonic whose dissonant seventh is well-predicated by the preceding ninth chord.

Amplified Chords

The dynamic forces at work in the excerpts adduced so far have been purposefully attenuated in order to keep focus on the static situation. Sharpening the focus further requires that dynamics be dampened to a minimum, which makes for admittedly artificial laboratory conditions. But this can give us a Pisgah view of an idealized overtonal statics, of integrated overtonal tonics whose structures need little support from dynamic contexts to stabilize as tonics. These *amplified chords* have an inherent static stability that mimics if not actually derives from that possessed by traditional consonant-triad tonics.

Figure 4.12 shows stages of tonic-chord amplification using the "note-value" notation for overtonal hierarchy introduced in chapter 2, keyed here according to the root and fifth, C and G. Any and all additional pitches observe what might be styled the *Pythagorean-Hippocratical imperative* of tonic chords: "minimize harm" to an already established concord by having new pitch classes fulfill conditions for chord emergence—be close enough to existing ones to fuse with them, but far away enough to avoid proximity dissonance. The first stage of amplification sets traditional modal color, either major (**M**) or minor (**m**), and its potential fills are shown as half notes, with stem direction correlated to mode. The second stage activates familiar seventh-chord formations with the selection of one of the three possible notes and—anticipating the effects of the next stage—a larger chord if the B♮ and A are sounded together. Quarter-notes show fills that honor the imperative best by introducing mild dissonance (ic2); the sixteenth-note value for B♮ marks the presence of a sharp (ic1) dissonance with the tonic note of the overtonal frame.

Various note-combinations from Stages 1 and 2 are detailed in the bottom system of Figure 4.12. These are graded from most to least stable constructions, as the notation suggests by means of both note value and stem direction. The major added sixth chord and its inversional partner, the minor seventh, need minimal dynamic (contextual) help to be proposed as tonics, and this feature can be encoded in abbreviation: **M+** for the former and **m+** for the latter. The next inversionally related chord pair, belonging to set class 4-27[0258], has a tritone in its interval vector (which the notation highlights with opposed note-stems). A traditionally unstable quality usually reserved for non-tonic functions, these chords can be easily stabilized by well-predicated placement in familiar locations for tonics in phrases, perfectly exemplified in the conclusion of Duruflé's *Requiem*, discussed above in connection with Figure 4.3. Nonetheless, we will mark such B-chords (as defined in chap. 3) in gray as configurations more easily adapted to non-tonic uses.

Figure 4.12 (a) schematic for amplified-tonic chords, showing four characteristic bands and "residue" notes (avoid tones); (b) Some pcsets that result from various band combinations. Gray pcsets are capable of being voiced as "B" chords (with tritone)

(a)

(b)

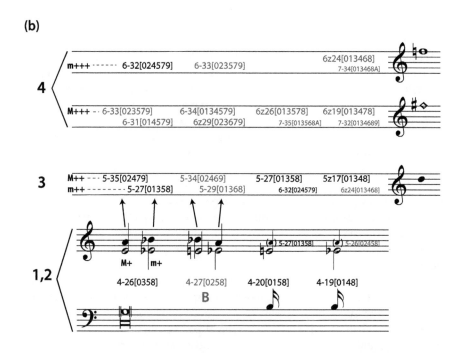

The final two chords are characterized by ic1 sharpness, with the last, 4-19[0148], also subsetting a difficult-to-stabilize augmented triad and, if two fills from Stage 2 are used, a tritone as well. Previous examples have illustrated the dynamic forces needed to stabilize these tetrads, such as the concluding rhetoric that sets up the major seventh chords in Figures 4.2(a) and (b). Such chords at the beginning of a phrase are comparatively rare.[16] Figure 4.13 shows a case from a

---

16. Examples from McGowan (2005, 88, 99, 101, and so forth), suggested by Chailley (1977 [1986], 10), all show concluding major-seventh chords.

Figure 4.13 James Pankow, "Colour My World," mm. 1–22

1970s pop ballad, where the major seventh chord is a pervasive accent in this passage, sounding not only in the opening, global tonic, but also in a local tonic (m. 9) as well as in a series of mid-phrase chords (mm. 5–7).[17] So marked, the chord attains a motivic status in the piece that promotes it beyond a simple colored triad. Even so, this status is not clear at the outset, and the arpeggiated major-seventh there seems too tensed to be a satisfactory tonic. Indeed, it is easily understood as an appoggiatura chord to the more phonologically relaxed A-minor triad in m. 3. The tonicness of the phrase-initiating major-seventh chord thus becomes clear only retrospectively, and it is gradually secured by its motivic quality.

The third stage adds a major ninth to both **M** and **m** types, creating **M++** and **m++** chords. D evenly fills the root-and-third pitch-class space for the former, successfully honoring the imperative by avoiding introducing sharpness to the resulting pentatonic chord. For the latter, both D and D♭ would appear to serve equally well, since either cannot help but to introduce sharpness. Yet, as noted in the previous chapter's discussion of harmonic fluctuation, the effect is noticeably mitigated if voiced as a major seventh over the chordal third instead of a (compound) minor ninth over the overtonal root. Thus, D♭ is ruled out as noticeably more "harmful" than D for amplified tonics. The lack of stem shows D's suitability for both modal types. Other combinations of fills, denoted as pcset classes, are shown in the relevant staff at (b).

The fourth stage, like the first, offers two options, though only F♯ suitably combines with other "down stemmed" notes from previous stages, as it evenly fills

17. McGowan (2005, 77), would understand the major-seventh "accent" as indicating a *principal dialect* of a larger language of dynamic consonance.

pitch-class space between E♭ and overtonal fifth, G. The dotted down-stem marks this preference, and the resulting amplified chord is m+++. In M types, by contrast, F♯ creates a detrimental (compound) minor ninth with the modal color note, E♭. For both, it can ambiguate the overtonal frame by attempting to suggest the root function for itself—the whole-note value symbolizes the close hierarchical relationship with the overtonal breves/double whole-notes. For these reasons, F♯ partly belongs to the final, "residue" section of Figure 4.12, which contains the remaining "avoid notes" of the chromatic collection. These dissonate as (potential) minor ninths with the overtonal frame and thus obscure it undesirably (see Tymoczko 2011, 354ff., for a sophisticated treatment of "avoid notes"). F♯, while topping the structure off with a tritone over the root, honors the imperative better than F♮ and can be fitted to either m or M types. If added to the "double plus" form of the latter, the resulting chord is M+++.[18]

The set-class results for various combinations of fills shown in the upper portions of Figure 4.12 feature scale and set structures familiar from other theoretical and analytical contexts, which shows that honoring the imperative enacts the functional equivalent of a progressive near-even division of octave space.[19] The best way to experience the plausibility of Figure 4.12 is at the keyboard, trying out various combinations for tonic-suitability for some putative overtonal composition. Various voicings and doublings will fluctuate in harmonic effect, with the principle of softening mild and sharp dissonances by compounding their intervals discussed in chapter 3 providing a useful way to keep track of this fluctuation. As should now be evident, the particular voicing of the chord in the figure was contrived to compound all mild and sharp intervals in order to "minimize harm" in a fully staged and amplified tonic chord.

One might very well question why a M or m triad is not taken as the starting point of an amplified chord (as it is for a colored triad, for instance). It is true that the overtonal fifth is normally filled in contemporary tonal composition—just as it is in music of the CP and a century or so before—and it is thus a default choice for many composers on grounds of familiarity. Further, an unfilled overtonal fifth is also difficult to use compositionally: like a hydrogen atom—which it resembles in its two-particle structure—the basic root and fifth seems to bond with another element more readily than to remain an unbound, single element. "Hydrogen-system" overtonality is thus rather rare outside of dronal contexts. Figure 4.14 provides an instructive example, wherein chords are either unfilled, as in the opening and final chords (cf. fig. 3.24), or filled with adjacencies instead of modal color notes, such as the second and third chords of the first measure, which form a colorless area of linear infill in which D and F pad the overtonal space

---

18. The structure of M+++ is identical to that proposed by McGowan (2005, 156ff.) for the set of scale-degree assemblies for tonic chords in tonal jazz. Borrowing terminology from Harrison (1994), McGowan individually names the fills in the amplification stages: Stage 1 contains the *modal agent*; the second has the *dialect agent*; the third, the *suffix associate*; and the fourth, the *Lydian suffix*—the last indebted to Russell (1959). See McGowan's (2005) Exx. 9(a) and (b), 77–78, for jazz-based correlations with Figure 4.12.

19. See Tymoczko (2011, 63ff., esp. Figure 2.10.3; cf. Figure 4.4.4).

Figure 4.14 Paul Hindemith, *Symphonie: Mathis der Maler*, "Grablegung," reduction of mm. 1–4

inward by a step, creating opportunity for some compositional elaboration (basically, neighbor and skip) with a weakly emergent pentatonic harmonic effect. An early and influential case of this kind of elaboration is surely found in the opening of Stravinsky's *Petrushka*, condensed and reproduced as an *aide-mémoire* in Figure 4.15. The overtonal D-A fifth is filled by a neighbor-note bandwidth trill, and the flute showcases the opportunities for skipping. This soundworld persists for quite some time, and while an eventual major fill (F♯) is predicted by B♮ and C♯ in the cello countermelody, mm. 6 ff., it fails to appear before the B♭ (in the key signature) is sounded with greater and greater force starting in m. 12, and the culmination of the passage—the grand chords of mm. 42ff.—are in an unambiguous G-dorian, with F♮.

The "added-sixth chord," M+, is a well-known tonic sonority from the early twentieth century, with origins apparently in French Impressionism; later, in the 1920s, it becomes a staple of jazz harmony.[20] This chord has already been encountered in Figure 4.2(c) (*Mackie Messer*) as a colored triad, in which the added sixth is understood analytically as a supplement to a major triad, or what Henry Martin (2005, 19), in his extended study of the chord, denotes as an "independent" sixth. In contrast, an amplified-chord M+ chord exemplifies Martin's "inclusive" sixth, in which "it is absorbed by the chord and often embedded in the chord voicing." We shall encounter an example in the opening of Duruflé's *Requiem* below.

While the M and m triads are related by interval inversion, the M+ and m+ chords are related by partial-order rotation, otherwise known as chord inversion. That is, both chords can be understood as instances of a minor seventh chord, with m+ in root position and M+ in first inversion. Unlike traditional chord-inversion theory, however, where the chord root remains invariant under rotation, voicing and arrangement can determine the root. In both current cases, chord root is allocated to the lowest note, thus making the chords nonequivalent in this important way.[21]

20. McGowan (2005, 86–87), cites a number of examples, the earliest being Debussy's "Le Jet d'Eau" from *Cinq poèmes de Baudelaire* (1887–89). Martin (2005) discusses extensively the chord's use in jazz.

21. In this way, the understanding of chord root is different from the traditional one derived from Rameau—although students of history will immediately recognize that Rameau himself found the *accord de la grande sixte* to be ambiguously rooted. It agrees instead with Hindemith's reading of chord roots.

Figure 4.15 Igor Stravinsky, *Petrushka*, synopsis of the opening

Overtonal Tonicity: Three Case Studies

Special Opportunities for Amplified-Tonics with Two Fills in Duruflé's Requiem

Figure 4.16 reduces and simplifies the opening of Maurice Duruflé's *Requiem*, op. 9 (the conclusion of the work was shown in fig. 4.3). An analysis of harmonic content is found beneath the staves, and the symbols are explained in Figure 4.17. This diagram uses the note-value system for representing tonal hierarchy (see fig. 4.12), in which square breves represent tonic, round breves dominant, and half-notes the modal third, with upstems for major and downstems for minor. The fundamental harmonic structure of the passage is an amplified-tonic chord, Dm+, and its triadic subsets, Dm and FM, are shown as the first two chords of the Figure, notated as (local) tonics. The third chord attempts to show the full amplified chord as a combination of its subsets, adding quarter notes to handle the second-stage fills (stems likewise indicating modal color), but the notation is crowded and over-weight; the fourth fuses the characteristic features of each into a single symbol. Square breves show the tonic attribute, round breves the dominant; the addition of stems to these registers the mediant attribute, depending on stem direction; and a fill of a stemmed notehead shows the second-stage attribute. (A single "stem column" serves all affected notes; noteheads to the right of the column are down-stemmed; those to the left are up-stemmed.

Three closely related nontonic sonorities used in the passage, shown at (b), are generated through neighboring motion; they are labeled N(1, 2, or 3). The first two involve activation of B♭, which whether functioning as $\hat{6}$ of Dm or $\hat{4}$ of FM, carries a subdominant charge. The fused symbol indicates both. N(2) increases the subdominant attitude with a G, shown as a fusion of $\hat{4}$ Dm and $\hat{2}$ of FM (i.e., the whole-note shape of the former and the filled notehead of the latter). While N(2) is characterized by its G bass, N(1) freely uses various chord tones in the bass, going so far as to arpeggiate through them all in mm. 8–9.[22] N(3) maintains the G bass, changes the tonic elements to Dm, and swaps

---

22. N(1) generally accompanies N(2)'s root, G, in a choral part, with A frequently heard as an upper neighbor or suspension. N(2) can thus be thought of as a stronger version of N(1), from which a root has been cast out to the bass.

in B♮ for B♭, changing the color of the chord noticeably away from minor hues. (The diamond notehead of the tritone of F is filled and upstemmed to show its major submediant attribute for D.)

The final section of the figure, (c), shows how a certain text-painting effect in the passage will be set up. The essential move here is activating and subsequently deactivating F♯ from F♮. This move is accompanied by semitonal contrary motion, using notes that are locally chromatic, E♭ and B♮. Given the text, which will be discussed shortly, I suggest that the most appropriate way to analyze the introduction of the F♯ is as part of a majorized, "shining" version of the local Dm triad that represents the fundamental tonic structure.

Returning to Figure 4.16, we see that the music setting the first two phrases of the *cantus firmus* (up to m. 11) is very lightly differentiated in its harmony, with m+ beginning and ending the unit. The understated N(1) is used in phrase interiors, while the more pronounced N(2) prefaces the notable tonic articulations of mm. 7 and 11. Further, the restricted range of the introit chant and the leisurely tempo help drain teleological dynamic from the passage, so that the basic overtonal statics are clear. The second half of the passage, mm. 13–22, is generally brighter in color than the first, with FM beginning and ending the unit and the conspicuously majorized N(3) of m. 12 prefacing it. Brightness is amplified by the "shining" tonic of m. 16, the contrapuntal dynamics leading to which were illustrated in Figure 17(c). This coordinated series of events is in service of the text—"may light perpetual shine upon them"—with the moment of maximum brightness occurring at the verb *luceat*. The shining, DM chord is a noteworthy harmonic contrast that is nonetheless strongly attached to the fundamental tonic structure, fusing the global root, D, with the local, major color. The contrast is underscored by the return of B♭ in m. 17, after which the passage harmonically darkens again, but only so far as to the FM triadic tonic subset, not back to the overcast Dm+. The momentary uncovering of light perpetual leaves a glow.

Considering the tight relations among tonic entities in the passage—the superordinate Dm+, its triadic subsets, and the "shining" version that fuses attributes of those subsets—it seems inappropriate to claim that the FM ending of the passage is the modulatory goal from an initial Dm colored-triad state. As was suggested above, the teleological dynamic here is noticeably attenuated, harmonic contrast and fluctuation achieved by subtle, low-energy means. FM and Dm seem rather to represent a single tonic structure of which a darker version is heard initially and a brighter version at the end. We are now at a crossroads with Robert Bailey's notion of *double-tonic complex,* which he first developed in connection with study of *Tristan und Isolde.* The original form of Bailey's idea (1985) involved a very tight tonal pairing of two tonic triads a minor third apart

linked together in such a way that either triad can serve as the local representative of the tonic complex. Within that complex itself, however, one of the two elements is at any moment in the primary position while the other remains subordinate to it. (122; Cf. Lewis 1989, 17)

Figure 4.16 Maurice Duruflé, *Requiem*, op. 9, "Introit," mm. 1–22, reduced. String figuration (mostly arpeggiation) and some chord doublings have been omitted in the accompaniment. The upper parts of the chorus vocalize on "ah"

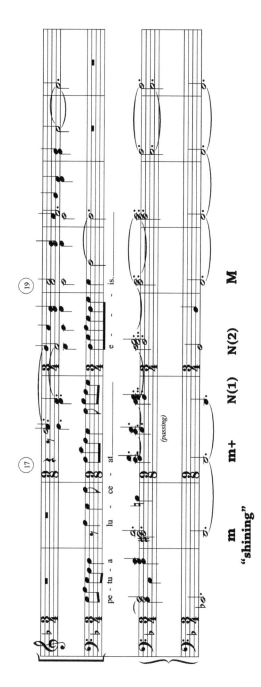

Figure 4.16 (Continued)

Figure 4.17 Key to analytic symbols used in Figure 4.16

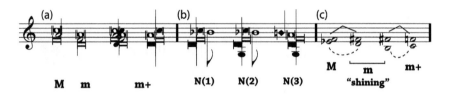

This is how Bailey had to explain the situation in *Tristan*—which is to say that Wagner's art did not recognize a fusion of the two triads into M+ or m+ as a possible tonic sonority. Such fusion, as I have argued, is a distinctive feature of contemporary tonal composition, a feature which arguably could be credited to French Impressionist harmonic styles in which Duruflé was thoroughly expert.[23] A rather different form of theoretical recognition of arguably the same phenomenon, though ostensibly limited to the music of Stravinsky, has been given by Joseph Straus (1982), who offered the *tonal axis* as a model of harmonic tonicity.[24] A structure that has the appearance of a minor-seventh or a major-seventh chord—in other words, of an amplified-root tonic with two fills or, in the case of the major-seventh, a colored triad at the very least—the axis

> must function in the piece as a referential sonority. It must occur prominently as a discrete harmony within the piece, particularly in cadential situations. It must be the essential harmonic generator of the piece; other harmonies derive from and relate to it. (Straus 1982, 265)

While not all uses of amplified-root chords with two fills, M+ and m+, in contemporary tonal composition involve techniques identified by Bailey and Straus, these structures are nonetheless uniquely qualified to use these techniques. A chord with more than two fills, as was pointed out above, can no longer rely on familiar advantages of pitch-class equivalence—octave doubling, for instance— that permit flexibility in voicing and voice leading. Extended chords with three or more fills and that consume up to two octaves of pitch space are thus more difficult to break into subset representatives that can themselves operate as overtonal tonics. For example, subsetting a four-band CM+++ chord into triads (i.e., CM and DM), seems to enable bitonal rather than double-tonic conditions, a suggestive point of contact between the two apparently theoretically distinct environments.

---

23. This feature of Impressionism has naturally attracted the attention of Bailey-inspired analysts, creating a considerable literature applying Bailey's ideas, especially to the music of Debussy. The earliest effort may be Crotty (1982), and the most recent (to date of this writing) is Pomeroy (2004).
24. Straus recently revisited this approach in Straus (2014), a far more comprehensive account with considerable implications beyond Stravinsky's music.

An Amplified Tonic with Coloring Agents in Steve Reich's Octet

A helpful consequence of having theorized amplified chords is that they can be understood to support more complex overtonal tonics. That is, their inherent static stability permits them to bear more coloring agents than less stable chords. The prototype case is, of course, the colored triad, but the larger amplified-root chords may also be colored. An instructive if confined case is offered in Figure 4.18, which excerpts the first two-measure cell of Steve Reich's *Octet* (1978) at (a)—repeated for some minutes thereafter—and graphically interprets the overtonal tonic at (b). The overtonal root and fifth are shown in the leftmost "column" of the analysis. The larger noteheads show the bass, root-space pitches, sounded in the left-hand of both piano parts, and the sustained violin notes in the treble. The smaller noteheads show intersections with overtonal structure of the right-hand piano 1 part, about which more below. The middle column extracts the coloration-band fills from the left-hand piano part, the first band shown with filled notehead and the second with open. (The downward stem signifies minor coloration.) The basic amplified-root structure of the tonic is thus **m+**.

A prominent coloring agent, D♯$_3$, is strongly attached as an *acciaccatura* to the modal fill, E$_3$. See the second, fourth, and fifth beats in the left hand of both piano parts, where sometimes D♯ neighbors melodically and other times sounds simultaneously

Figure 4.18 (a) Steve Reich, *Octet*, mm. 1–2; (b) harmonic analysis; (c) analysis of overtonal hierarchy

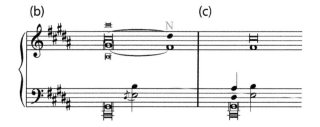

with E. More than a simple accent, however, the D♯ is a symptom of a kind of "hyper-overtonal" condition exhibited in the opening tonic in which the perfect-fifth rooting interval is reduplicated elsewhere in the harmonic texture in ways that do not reinforce the C♯ root. Which is to say that D♯$_3$ appears to be generated as a duplicate fifth, stacked as surplus on top of the foundational C♯$_2$–G♯$_2$ and thereby imparting to the tonic chord characteristics of "interval-inflation" construction discussed in connection with root-representative structures above. That *acciaccatura* quality of D♯$_3$/E$_3$ audibly marks the site of conflict between two chord-structure ideals: interval inflation by perfect fifth vs. root amplification by coloration-band fill. A more prominent (if less acute) symptom of hyper-overtonality is the right-hand part of piano 1, which "doubles" the left hand-bass at the upper twelfth (i.e., fifth)—in effect, droning an entire line with the fundamental overtonal interval, not just a bass note. This technique adds F♯ and A♯ coloring agents to the C♯m+ mix as well as another D♯. Of the three, only A♯ is uniquely generated from the linear drone while the other two have additional sources and registers.

The results of a tissue culture, as it were, of the piece's hyperovertonality are shown at (c), which accounts for all the notes used the passage. The m+ chord is shown broken down into two components: (1) the C♯–G♯ overtonal fifth, over which are two surplus fifths, G♯–D♯ and D♯–A♯; and (2) the two fifth-related fills, E–B, over which are also two surplus fifths, B–F♯ and F♯–C♯, the last of which resounds the tonic pitch class and thereby seems to complete the structure.[25]

The view of the material presented at (c) is entirely from the perspective of the piano parts. Working much the same pitch classes but with quite a different rhythmic idea is the violin, which the analysis at (b) takes into account. There, in the third column, we see the coloring agents D♯ and F♯ again, this time as melodic neighbors to the overtonal G♯–C♯ pair. The undulating neighbor motion is reminiscent—though obviously not in tempo—of the opening of *Petrushka* (fig. 4.15), where the overtonal interval was elaborated similarly. There, however, no first-stage fill was present, and the passage was modally uncolored as a result. Yet in the present case, where both first- and second-stage fills are present, as well as coloring agents, the marked prominence of the violin figuration puts some pressure on the structural claims of the amplifying fills, which is to say that another viable way of hearing the opening tonic is as a "hydrogen-system" C♯ with a slow-moving trill, the remaining notes being heard as more or less ephemeral coloring agents resulting from hyperovertonality, two of which happen to resemble notes from amplification stages.

Pentatonic Ambiguities in Marcel Dupré's Prelude in B major, op. 7 (1912)

Marcel Dupré (1886–1971) was the leading symphonic-organ virtuoso of his day, continuing a tradition of brilliant composition for that instrument whose best known exponents were César Franck and, from its final generation, Olivier Messiaen. In fact, Dupré was Messiaen's organ teacher at the Paris Conservatoire,

25. Given the hyperovertonality, it should hardly be surprising that the notes of Figure 4.18(c) form pitch-class set 7-35: the diatonic collection.

under whose tutelage the latter won a *premier prix* in 1928. (Dupré himself won multiple prizes while a student, including the *prix de Rome* in 1914.) Dupré's beneficent influence on Messiaen's musical life was sufficient to have set him at the organ console of *Sainte-Trinité* in Paris for over sixty years.

The first section of Dupré's B-major Prelude, mm. 1–25, is shown in reduced and condensed form in Figure 4.19. The brilliant, *toccata-sortie* manual

Figure 4.19 Marcel Dupré, Prelude in B major, op. 7, mm. 1–25

figuration—perhaps a model for "Dieu parmi nous" from Messiaen's *La Nativité du Seigneur*—draws immediate attention, but its tonal relations are quite complex and not disclosed without preparation. An easier way in is offered by the pedal tune, mm. 3–13, which is segmented into three units, mm. 3–6, a varied and transposed repetition in mm. 7–11, and an intensifying transition, mm. 12–13. Figure 4.20(a) extracts the notes from the first two units (sourcing is shown beneath the staff) and collates them in descending scalar order, which reflects the general contour of the tune. Highly placed notes in the overtonal hierarchy are marked for a basic analytic orientation, which is clearly in a line from F♯ through the ostensible B tonic and directed at E. Indeed, B is such a light chordal skip from the emphasized F♯ in the opening phrase that it doesn't appear in the extract. As the dotted slur shows, the melodic figure there descends through an 3-7[025] pcset and rests on C♯—pointedly failing to resolve to B tonic. The second phrase begins similarly to the first, with B seeming to be the fifth of E and not a root in its own right, but it ends rather differently, passing through an inverted [025] so to touch upon G♯ on its way to arpeggiating towards and—unlike the previous phrase—actually reaching local tonic, E in this case. The general tonal motion here thus sideslips relative to the global tonic B, skewing away from an overtonally reinforcing root and fifth (B & F♯) and apparently towards root and fourth (B & E), a circumstance that greatly strengthens E as tonic at the expense of B.

Considering the notes of Figure 4.20 as a scalar aggregate substantiates the tonic claims of E. Comparing these with the notes of a BM++ chord shown at (b), we discover that the scale lacks D♯ but has an E. In other words, the putative B tonic chord appears to be built from the notes of (c), not (b). Given the power of basic overtonal relationships, the notes of (c) affiliate into the hierarchical relationships shown at (d), a permutation of an EM++ chord. In other words, for reasons of harmonic statics it is easier to understand E as tonic of the mm. 3–13 pedal tune rather than B.

In this light, critical features of the manual figuration, schematized in Figure 4.21, can now be appreciated. In particular, the "fourthiness" of the overtonal environment is intensively underscored: nine out of twelve dyads in the first

Figure 4.20 (a) Analysis of pedal tune, mm. 3–13; (b) Putative BM++ tonic apparently underlying the passage; (c) Actual configuration of notes; (d) Reinterpretation into E tonic

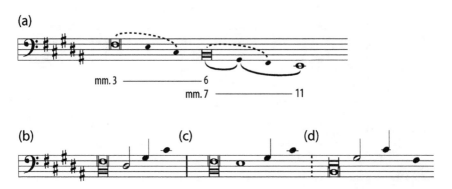

Figure 4.21 Dupré, analysis of manual figuration, mm. 1–13

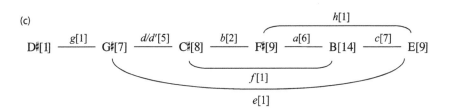

analytic measure of (a) are perfect fourths, as are ten of twelve in the second measure.[26] (For ease of reference, the dyads are labeled with italic letters and slurred according to beat.) The aggregate pitch content, essentially the same as found in the pedal tune, is deployed in harmonic configurations that bring out the overtonal configuration of Figure 4.20. This is especially evident in the dyadic string ⟨*c d e f*⟩, which creates a harmonic syncopation emphasizing EM+ in the first measure.[27] But there is palpable resistance by B to the tonic claims of E, most notably by the persistent sounding of B throughout the measure, a feature symbolized by the elongated B tonic-breve. Note also that the light chordal skip to B in the pedal tune (see m. 3 of fig. 4.19) is harmonized by dyads *a* and *g*, which form BM+, thereby briefly introducing the "missing" D♯ into the scalar composite.

In the second measure (displaying the figuration of mm. 7–11) the situation is somewhat different. The density of E-oriented dyads increases: four *c* dyads (vs. three in the first) and three forms of *d* (vs. two in the first), an increase that supports the explicit resolution to E in the pedal tune discussed above. In addition, the metric grouping of the dyads becomes consistent, with each group of four beginning and ending with the same dyad type: *c—c*, *d—d*, and *a—a*, the first two of which are strongly E-based. The last, however, points back to B, so that the end of the measure, with its ⟨*a b c a*⟩ echoing the opening bit of the first measure, seems to re-energize B, though E-ness is hardly lost.

26. Tymoczko (2004, 230) rightly recognizes these as "pentatonic thirds."
27. A firmer if more subtle tonic anchoring on E is created by the set of top notes of the odd-numbered dyads (= those on strong pulses at the eighth-note level) in the first measure, $\langle B_4, E_5, G\sharp_4, B_4, E_4, G\sharp_4 \rangle$.

A different way of organizing the figurational material is by a network representation, Figure 4.21. The notes figurationally yoked into dyads are strung along a line of fourths, reading left to right, with the number of occurrences shown in brackets. The dyads themselves label the lines of linkage, and their number of occurrences is likewise bracketed. It is clear at once that D♯ is an outlier both statistically and physically, the equivalent of a nonstructural lower neighbor to the E of Figure 4.20. At the other end of the line, we can see the tension between B and E played out. As a pitch class, B dominates in the passage, sounding fourteen times within the two figuration-pattern measures. Whether it is root or fifth is clearly at issue, as the overtonal element that would clarify the question is deadlocked: F♯ sounds as often as E, both nine times each. Breaking the tie is the first coloration band-fill: the seven attacks of G♯ overwhelm the single one of D♯, and via *e*, it is explicitly attacked as M3 of E. Finally, there is the matter of precedence, of how the dyads are ordered—especially in the first measure—in which the claims of B are advanced before those of E. The linear ordering ⟨a b c d e f⟩ of Figure 4.21 is shown at (c) to have a particular design that expands from and contracts to B. Considering each dyadic fourth as a linear transposition and fixing dyad *a* as T_0, we note the following T-values for dyads ⟨a b c d⟩: 0, −1, +2, −3. Dyads *e* and *f* work back towards B, but not by fourth. Dyad *e* sounds the extreme notes implicated in the linear transposition, G♯ and E, and dyad *f* then sounds the next inner pair, C♯ and B. This accordion-like behavior occurs at the beginning of each bar in mm. 1–6.

We have gone into some detail on the issue of overtonal tonic in the opening phrase in order better to appreciate how it will be eventually cleared up. From a situation of studied ambiguity in the opening section, mm. 1–13, the music will subtly declare a favorite in mm. 14–17, and then more obviously shift the tonal center to a new but not unexpected place in mm. 18–24. The score of Figure 4.19 should be sufficient to follow the remainder of the discussion.

Measures 12–13 restore the opening manual figuration while offering a new pedal line that seems to be energizing a transition. This line contains all the notes analyzed in Figure 20(a) as belonging to EM++, but which are now organized melodically according to the harmonic dyads of the figuration. That is, the pedal notes beamed together beatwise in m. 12–13 express dyads *b, e,* and *f*. In m. 14, this dyad progression is reversed and rhythmically augmented: *f, e,* and *b* sound as quarter notes. (The melodic order of *f* and *b* is reversed as well.) Both changes significantly boost the tonicness of B; the augmentation places B on downbeats in mm. 14 and 16, with the reversals of dyad properties giving a strong F♯-to-B downbeat accent at the latter place. Over this activity are three other layers. Reading upwards, they are (1) a "fourthy" pattern built from EM++ that continues the established sixteenth-note pulse; (2) a tetrachordal melody that travels between F♯ and B in the fifth octave, with an important A♯ working on behalf of B; and (c) the head motive of the opening pedal tune, outlining the B-F♯ overtonal fifth. Notwithstanding EM++ as still the basic pitch source of this section, the move towards a solidifying of B as tonic is unmistakable. The second part of this transition, mm. 18–19, confirms this. D♯ now enters to transform E from weakened pretender to Î into an acquiescent 4̂. Indeed, the harmonic signal of those measures, in contrast to the distortion of the opening, is received clearly as something like T_3–$S_{4,2}$, colored as diatonic seventh chords in B-major.[28]

At mm. 20–21 is the deeper scheme of reversal and augmentation truly revealed, as prominent E♯s announce a shift towards F♯ tonic, which is attained in m. 22. That is, considering how Figure 4.20) suggested an immediate orientation from F♯ through the ostensible tonic B and directed towards E, we now can see that the larger orientation is, in fact, the reverse, from a surprisingly strong EM++ (mm. 1–13) through a passing B (mm. 14–19, in the harmonic configuration of fig. 4.20[c]), and directed towards a clear F♯ of m. 22—initially lacking fill in its first band, but then receiving it triumphantly on the downbeat of m. 24 and celebrating with a flourish into the next bar.

Dupré's piece, especially its opening, is a useful reminder that the theoretical representations of amplified tonic chords, such as that of Figure 4.20, are no more compositionally normative than the representation, typical of a textbook on CP harmony, of some tonic chord as treble-cleffed whole notes in close position. In both cases the representation makes certain basic structures fully clear and uncomplicated, such as the claim that a CP tonic chord is built as a "stack of thirds"; the representation need not handle questions about voicing and arrangement. Abstraction to simplicity can be useful. The schematic representations of M++ chords show these structures in their most stable and coherent forms— clearly rooted and at maximum harmonic density (i.e., close positioned). These forms, as mentioned above, are most useful for conclusions, where the qualities of density and stability are most prized. Dupré's achievement in the opening of the B-major Prelude is to deploy the M++ elements in a very unstable and rather porous configuration, a redistribution of the chord's ideal static load to a point near failure. This is virtuosic handling of pitch material that goes hand in glove with the virtuosity demanded of the performer in playing it.

Antitonics and the Ends of Harmonic Function

A review of the amplified-tonic chord hypothesized some pages ago (fig. 4.12) is in order at this point if chords having other functions besides tonic can be defined. If nine or possibly ten of the twelve traditional pcs can be used in a tonic chord, how are non-tonic chords possible, if pc exclusivity that characterizes the three-functioned Riemannian model is not operative? Further, as many previous examples have suggested, contemporary tonal composition can replace harmonic functional progressions with other shaping techniques, such as fluctuation or various styles of modulation. And even when progressions are active, they can operate in novel ways. The distillation of function into pure bass-line activity, for example, is a leading feature of excerpts from *Mackie Messer* (fig. 4.2[c]) and "Human Heart" (fig. 4.9), as well as in other situations where root-representatives predominate. What happens to harmonic function when dissonances are emancipated?

---

28. The functional notation T_3–$S_{4,2}$ is equivalent to the Roman-numeral representation iii[7]–ii[6][5]–ii[7].

Elsewhere, I have suggested that these conditions collapse the three traditional functions onto two, tonic and antitonic (Harrison 2011, 553–64). The latter is hypothesized to be a compounding of 3-8[026] essence, and the resulting
chords grow into whole-tone formations. This is in distinction from the composition of tonic, which tends towards the diatonic. In this way, harmonic function
can be reinscribed as collectional (and even macroharmonic) contrast rather than
pc exclusivity. In compositions without much tonic amplification, pcs in the later
stages need not be embargoed from other functional duties, and a version of the
Riemannian functional categories can be constructed from them. Figure 4.22 gives
the details, reprising the tonic and adding details for antitonic (notated as ~*T*) and
showing the possible configuration of subdominant chords.

Figure 4.22 Tonic and antitonic amplified chords

The stages of antitonic amplification contrast with the situation with tonic. There, doing least harm to the overtonal frame means favoring ics 3, 4, and 5 at the expense of ics 1, 2, and 6. Antitonicity, in contrast, is based on a tritone frame formed from elements of the (collapsed) D and S Riemannian functions. Stage 1 roots the frame and/or fills it with one of three pcs within the "bandwidth"—in traditional terms, with either lowered, natural, or raised $\hat{2}$. The natural version is most relaxed, with the others creating germinal 3-8[026] trichords, mildly tensed. The turn symbol acknowledges enharmonic potential for *functional-mixture* chords, where scale-degrees associated with different attitudes are assembled.[29] These are articulated rather than integrated chords, wherein a pc is heard either to anticipate or preserve some other harmonic state. In the style this chapter has employed, they are chords with significant coloring agents, and the essence of their enharmonic transformation lies in how the pcs in question are heard—whether as so tensed toward major $\hat{3}$ that it is functionally identified by it (that is, $\sharp\hat{2}$ = magnetic-to-$\hat{3}$)[30] or whether tensed as a suspension or anticipation of minor-tonic $\hat{3}$. To be sure, the antitonic frame is already a functionally mixed structure, a compound of subdominant base and dominant agent. Aside from grounding the chord in a dominant base and, potentially, its associate, Stages 1 and 2 mix in minor-inflected degrees characteristic of traditional subdominant in both its plagal and authentic functions: $\flat\hat{2}$ (the "agent of the agent"), $\flat\hat{3}$ (via enharmonic potential), the agency around both modes of $\hat{6}$. The enharmonic possibility of the modally unmatched dominant agent, $\flat\hat{7}$, closes out this roster of downward tending pcs. Stage 3, on the other hand, clearly mixes in major $\hat{3}$ and shows the limits of amplification as a chord-building strategy.

Tonic and antitonic can be deployed according to schemes of harmonic fluctuation where the presence and absence of tritones in a chord is tracked (e.g., Hindemith's system). To use subdominant function for a more conservative compositional design, as in Duruflé's *Requiem*, the base and agents form the frame, and the remaining elements accrue as shown. Note, however, the comparatively large number of residual "avoid tones."

29. This term refers to Harrison (1994, 64ff.), but (as discussed there) is basic to Riemannian thought and reaches a logical conclusion in the work of Erpf (1927 [1969]).
30. The idea that an insuperable tendency tone is functionally indistinct from its resolution is Ernst Kurth's. Rothfarb (1988, 176ff.) provides a clear summary. Silberman (2006, 73–79) suggests a way to formalize such intuitions.

CHAPTER Five

Styles

The odd-numbered chapters of this book have put compositional materials and techniques into the hands, and lives, of composers and their audiences. They are an attempt at a human geography of contemporary tonal practice. The even-numbered chapters—examining the properties of those materials and techniques—propose appropriate analytical procedures, offered as a suite of extensible, "open source" applications adaptable to different stylistic situations and tastes. The occasional analytic vignette in all chapters illustrates possible interpretive uses, poses additional pertinent questions, or otherwise attempts to enrich musical appreciation.

This final, odd-numbered chapter undertakes a more nuanced survey of overtonal settlement. Boundaries having been sketched in chapter 3 on geography, patterns of habitation are characterized in this chapter on style—the "replication of patterning, whether in human behavior or in the artifacts produced by human behavior, that results from a series of choices made within some set of constraints," according to Leonard B. Meyer (1989, 3). The material in this chapter is a "stress test" of Meyer's program, enacting it under compositional conditions where "some set" of constraints has become "many sets" of constraints. It takes particular interest in composers who experienced the release of the CP enclosure and the "land rush" into exurbia that followed, a disquieting time for those musicians who would live long into the new settlement. Following Richard Taruskin's example, I'll refer to them as the "Class of 1890." Among its members whose works have been analyzed previously in this study (or are proffered in this chapter) are Frank Martin (1890), Sergei Prokofiev (1891), Germaine Tailleferre (1892), Darius Milhaud (1892), and Paul Hindemith (1895). This generation was expertly trained in CP techniques, but they also understood that the innovations of Debussy, Schoenberg, Stravinsky, and others each offered new sets (not necessarily disjoint) of constraints on compositional structuring and arrangement. A special case study beckons here for furthering the inquiries into psychology, history, and analysis that Meyer so powerfully developed and promoted, as musical styles produced under these conditions might be analyzed generally as responses to the psychological stress of accommodating rapidly changing conditions of artistic production. The subsequent influence of these early styles (behaviors) has been long-lasting and self-reinforcing; the "many sets" condition that the Class of 1890 first experienced still holds even now, and choosing among models for inspiration in developing a distinctive compositional voice has, for today's composers, hardly changed since then, even though the adaptation over time has made the process normal and expected, rather than fraught and extraordinary.

The matter of style in contemporary tonal music can thus be joined here—with a survey of the cultural and artistic conditions that initially shaped contemporary tonality. These conditions direct attention on a few general concerns that have directed compositional styles in various ways from the Class of 1890 on, which are here analyzed in short pieces or representative sections of larger ones. These are intended more to illustrate analytical possibilities than to detail musical structure exhaustively. The reader is invited to investigate such details, and with as many additional pieces as curiosity and interest bring to mind.

Peak Common Practice: An Institutional Curriculum

Despite well-known experiments and innovations, music composition until the last quarter of the nineteenth century relied upon settled principles whose origins seemed ancient and obscure—as if it were a natural language, ethnic costume, or local cuisine. While composers worked in stylistically individual ways (and, moreover, could imitate the ways of others), accepted principles of pitch structuring were apparent to all concerned. Further, they were widely discussed, analyzed, normalized, and arguably even epitomized in music theories—Heinrich Schenker's chief among them. In chapter 1, on the inheritance that subvents contemporary tonal composition, the guild-like qualities of this social situation were made clear, with a barrier to entry that for many required a start in early-childhood in order to surpass. Once inside, discourse relied heavily on jargon, abbreviations, and other tokens of long training and association among people like themselves. This led to "economical, fast, efficient, and satisfying" interactions (Hall 1976, 101). All this is to leave aside the outstanding fact that the written forms of musical ideas (whether staff notation, tablature, or other code) was and remains indecipherable to outsiders. These social conditions encourage mutual reinforcement, complex tacit understandings, and a large set of constraints that can be variously negotiated and endlessly played with.

By the middle of the nineteenth century, an international consistency of higher musical training in state-run conservatories became possible and was vigorously pursued. In this music lagged behind painting and sculpture, which became highly academized earlier in the nineteenth century (Gjerdingen 2013). Musical composition became a taught, "blackboard" subject throughout Europe and her cultural satellites, supported by textbook-training in harmony, counterpoint, orchestration, and the like. Musical instruction aspired to be scientific, modern, and efficient, with institutionalized competitions and prizes becoming regular means of identifying and rewarding talent. In Paris, the situation is clear: its *Conservatoire* was the clearinghouse for musical education throughout the country. The standard precepts of its technical classes are thoroughly documented and even have been studied as keys to the styles of techniques of individual composers.[1] London, by the end of the century, had seen the establishment of the Royal College of

---

1. For example, (Clevenger 2002). Cf. Groth (1983) and Peters (1990).

Music and the continued success of the Royal Academy of Music. Authors such as Ebenezer Prout set the established line on theoretical questions. The strong regional music schools in Germany, already enrolling more students from other states and countries by the later 1860s, certainly after 1871 became attuned to a national instructional market, which enabled pedagogues like Hugo Riemann to become highly influential. His system of harmonic analysis was a curricular lingua franca in North-central and Western Europe by the beginning of World War I, and largely remains so to this day.

This centralization of higher musical instruction is something that might be attended to as decisive in the later history of the CP. The change from the unsystematic training of guild apprenticeship to the prescribed and vertically integrated curricula of the state music school is nothing less than the transformation from high-context relationships to ones that are explicit, spelled-out, and officially certified. The history of the fugue is an instructive case. Originally a significant milestone in both *partimento* and species-counterpoint instruction, it was the subject of scholarly and academic interest already by the 1750s (Bach's *Kunst der Fuge*, Marpurg's *Abhandlung von der Fuge*), and by the end of the nineteenth century it may have been the most abstracted, pedantic, and conformist genre demanded by state-conservatory examiners, Paris being most notable for its *fugue d'école*. Discussions of the "academic fugue"—even by those sympathetic to it—make all this clear.[2]

For good musicians who were artistically restless, ambitious, or free-spirited, experiencing this change in context must have been disorienting—disabling to some and stimulating to others. On one hand, the secrets to mastery of musical composition were being passed on so efficiently and explicitly that pedants, epigones, and even mediocrities (hacks!) might practice at rather high levels; on the other hand, new and clearly distinctive practices were needed if brilliant talent was to be identified and developed. Given circumstances like this, one surmises that practice of common overtonality didn't so much "exhaust" itself as became overly explicit in the hands of pedagogues, and thus boring to its most imaginative students.

Reading "radical" early twentieth-century compositions as reactions to this lowering of context sheds new light on works by Debussy, Stravinsky, Schoenberg, and others, which quickly acquired, individually and jointly, a carapace of paratextual explanation—critical essays, apologias, manifestos, analyses, and the like. These testify to how vastly the load increases on the individual utterance if no support comes from a common background that elevates its context.[3] Though these are also signs of parties, polemics, and posturing, all of which have a long history in music ("Brahms v. Wagner" being a recent one at the time), they are also more than that, since few controversies penetrated to the fundamentals of

2. See esp. Bullivant (1971, 175ff.) Gjerdingen (2013) values its "artisanal" roots and place in a fully developed compositional curriculum, which included orchestration and other "design" studies.

3. Hall (1976) suggests that when high-context cultures lose cohesion, the change is rapid and dramatic: "because bonds between people are so strong there is a tendency to allow for considerable bending of the system. When the explosion comes, it is likely to come without warning. When the boundaries are overstepped, they must be overstepped so far that there is no turning back" (111). This general description harmonizes perfectly with the context-lowering experienced in musical composition 1910–20.

compositional technique like the early-modernist worry over the nature, future, and procedures of tonality. So basic were the issues involved that an entirely new kind of music theory was called for and subsequently developed (over a fifty-year span) to explain the structure of atonal music.

By the turn of the twentieth century, the operations of the state conservatories reached a first peak of efficiency, giving the Class of 1890 unprecedented educational advantages. For few, if any, did the efficacy of instruction leave no permanent, positive marks upon musicianship, even for those who were not model students. (Bohuslav Martinů, for example, was kicked out the Prague conservatory for indolence.) These composers completed basic training just as artworks that explicitly questioned the value and point of their schoolwork were being made, promoted, discussed, and celebrated. Debussy's techniques, for example, seemed well beyond what the classroom could comprehend.[4] Stravinsky, in the *Rite of Spring*, had clearly bemused the professors of ballet in addition to those of music. And how exactly was one supposed to enjoy fruits of the harmony study in puzzling works like Schoenberg's op. 11, no. 2? (Recall that Busoni's response, discussed earlier (see chap. 3), was essentially to *correct* it!)

The *outré* and experimental aside, most composers' distinctive solution to these problems was to maintain, adapt, and reuse the received compositional techniques, incorporating as needed any "specialty" effects produced by emancipated dissonances—nonresolving suspensions, unbound nonchord tones, clusters, and the like. This feature shows that the changes in style-constraints negotiated by the Class of 1890 involved a greater number of choices themselves rather than a swap of one set of choices for another, roughly equal in scope. Swapping of this kind is registered in music history in familiar binarisms *ars nova/antiqua, prima/seconda prattica*. Eventually, the older in these pairs became consigned to the schoolroom, then the antique store, and, ultimately, the trash heap. In contrast, CP techniques have persisted into this twenty-first century, whether artisanally combined à la carte into distinctive statements or packaged in the familiar rhetoric of inner-ring suburbia.

While preservation of hard-won "marketable skills" is an entirely understandable explanation for the continued relevance of CP technique after other options were offered up, its century-long persistence speaks to something else. The philosopher and music critic Kenneth Burke (1897–1993) observed that the heavy investment of personal resources needed to participate in a high-context culture—time to learn it, attention paid to its subtleties, and adequate performance of its rituals—can create in its wake a deep loyalty to that culture and to its core symbols and beliefs, particularly those held since time out of mind (Burke 1935, 95–106). This loyalty provides a "schema for orientation" and is a font of personal judgment and tastes. Noting the clear connection to religious practice, he identified it as *piety*, a certain sentimentality about "the old religion" and its rituals. In the art of music, piety is extremely influential, as the "old religion" is still expertly performed, practiced,

---

4. Debussy the journalist-critic made clear his opinion of the aridity of the educational establishment. See Debussy (1927 [1962]).

celebrated, and powerfully reasserted. How else can we explain the loyal mainte-
nance of the great CP standard repertory in concert, recital, and opera programming (not to mention recordings and, for that matter, scholarship)? And surely
piety is the main support for curricula in which tonal harmony and counterpoint
are taught, even though the kit of aspiring composers no longer requires either.

This persistence supports considering the stylistic behaviors of the Class of
1890 over and above a regular load of "choice making within constraints," and
as conditioned by a determinate stress arising from a rapid increase in the numbers of creative choices to be considered, sorted, tested, and (ultimately) made.
This stress can be registered as *choice anxiety*—an influential director of human
behavior in general, and, in this case, artistic production.[5] Choice anxiety is the
experience of discomfort with the gap between (1) an optimal process for decision analysis, and (2) the time and resources required to undertake it. Familiar to
people in contemporary consumer societies, it arises when a range of, say, health
insurance plans is offered, the differences among which are subtle and indistinct
and/or the respective predicted consequences cannot be assessed without study.
Which one is best? For important choices, the stakes are deemed high enough that
a more or less formal decision analysis takes place, often mediated by specialists.
(Medical treatment is a central case. Financial planning is another.) For others,
best guesses are made; some might be made without even that but rather on the
basest of instincts. Choosing can be fatiguing and annoying business if what had
previously involved relatively simple decisions now requires many. If the old setup
was inefficient or bad, choice is welcomed and perhaps even savored. If, however,
it was adequate, only mildly irritating, or simply not important enough to warrant
the effort, then the prospect of its replacement is an annoyance, a potential over-
load, or, worse, an occasion of high anxiety.

As long as CP technique is maintained through piety, choice anxiety will surely
play a role in deciding what other techniques to adopt, and both psychological
states will converge on the project of developing individual composers' personal
artistic missions, where taste and style preferences are the "schema for orientation"
when choosing among the many new options. For the artists in the Class of 1890,
I propose that the heightened pressure on this project engendered "coping behaviors," which their compositions document and model for their successors. While
specific and nuanced at the level of the individual composer, the behaviors nonetheless seem to address a few leading themes, and do so consistently from the early
post–Great War period on. They play a role in musical life even today, though differently and modified by more recent thematic concerns. In what follows, they will
be portrayed through analysis of *attitudes* that composers take toward them—read
in both their works and in their biographies—of habitual dispositions of material
and technique that mark, and make, musical styles.

5. Because choice anxiety has commercial effects in the modern mass consumer market, the best
introductions to it are trade books such as Easterbrook (2003) and especially Schwartz (2004),
which frame the relevant issues vividly and are based on academic work in the applied social sciences devoted to psychology, business administration, and organizational management.

Irony and Sincerity: Contrasting attitudes toward tradition

Responses to the urges of piety and anxiety about choice can be read in a few dimensions, one of the most far-reaching of which concerns attitude toward the common-practice inheritance. The respective behaviors expressed here cluster around the style traits of *irony* or *sincerity*.[6] Are CP techniques toys for new play, or are they tools for new construction? Are pastiche, unexpected juxtaposition, and meandering modulation the leading techniques, or are shaped continuity, focused phrases, and suitable cadences? In the former we can hear irony and play; in the latter, sincerity and earnest purpose.

To illustrate, let us consider a well-known, telltale trait of irony in so-called wrong-note music—a technique characterized by nudging the "notes" out of expected paths of continuation, in most cases preserving traditional meter, rhetoric, and melodic ductus, with the nudged "wrong note" felt as a bump in an otherwise traditional environment.[7] Writing wrong-note music requires the kind of traditional rhetoric (meter, phrase, form) detailed in chapter 3, as well as diatonic or near-diatonic scales (i.e., strong linearity). Harmonic fluctuation, in all likelihood, operates indifferently if not accidentally over short-to-medium spans of music. In general, the overtonal environment is sufficiently traditional that purposeful solecisms—wrong notes—can be read ironically. (Prokofiev's *Classical Symphony* epitomizes this sensibility.) In less traditional overtonal settings, wrong-note irony is more difficult if not impossible to employ, and different techniques mark the ironic sensibility. Stravinsky, for example, frequently employed linear *ostinati* in which the notes may be right but the line is "wrong" (see Horlacher 1992). That is, the linear immobility of the pitch cell over the long term is an ironic trait. Minimalist music pushes this technique to the extreme.

In contrast, a sincere approach to the inheritance not only eschews wrong notes but also attempts to convey the impression that every note is "right," that the music is unfolding naturally and that the composer is seeking the most logical and smoothest flow. Instead of setting up opportunities to intervene and draw attention to some manipulation, the sincere composer seeks to respect and leverage inherent properties of tonal relationships—even if such properties are contingent, invented, or even dogmatically imposed. An important technical mark, then, of a sincere attitude is a degree of systemization and limited-choice continuity in composition, in which respect it resembles CP sensibility. As a result, such music welcomes and indeed invites music analysis, since it is generally carried out as a serious endeavor in itself. (The sincere composer and the music analyst could even be said to have similar personality types!) In this connection, another telltale trait of sincerity is the production of theoretical works as compositional paratexts. (Hindemith is a central case,

---

6. Allport (1937, 293ff.) ventures to distinguish between traits and attitudes, with the latter being, I believe, the better term for what is at stake in this chapter. However, attitude as Allport understands it is a ramification of his ideas about traits, and for that reason I prefer to use the more general term as the index of reference.

7. A survey of the contexts that enable "wrong-note" effects is undertaken in Rifkin (2006).

but also Messiaen, Schoenberg, Serly, Tcherepnin, et al.[8]) An earnest attitude toward material seems to correlate with noticeable effort when dealing with serious genres or subjects, with sacred music being an especially interesting site. Thus, in contrast to Prokofiev's symphony is Messiaen's *Apparition de l'église éternelle*, an organ work whose subject matter asks us to consider Messiaen not so much as a mundane "composer" but as a spiritualized "medium," translating a solemn and prophetic vision of heaven into music. All notes must be right.

Prelude and Interludium

To clarify these ideas, I propose to analyze Shostakovich's Prelude in E♭ from op. 87 and Hindemith's E♭ Interludium from *Ludus Tonalis* as a contrasting pair, highlighting their treatment of materials and apparent dispositions toward them. Hindemith's piece is a march, but an ironic one; Shostakovich's is through-composed as a dialogue between a duple-metered *solemn chorale* of *mezzo forte* chords and a triple-metered *impish interlopation*, always *piano*—"a puck-ish, chromatically slippery woodwind-like duet," in Mark Mazullo's (2010, 208) description. The irony of Hindemith's wrong notes, as we will see, is needed for the piece's character, suggestive of a somewhat chaotic and even comedic parade ground, definitely unmilitary in bearing. (The ten bars repeated of Trio in mm. 21–30, however, are in good order.) It does not penetrate to deeper structures, as it is held in check by Hindemith's respect for traditional march form, genre, and rhetoric and his usual habits of compositional planning. Shostakovich's Prelude, on the other hand, ironically misaligns tonal markers for significant stretches, as seen in Figure 5.1, a linear and tonal analysis of the chorale passage of mm. 40–68. Fundamental overtonal degrees are established by the bass articulation of E♭, B♭, and A♭. At m. 45, D♭ pronounces movement out of the E♭ major collection, and at m 47, the destination is reached: a seven-measure articulation of wrong-note overtonal degrees E♮, B♮, A♮, which cast a shadow back upon the E♭ overtonality (see descriptions in Bass 1988). (The note-value notation for an E♭ hierarchy is retained, emphasizing the semitonal displacement of its members.) Meanwhile, the upper voices extend through a large H-line, embedding motivic H-line thirds, smoothing out the "bump up" to E♮. At m. 54, return movement to E♭ can be sensed, and from m. 58 on, a loose retrograde of the main opening events through m. 47 unfolds, culminating in a slightly deformed yet still recognizable perfect authentic cadence at m. 68.

If the chorale sections of the Prelude demonstrate Shostakovich's best technique in solemnizing overtonal irony, the interloping imp sections undercut any pretense to solemnity while emphasizing the irony. Figure 5.2 interprets the first

---

8. Messiaen (1956) is a leading example, as is Schoenberg (1912 [1978]) and elsewhere, especially in Schoenberg and Stein (1984). Serly (1975) was written by a student of Kodály and friend of Bartók. The interesting work in Tcherepnin (1962), never published, has been made available online, available at http://www.tcherepnin.com/alex/basic_elem1.htm.

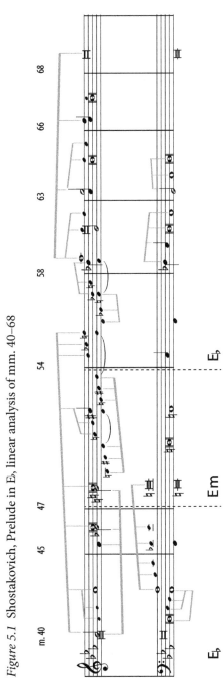

Figure 5.1 Shostakovich, Prelude in E♭, linear analysis of mm. 40–68

Figure 5.2 Shostakovich, Prelude in E♭, linear analysis of mm. 16–37

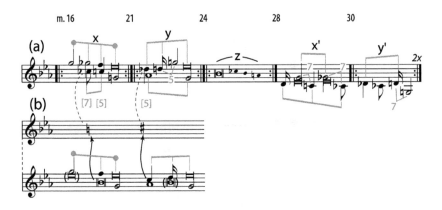

one, from mm. 16–37. The imp prances in over an E♭ pedal tone (not shown in the figure) that is left over from the end of the chorale in m. 14 and allowed to decay *quasi niente* during the episode. Light re-strikings at mm. 22 and 29 keep some vibration in the air, though by the end of the passage at mm. 37–38, they are too weak to be heard. The main activity is in the upper part. Repeated motives x and y focus on E♭; a meandering middle around B♭, z, also repeats, followed by a single foreshortened rearrangement of x, finally spinning down into foreshortened rearrangement of y, repeated twice. The opening motives are deformations of ideas shown at (b) in the figure. Motive x derives from the venerable horn-fifths topic, with B♭ displaced upward to B♮, while y connotes a small-scale S–D–T **cadential** discharge, with a normal C displaced upward to D♭.

The greatest point of interest in this passage is the explicit play with i[5] and i[7] intervals, both harmonic and melodic; the annotations on the figure highlight the relevant passages. The final pitch event before the *fermata* over *niente* of mm. 38, not to mention the puzzling extension into the downbeat of m. 39, is somehow a pointed reminder to the pianist that *something* is still happening down there at E♭$_{1,2}$, even if below the threshold of hearing.

Following this enigmatic moment is the chorale section analyzed in Figure 5.1—the two figures together analyze mm. 14–69, a significant portion of the piece's 133 measures. This unit fits into the whole according to the scheme proposed in Figure 5.3, where the four chorale and imp dialogues are grouped into two larger units (quatrains). The dialogues are centered on the seams where the imp follows a chorale, a layout that emphasizes difference in how long each interlocutor "holds the stage" for any dialogue couplet. Indeed, the whole design of the work looks like a transcript of a conversation with a little bit of heat in it. That is, the four dialogues together read as if (1) the chorale proposes something, and the imp then responds at length; (2) the chorale explains in more detail, and the imp responds but somewhat more curtly than before; (3) the chorale offers more, but the imp overtalks and preempts the conversational initiative; (4) the chorale tries

Figure 5.3 Shostakovich, Prelude in E♭. Formal layout by couplet and character

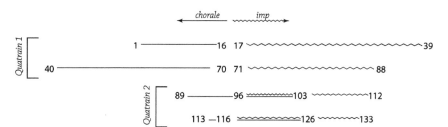

once more but is quickly overtalked, and the whole topic ends up holding no further interest and winds down into the second octave, *pianissimo* and lapsing into fragmented phatics. The organizing of the dialogues into quatrains marks important change of conversational behavior, when respectful back-and-forth gives way to overtalking and insistence, signs of increasing discursive heat.

The embedding of motive x in an inner voice in this following passage (which was marked in fig. 5.1) is suggestive of serious thinking about motivic unity in this work. More evidence is shown in Figure 5.4, which analyzes the opening chorale, mm. 1–16. The first four measures feature an old construction: expanding tonic through parallel 10ths over $\hat{1}$–$\hat{2}$–$\hat{3}$ with a "stationary seventh"; the analysis in the figure could just as well be purely Schenkerian at this point, since the main motion is an S-line. The doubled leading tone of m. 4 is, to my ear, a subtle and clever clue that the music is not to continue as classically built as the opening suggests, and the uncertainties of m. 5, followed by a retrogressive harmonic move at m. 6, confirms this change of technical venue. The appearance of IV⁶ in the next measure discloses an emerging descending bass line of at least H quality and, if reaching B♭, then an S—a Schenkerian linear progression. This possibility is sidelined by the events in m. 8–16. The top voice continues properly to D, the bass reverses direction and retreats to leading-tone, D. This produces a much stronger "doubled-leading tone" effect, and sets in motion a transitional ascending S-line, extending toward a reattained $\hat{3}$ at m. 11. Here, structure is nudged, and G is depressed to G♭—the essential move of motive x, capsuled as x′ earlier in Figure 5.2. Also analyzed in that figure was the essential move of motive y, identified as the juxtaposition of D♭ and D♮, noted as y′. Its operation in absorbing the displacement at m. 11 is sketched in Figure 5.4), with the doubled-leading tone effect perhaps a portent of further motivic function.

More rewarding engagement with this piece is promised by the analysis so far. More motivic interaction—such as the z-like affinity of the inner line of mm. 11–13—is evidence of shared "genetic material," suggesting the interlocutors to be members of the same family, which explains how the rise in "discursive temperature" seems not to be the discourtesy it would be among strangers, but the habit of family and friends. The specific motivic points argued, mostly by the imp, also repay study, especially repetitions of motives z and x, sometimes varied as if "putting something a different way" would somehow move

Figure 5.4 Shostakovich Prelude in E♭, analysis of mm. 1–16

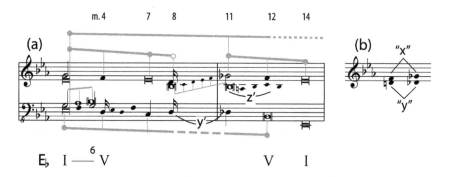

the discussion along. The significant upward nudge in the coda, starting in m. 116, reactivates E♮, which was marked at m. 47 for significance. And how all this might relate to the fugue that follows is of considerable interest. I invite the reader to continue analyzing as curiosity dictates, since Hindemith's composition now beckons.

If Shostakovich's Prelude is specially formed around the conceit of interlocution, Hindemith's Interlude takes the form of a traditional march, with a main section (including a repeated first "strain"), a repeated Trio, and a shortened reprise (with adjustments of the main section. Figure 5.5 shows the particulars. The clearest articulation is at mm. 20–21, at the onset of a trio section in everything but title. Below that level, the figure shows the smallest unit of continuity that can be analyzed in the piece. Measures 1–2, for example, executes a contrapuntal wedge shape and a strong circular bass motion around E♭. The following pair of measures is even clearer—a bass line of trilled quarter notes that quits at the end of m. 4. Together, these two pair combine to set a duple hypermeter, open a march topic, and enact a statement/response rhetorical scheme.[9] In contrast, the following section, mm. 5–9, takes longer to unfold and is not divided internally. The situation with the rest of the piece can be read from the figure.

The trio, mm. 21–30, is characterized by a change of tonal focus from E♭ to A♭, and also by a *staccato* walking bass that never rises above the second octave. Above, a smooth curvilinear tune sounds in the third octave and only breaks into the fourth at m. 28, the beginning of another wedge-shaped sectional close. The figure makes clear differences in formal organization between the trio and main section, with 2 + 2 + 2 measure grouping of mm. 21–26 contrasting with the 2 + 2 grouping of the refrain that bookends the sections, *Ref*, mm. 1–4, 16–20, and 31–34.

Figure 5.6 shows the linear construction of the trio, with a focus also on harmonic fluctuation. Since the main impression of the bass is on *the fact* of line rather than *the structure* of it, analyzing most of its activity as K-lines—unpredictable

---

9. Looking back at the Shostakovich prelude, we can appreciate an affinity between the imp and the trilled quarter-note.

Figure 5.5 Hindemith, Interludium in E♭, formal structure

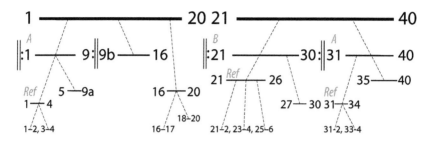

linear stretches punctuated by leaps—seems the best approach. The first one, in m. 21, is comprised of two disjunct S-lines, 8̂–5̂ and 3̂–1̂, which establish the A♭ tonal center. This is immediately complicated by harmonic-interval relations with the second line, consistently flavored mild with some passing sharpness, and with tritones punctuating the phrase end in the middle of m. 22. The increase in harmonic tension perfectly accompanies the deflection of the upper line there first to D♮ and then to B♮ at the end of the gesture.

All this and more can be shown in the middle staff of the figure, which is inspired by Ulehla's layout but modified in light of general improvements made to interval/chord tension metrics in chapter 3 (p. 59). Characteristic dissonances are marked, with mildness registering in the bottom half of the staff, at three levels of intensity increasing with height; sharpness likewise in the upper half. Because the texture is generally thin until m. 26ff., sensitivity to changes in fluctuation can be set very high, at every eighth note. At this level, interpreting singletons, like the i[10] strike in m. 21, can be a challenge—though here it may function like the "double leading tone" did in the Shostakovich Prelude, as a subtle signal of contemporary composition to be confirmed by upcoming events. But the following measure is suffused with mildness with a sharp spike preceding the last three notes of the melody. This change is capped off with an inflow of i[6] to mark the phrase boundary.

The second pair of measures, mm. 23–24, employs a different fluctuation scheme, though deployed similarly to the second half of the gesture, and also with concluding i[6] markers. It's difficult to know when to "connect the dots" when marks are close but not adjacent, as they are here in m. 23. The arrangement and spacing of marks—a line from extra sharp i[13] to very mild i[10] is enough, I think, for readers to draw their own conclusions. In both pairs, the first half is generally clear of tensive effects while the second uses them noticeably, finished off with tritones.

The outlines of sentence organization for the Trio can be felt in the harmonic fluctuation of the passage up to this point. Inspection of the remainder of the trio reveals a magnified version of the scheme, where tritones are withheld for the first part, mm. 25–26, but cluster in the second. The mild and sharp profile is similarly enlarged, with a single "uptick" gesture marking the phrygian move at

Figure 5.6 Hindemith, Interludium in E♭. (a) Analysis of pitch relations, mm. 21–30. (b) Neighbor space in mm. 21–22

m. 26. Thereafter, thickening texture creates more dissonances, including tritones, with "patterned" strikes around m. 28, a rest heading into m. 29, and then a final pulse of tension before relaxing into the final two chords of the strain, G♭M and tonic A♭M.

If the bass primarily moves through K-lines, broken up occasionally by arpeggios, the upper part has a deliberate linear design. Measures 21–22 are a dense *neighbor space*, where a set of overtonally stable tones are relieved by a set of its neighbor notes.[10] These are shown as *Stable* and *Neighbor* in Figure 5.6). The highlight on the far-out tritone of the local tonic, A♭, is noteworthy, as D♮ neighbors all the elements of *Stable*. The initial movement in the upper lines, then, is a rectilinear oscillation *Stable–Neighbor–Stable–*, with the promise of another *Neighbor* in m. 24. The result there, however, is more like an adulterated *Stable*, a displacement only of C to B while D♭ and E♭ are reinscribed as C♯ and D♯, respectively. Even so, the C–B change produces a significant color affect, one which was also part of Shostakovich's design for motive x in his Prelude.

After a final adulteration of *Stable* going into m. 25 (D♮ is swapped in for D♭), a substantial ascending H-line takes shape that targets B at m. 26. A longer and more surely directed H-line stirs in mm. 27–8 before proceeding downwards from D♮ to nadir G♭ at the end of m. 29. It cannot escape notice that ascending K-line activity in the bass is intense during the descent, and that elements from *Neighbor* are prominently featured. In contrast, during the period when the line gathers energy (mm. 26–8), the remarkably long K-line in the bass supports the preliminary neighboring between D♮ and C♯ above.

For comparison, the structure of mm. 1–9 (in the main section) is graphed in Figure 5.7. H-lines abound and move between overtonally important pitch classes, especially evident in the first two measures. As also heard in the opening K-line move of the trio as well as in its final chord succession, the tonic in this work is habitually fitted with a whole step below it rather than a traditional leading tone, meaning that all Ds in mm. 1–4 are flatted. The passage to m. 9a that cascades downwards by thirds also targets D♭ at m. 8. H-lines resume and move towards arrival on FM in m. 9; the emphasis on the top line's A♮ provides a suitable hierarchical contrast as the tritone to the tonic degree, which the hexatonic-pole embellishment only underscores—a wrong-note substitute for a traditional dominant. However, the overtonal focus of those measures is strongly affected by spike in chord tension at the end of m. 8, where an 3-5[016] trichord in the right hand voices both i[11] and i[6] while B♭ in the bass makes i[14] with the top-voice C.

The quick release onto a major triad, accomplished by rising fifth motion in the bass suggests a more protean read of the modulation, shown at (b) in the figure. There, the bass motion is interpreted plagally, with the F arrival receiving tonic accent. The end of m. 9a uses an authentically-related B♭M chord to regain, by another authentic motion, the E♭M tonic of m. 1. The complicated reinterpretations in the right-hand part are condensed in the staff above, where note shapes have been specially combined to show the hybrid nature of the chords—the sixteenth-note flag on an upstem signals leading tone "exit" for A♮ from an entrance on open-notehead major $\hat{3}$; the round breve of the entering $\hat{5}$ is filled to signal exit as $\hat{2}$.

The situation at the second ending, m. 9b, is different since music will continue in D♭ rather than loop back to E♭, but it can be symbolized similarly, as at (c). A♮

---

10. The neighbor space is defined formally in Silberman (2006). Silberman (2008) provides an introduction to the concept.

exits as ♭$\hat{6}$ onto A♭, with a change in flag and stem direction indicating the change. The round breve receives an upstem with two flags, showing its exit to be the leading tone, $\hat{7}$, and the upstem grafted onto the square breve shows its transformation from tonic degree to major $\hat{3}$ of D♭.

In sum, the shaping of phrases, lines, and harmonic fluctuation in Hindemith's Interlude is strongly influenced by the formal articulations identified in Figure 5.5 and by standards for the march genre. In this it is different from Shostakovich's Prelude, where form reflects a comparatively specific situation, which also dictates affective differences in content between solemnity and playfulness. This is a more playful, adventurous, and ironic setting of inherited technique than Hindemith's, which uses these elements to make fun of the hint of military menace a quick-tempo march can give, especially from a German veteran of World War I. The larger frames of the two works amplify this difference. Whereas Shostakovich's collection of Preludes and Fugues, op. 87, is put together with no more than the requisite effort to align it with previous collections, of which the Bach's *Well-Tempered Clavier* is the standard, Hindemith's *Ludus Tonalis* earnestly re-enacts the didactic and theoretically illustrative purposes of the WTC—in this case offering an extended study in "*kontrapunktische, tonale und klaviertechnische Übungen*," as the subtitle puts it in very Bachian terms, with pieces arranged according to Hindemith's Series 1 order. The Latin titles—*Fuga* and *Interludium*—further emphasize the seriousness of purpose in this project. The contrast with Shostakovich's "packaging" of his work, in "Chopin" rather than "Bach" order (i.e., by progression through key signature, rather than through a scale), bears notice here. The open and very pious reference to CP inheritance can make Hindemith's "WTC" seem pedantic in a way Shostakovich's does not—despite moments of expert pedantry, drolly displayed, as in the C-major fugue: a *ricercare* on the diatonic scale, sounding the subject on all its degrees without using any accidentals. Indeed, pedantry can easily be heard in the solemn chorale of the E♭ Prelude, which the interactions with the imp make comic and tolerable. All of this is to say the sincerity is situational and comic when Shostakovich composes it, but systemic in Hindemith's work.

Pop and Art: Preferences about register and audience

The excerpts cited in the opening of chapter 4 also served as a reminder about unprecedented options given the Class of 1890 and its successors, thanks to generally rising living standards, to make increasingly viable middle-class livings in what was originally thought of as "light" as well as "serious" settings (e.g., in operetta). The possibilities were already evident in the careers of, for example, the Strauss family of Vienna, Sir Arthur Sullivan, Victor Herbert, and Emile Waldteufel—the composer of the memorable tune from *The Skaters* excerpted in Figure 4.1(a). The new options which developed after World War I involved very different techniques from those of "light" music, which are generally those of the CP. Jazz and other non-European styles became available and of interest, and "serious" composers

Figure 5.7 Hindemith, Interludium in E♭, linear analysis of mm. 1–9

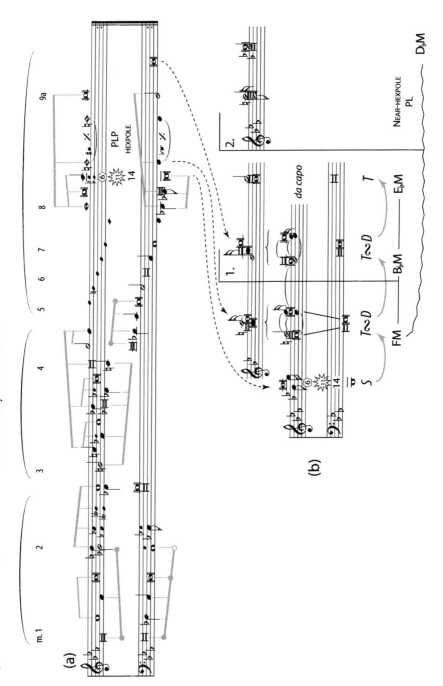

began to work with them from the 1920s on. Milhaud's contributions are exemplary here, since he engaged genres and techniques from both North and South America, the former in works such as *Création du Monde* and the latter in *Saudades do Brasil*, featured in excerpt as Figure 4.7. A survey of Kurt Weill's compositional toolkit during the 1920s shows mastery of modernist composition in a fascinating concerto for violin and winds as well as the new cabaret style in "Mackie Messer" and the equally effective "Surabaya Jonny" from *Happy End*. In sum, just as technical options increased *within* the European art-music tradition, options *outside* that tradition also became viable within it.

Sifting through contemporary overtonal technique, genre, and style for pop and art traits produces both well-known and suggestive correlations. Target audience, for example, is strongly implicated in a composer's *modus vivendi* with pop techniques and allusions, not to mention overtonality itself. A small elite of knowledgeable listeners can be the only audience for an "inaccessible" and definitely unpopular expression, while a wide audience must—almost by definition—be appealed to with widely understood gestures. In this light, the financial stake involved in opera production, for example, makes demotic musical technique an attractive option—though that is but one variable among many in the appeal of that complex art form. More clearly, functional liturgical music registers strong preference for popular compositional techniques, with developments during the last fifty years being particularly noteworthy in various traditions, Roman Catholicism especially. All of this was forecast in chapter 3's discussion of the innermost and most densely populated ring of CP suburbia.

Simple Songs

We can pursue these matters further in Leonard Bernstein's "A Simple Song," from *Mass: A Theatre Piece for Singers, Players, and Dancers* (1972). Bernstein's compositional profile resembles Weill's to some extent, in that he was recognized as a "high art" musician who made his reputation and fortune in musical theater. Bernstein was also heir to an American "cross-over" pattern modeled most successfully by Gershwin. Thus, his compositional work in general is pitched for a broad audience, and genres associated with "boutique" chamber venues are hardly represented in his output, especially after the 1940s. It offers a rare opportunity to analyze pronounced pop and art impulses concurrently in individual works.

In "A Simple Song" and throughout his *Mass*, these impulses are pitched at an unusually high level. That it uses the Rite of Mass as the formal scaffold testifies about its artistic register; while Bernstein was drawn to religious subjects in composition, they were largely congruent with his Jewish ethnicity and arranged for concert rather than liturgical performance.[11] The Mass, in contrast, is both outside his

---

11. See Copeland (1998) for background on the interest in sacred subjects in Bernstein's work. An exception to this generality is the late *Missa Brevis* of 1988, a reworking of incidental music for a 1955 stage drama about Joan of Arc and composed as a retirement offering for the noted choral conductor Robert Shaw.

tradition and a venerable "premier genre" of European art music. By the early 1970s, after the liturgical innovations of the Second Vatican Council had begun firmly to settle in, the inroads popular music made into the rite allowed Bernstein to approach it (impiously, as Burke might see it) for appropriation into a secular theater piece.[12]

Bernstein's popular-music techniques, rooted in conventions of the 1940s, are also put to critical test in this work, which debuted during a period in cultural history where "youth" music (i.e., rock) first attempted to satisfy higher-art ambitions and, thus, to be taken seriously by elders and elites—something Bernstein himself had recognized and promoted as early as 1967 in a revealing television documentary for CBS News, *Inside Pop—the Rock Revolution*.[13] Sympathetic and engaged with the music, Bernstein plays the part of bemused adult, trying to understand the kids—patient and didactic.[14] But the implications for Bernstein's own suite of compositional techniques are clear if unstated: How could he "stay current" in popular techniques if he was too old for them? *Mass*, and "A Simple Song" in particular, show him working through this question.[15]

"A Simple Song" is the opening song of *Mass*, and is part of the celebrant's preliminary devotions before the public portion of the liturgy.[16] Bernstein styles it as a two-part "Hymn and Psalm." Musically, this idea is arranged as a standard American popular song: an AABA form for the Psalm, preceded by a sectional verse for the Hymn.

Stephen Schwartz's lyrics have three distinct constructions. The main body of the song quotes *characteristic* verses from Psalm 121:1, 5b–6, but these appear in the bridge, traditionally a site of transition rather than statement. The A music, in contrast, strings together *generic* verses and images found in multiple places in the psalter. The opening lyric, for example ("I will sing the Lord a new song"), can refer to Psalms 96:1, 98:1, 33:3, and 144:9. The opening lyric of the second verse ("Blessed is the man who loves the Lord") appears to rework Psalms 128:1 and 112:1 with "loves" replacing the original verb, "fears," a theologically significant change consonant with the rest of the work.[17] The curious inversion of lyric function—the bridge is characteristic and liturgically traditional, while the A section has generic assemblages, theologically tweaked—is underscored when the verse is taken into account. Here, Schwartz's contributions override allusions to the psalter, and contemporary theological ideas come clearly into view—underscored by the title lyric ("Sing God a simple song"), which appears only in the verse and

12. Sheppard (1996, 470ff.) provides a comprehensive account of the work and its context.
13. Currently online at: http://youtu.be/afU76JJcquI.
14. One Internet headline writer put it: "Leonard Bernstein explains the rock revolution to squares."
15. The unresolved compositional stress in this work is likely behind its failure as a "big statement" that writing a Mass setting promised. Bernard (1998, 539) finds the work to be "affected [and] even self-indulgent."
16. Sheppard (1996, 488ff.) provides a useful annotated scenario of the work. The position of the "overture" in *Mass* is taken by an "Antiphon–Kyrie Eleison," which is delivered in total darkness by prerecorded voices increasingly manipulated toward a final cacophony, which "A Simple Song" suddenly breaks in upon.
17. Another example of generic lyric sources in the psalms is the opening of the second verse, "I will sing His praises while I live, All of my days," which references Psalms 104:33 and 146:2.

not in the main body of the song. The combined effect is of a nonbiblical and contemporary, youth-inflected theology proposed in the verse, an accommodation of this vision to generic images in the psalter in the A music, and finally only a transitory engagement with the text of Psalm 121.

An analytical synopsis of the verse is shown in Figure 5.8. A strong, nearly dronal overtonal foundation is announced at the beginning with strummed root and fifth in G, and the bass motion of the first phrase, mm. 1–4, is functionally clear, supporting an octave S-line spanning D_5 to D_4. Two scale-degree inflections are noted that prevent GM from consolidating. Though possible to conform these to an underlying diatonic scale (F♯m, perhaps) or to conjoint diatonic tetrachords, hearing them in relation to G root is instructive. C♯$_5$ (tritone) announces initial denial of GM, and G♯$_4$ forecasts a transformation of the root degree that is realized at the "second ending," m. 8, where a general upward pitch deflection occurs. As in Figure 5.1, which illustrated the same "wrong note" technique in the Shostakovich E♭ Prelude, sharp-side accidentals applied to the "open notehead" degrees symbolize the change of pitch height but not of underlying degree identity. In m. 12 the bass relaxes back into overtonal G♮ and stays there for the rest of the verse. The vocal line, though repeating its material of m. 10, is pulled back enharmonically as well, a reorientation completed by the "second ending" of m. 13. For the basic theological claim of the verse, "For God is the simplest of all," Bernstein brings GM gradually into focus, correcting for C♯ and G♯ of the beginning, and ending first on Em as relative of GM (m. 16), and finally arriving at GM itself in m. 19, emphasized litotically by a "missing" bass register.

As the continuation of the song into Figure 5.9 shows, the GM finally attained is made to yield as overtonal fifth to the CM of the main body. (The conjoined square/round breves at the end of fig. 5.8 symbolize this upcoming change.) Setting the verse of a popular song in the dominant key of the chorus is unusual if not unprecedented.[18] The effect here is to introduce the main body with a colon punctuating the Hymn and the Psalm, making the latter the nominal "simple song" announced in the verse.

With this relationship in mind, the most significant detail of the combined linear analysis is the H-line connection from C_5 in the verse to F_5 in the chorus, m. 24, explaining this upper neighbor to the tonic major third as something other than a wrong note—a reading which the intervallic sequence of the bass vamp, mm. 20–21, strongly conditions. (Octave leaps there are split 3rd/6th; the celebrant is thus presumed to be aiming for E_5).

Thanks to strongly projected S-lines, the overtonal linear structure of the passage is clear and specific to CM. We readily identify significant "blue note" coloration in the vamp (mm. 20–21) and concluding flute line (m. 30), and a prominent F♯ at m. 26, a "lydian fourth" also characteristic of the verse. This pointedly replaces F♮ of m. 26, then is retained in m. 28, and is not naturalized for the rest of the section.

---

18. "How Come You Do Me Like You Do," by Gene Austin and Roy Berger (1924) has this structure. It is also found, in magnified form, in the American march form, where the opening strains are in the dominant key of upcoming the "big tune" in the trio.

Figure 5.8 Bernstein, "A Simple Song," analysis of the verse, mm. 1–19. The two bass staves show first- and second-ending differences

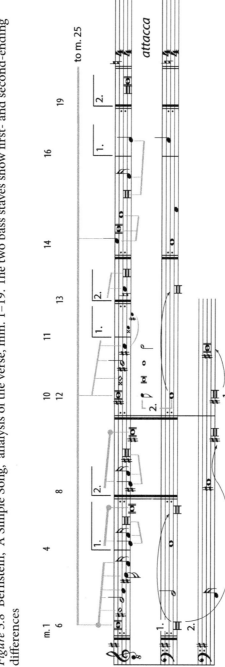

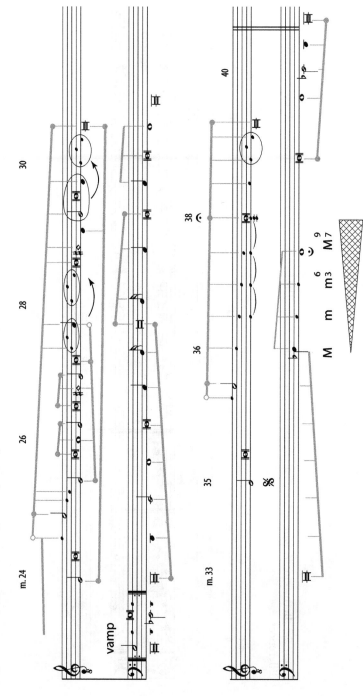

Figure 5.9 Bernstein, "A Simple Song," analysis of the main section, mm. 23–40

Repetitions of figures take place at the local scale (rather than in sections, as the analysis of the verse suggested), with two related gestures (circled) repeated and extended forward. The extensions advance the S-line to strongly overtonal degrees: tonic C_4 at the end, where all lines converge; dominant G_4 at m. 28; and then immediately to Bernstein's motivic lydian F♯—his event-hierarchical intervention that puts a sharp on the subdominant breve in the Celebrant's tonal hierarchy. F♯ is quitted by leap into D_4, stopping the upper line while making a move on a lower one. The repetition scheme here—the first time delays, the second repeats and completes—is a recognizably traditional *anadiplosis* (when the last word of one clause is repeated as the first word of the following clause).

The compositional technique discussed so far places this piece well into the innermost suburb: S-lines predominate; meter is regular and hierarchically organized; and expressive gestures are conventional. Harmonic fluctuation is artfully managed to support phrase structure, activity on the S-lines, and dramatic expression. The wrong-note F♮ at the beginning of the main section is a good example—sharply off-target, it spikes the start of the lyric—though not very high, since the bass harmonizes it as a triadic consonance over D. Measure 25 sees melodic resolution to E_4 while bass reaches F_2, registering another ic 1—though dulled by deployment as i[11] over F and filled with A. Mild dissonance comes to the fore in m. 26, before a B-chord tritone marks the lydian effect. Thereafter, no significant fluctuation occurs until the flute's blue note rubs with the CM tonic chord at the end of the verse in m. 30. And, again, the softening agents here are powerful: not only is the sharpness expressed at a three-octave remove, but the flute is offstage and *piano*.

In relief from considering more details of pitch structure, Figure 5.10 diagrams the form of the work. Progress is read in rows, and columns show repetition; the end of one row connects with the beginning of the row below. Arrows guide the eye at three important returns. Columns are headed by thematic ideas named there: the main body begins with a "wrong note" hook (cf. "Maria" from *West Side Story*), which in the second verse gets an intensified repetition (mm. 35–38). The first and last rotations through A have a middle passage, and all end with the same tag, set to one of two rhyming lines, "All of my days," "And walks in his ways."

The B music is lightly sketched in Figure 5.11. Of particular note is the "overshot" tonal center; instead of veering into subdominant F at the start, Bernstein backs into it from F's subdominant, B♭. (The note-values in the figure are denominated in F.) Other breaks with A are equally marked, such as the clear ascending H-Line contrasting with generally descending upper-voice vectors in the other parts of the song. The two endings enact another *anadiplosis* scheme, the first by repulsing the H-line back to the start of the Bridge, and the second by completing it and then breaking through to A's intensive hook at m. 57. An instrumental rotation of A in A♭M covers stage action: the investiture of the celebrant. The Bridge is reentered at m. 71, but freely in cadenza, and discharges into the final tag of m. 72ff., accompanied by blue-note flute.

A "simple song" it is not, especially in its studied use of *anadiplosis*, its brightly lit motivic network, and its well-articulated linear structure. Even though *Mass* can be regarded as an ironic profanity of a sacred rite, the sincerity of Bernstein's

Figure 5.10 Bernstein, "A Simple Song," Formal analysis

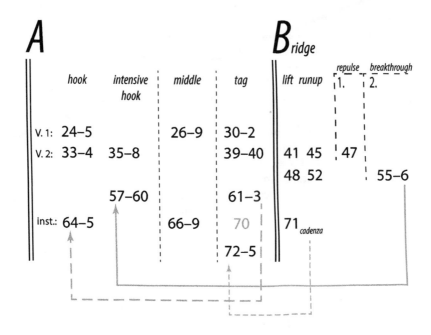

Figure 5.11 Bernstein, "A Simple Song," Analysis of Bridge, mm. 41–55

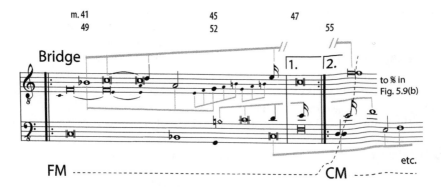

cultural engagement is palpable enough to wave off protests from all but the most pious and conservative. As in the television special about the "Rock Revolution," Bernstein adopts an earnest, respectful, and anodyne attitude toward the pop-music elements in his composition. That young pop-musicians of the day were rejecting these behaviors is an irony—but one that attaches only to Bernstein's artistic judgment, not to his composition.

One scene from Bernstein's television special is Brian Wilson of The Beach Boys performing a demo version of "Surf's Up," an ambitious, episodic, carefully worked, and sincere song described approvingly by Bernstein as "poetic, beautiful even in its obscurity." "Surf's Up" is an attempt at an art song by a pop composer. As such, considering it alongside "A Simple Song" makes a natural pairing, especially since it is far from simple itself. But both are very sincere compositions, and a wider-ranging contrast can be obtained by a brief analysis of a song Wilson composed the year after the television show, "Passing By," from the album *Friends* (1968), a song that gently ironicizes certain conventions about high-art harmony. Whereas "Surf's Up" strains to be an artistic statement, "Passing By" achieves this state as a mere simple song.

This delicate composition was designed for embryonic lyrics that were either not developed further before the song was recorded or were omitted for other reasons: "While walking down the avenue / I stopped to have a look at you / And then I saw / You're just passing by."[19] This wistful reflection on an unreturned gaze is responsible for distinctive modal treatments in this piece. As sketched in Figure 5.12, the first couplet is set to a carefree, hopeful major-pentatonic melody shown in the first two analytic measures. After this is repeated, an infusion of flat-side accidentals G♭ and D♭ at the third ending seems a particularly poignant sign that what captured the narrator's attention (so much so that he stopped walking) will not stop in return but pass by and pass on. These accidentals are resisted and overcome, first by the refusal to "accept" G♭ at m. 4, then by the subsequent sharp-side lift into A♮. This activates "double-headed" notes in the figure, which, as in previous graphs, show degree-reassignment suggested by modulation—in this case, from E♭M+ to a modally undetermined B♭. In the *dal segno* ending at m. 5, B♭ minor is sounded, completing the tonicization, but the subsequent resetting of D♭ back to D♮ reenergizes the dominant for a turnaround into the next rotation.

As the figure documents, these events map perfectly onto a sentential, SRDC (Statement–Restatement–Departure–Return) organization, with some overlap of the final two zones (see Everett 2009, 140). This organization rules the overall form as well, and the scheme presented in Figure 5.13 gives the details, scaled mostly at two-measure units. Two verse rotations are followed by a bridge, and then that structure is itself repeated: AABAAB, followed by an A′ alteration for the outro. This form is heavy with A, a module itself laden with internal repetition. The regularity of rotation in "Passing By" puts the fragmentary lyric into new light: the "you" may well be plural. The scene comprises not just one passing episode but many. The song may tell a sad tale of a noticer never being noticed.

If the A music records the quick "write off" of the lyric—a rejection occurring without delay—the bridge at B describes a slower-to-develop episode. Fulfilling the potential for the third ending to modulate to B♭M, it begins traditionally in that key before remodulating back to E♭, developing the first H- and S-lines in the piece longer than a single step. A new groove accompanies this change—more toms and fewer snare hits, and an organ taking the lead from the wordless vocals. The phrase initially develops very traditionally, with a regular-sized opening module that promises a like-sized consequent. This expectation is dramatically altered when

---

19. There is a possibility that these lyrics were fitted afterward, perhaps as long as several years, in preparing the publishing company for sale. Their provenance is unclear.

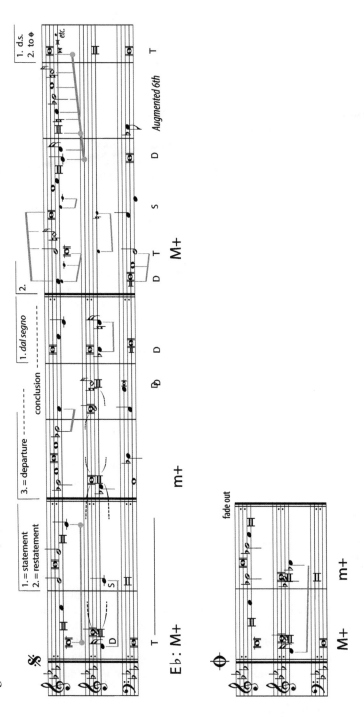

Figure 5.12 Wilson, "Passing By," Analysis of entire song structure

Figure 5.13 Wilson, "Passing By," Formal layout

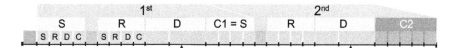

Wilson stages the sudden entrance of a harmonically immobilized augmented-sixth chord—a touchstone sonority of psychological import in art-music song, over which a near-chromatic H-line rises, slowly and expectantly. The encounter described here *might not* end in rejection after all.

But it does, and a second rotation of AAB ensues. Conventions of song arrangement come to aid the interpretation of this large-scale repetition. If the bridge episode ended in disappointment, it is not hopeless. A simple guitar countermelody from the introduction accompanies the lead, as if to represent the narrator's optimism after the events of the bridge. Yet during the restatement phase of the rotation, a strange and ominous buzz takes over the bass line, growing ever louder until suddenly cutting out at the beginning of the second bridge. At the augmented-sixth chord, however, it reenters and remains, noticeably but unobtrusively. The bass harmonica that Wilson calls for here is a symbol of doubt, anxiety, and defeat.

These fears are well founded, as the second bridge realizes them by repeating the sequence of the first. The result this time is not another rotation in the hopeful tones of the original A, but an outro coda that cycles through an irreversibly saddened A with an E♭m+ tonic, accompanied by a *mezzo piano* bass harmonica. (See ✿ in Figure 5.12.)

It's curious that the lyrics for "Passing By" developed no further than the scenario sketched in a single quatrain of poesy. The limitations of the arrangement may be responsible. Wilson's repetitive chord oscillations in SR modules both small (2 mm.) and large (8 mm.) direct lyrical thoughts toward the depressing repetition of missed opportunity and dampened hope. And the outro is a downer. Had the program for "Passing By" been produced a year or two earlier in Wilson's career, the results would surely have been more ambitious (along the lines of "Surf's Up" but darker) or a scenario-driven story of constant personal rejection, done lightly, possibly with sound effects (speech, for example—especially during the augmented-sixth drama), and describing it all in innocuous, teenagery terms. A year or two later, however, this program might not have been allowed by the other Beach Boys to be recorded under their name. In 1968, "Passing By" received an understated and suggestive arrangement as a song-without-words (but whose program is known) that leaves the level of interpretation up to the listener.

The structural analysis in Figure 5.12 makes the overtonal foundation of the piece very clear. The preponderance of open noteheads in the graph is one indication. The presence of H- and especially S-lines is another, as are motions by fifth in the bass line. The contemporary tonal touches are equally as clear. Rectilinearity predominates, especially in the repeated-chord accompaniment of A. And the harmonic vocabulary is primarily colored chords working around an integrated E♭M+ tonic—darkened in the outro, as already noted, to E♭m+. Brian Wilson's penchant for voicing unusual chordal inversions is also in evidence here, with the opening tonic colored as a major-seventh chord in second inversion being particularly conspicuous. The B♭ bass there mutes the sharpness of the i[1] in the accompaniment's fourth octave, giving it something of a foundation. The relaxation of tension into m. 2, which has a very mild i[10], is nonetheless palpable, and the oscillation between those two states during the SR phase of the sentence has an active yet calm character.

The most significant element that does not fit with the previous description is the augmented-sixth chord passage. This is ostentatiously inserted as an indivisible four-measure unit into an otherwise regular two-measure hypermeter, unbalancing the B section into ten measures of (2 + 2) + (2 + 4). The harmonic seam at the insertion is jarring: a deceptive cadence supercharged by an unexpected modal change—aptly marked by the flagged C♭ bass note. Further, the long melodic ascent here constitutes the only extended line of the piece; the A music generally oscillates or arpeggiates, and the opening of the B section, while a bit more expansive, does not promise a line of the size that eventually develops. These features effectively put quotation marks around the passage, referencing the kind of subtle psychological play with augmented-sixth chords found in romantic art-song.[20] That Wilson's deployment is hardly subtle makes the connection all the stronger. It comes off as ironic play with convention, as a connotatively rich interpolation into an unpretentious, light, and overtonally simple pop instrumental.

Whereas Bernstein earnestly works to erase any quotation marks around his popular stylings in "A Simple Song"—developing particular motives and finding an interesting way through the AABA form—Wilson uses them on one chord to deepen the tone of his artistic discourse, to complicate an otherwise simple double rotation of repetitive modules, and to complement the other modal activity in the song. Both "Passing By" and "A Simple Song" mediate art and pop through separate negotiations. Bernstein uses pop with the kind of bemused sincerity he portrayed in the TV special, while Wilson stages an "art event" in his song with the guileless irony of a child.

Global and Local: Allegiances to imagined communities

The huge enlargement of the central European cultural franchise during the nineteenth century—first eastward toward Russia and later the Americas—tapped new regional sources of talent and styles, many of whom inflected their CP training with markers of regional, national, or ethnic identification. Among Chopin's many Polish signifiers, for example, were genres (e.g., Mazurka, Polonaise) and modal effects (e.g., lydian). Liszt had much the same at his disposal, augmented by his choice of Hungarian-themed subjects for tone poems and other programmatic genres. Grieg's style can be viewed the same way, switching out eastern for northern European markers. By the end of the century, even British and Spanish composers

---

20. Schubert's examples are ubiquitous (e.g. "Die Neugierige," from *Die Schöne Müllerin,* mm. 33–43). For a detailed study of the chord's role in a Brahms part song, see Harrison (1995, 189ff.).

found a place on standard-repertory programs (Elgar and Albéniz, respectively). By the beginning of the First World War, the sources of regionally inflected compositional materials reached around the globe, certainly as an interconnected network from the Urals to the Atlantic, newly linked to North America, and with South America about to come online. Among its other distinctions, the Class of 1890 was the first to have significant numbers from outside the European continent.

Contemporary composers, in addition to negotiating and choosing among various abstract techniques, also contend with provenance and geographical situation of those techniques. One tendency—a strong expression of cultural piety—roots them in the world of specific places and peoples. Another deracinates them for a discourse generalized, often hopefully, to humankind. The first, if indulged regularly, results in works contributing to a "national" or ethnic art. Joaquin Rodrigo's *oeuvre*, for example, is firmly located in Spain, where it enjoys its greatest appreciation. The same could be said of Aram Khachaturian and Armenia, Heitor Villa-Lobos and Brazil, and Howard Hanson and the United States, and others (and all to varying degrees, of course). The second may identify with transnational institutions (such as Messiaen and Catholic Christendom), with aesthetics of common forerunners (such as read from Stravinsky's neoclassic works), or with some other aspiration to universal meaning (such as Schoenberg's pointing the way toward a music entwined with mathematics.) At its "art for art's sake" extreme, composers can position themselves as Citizens of the World and their works as contributions to a general fund of human culture. Milton Babbitt's "research based" program strongly expresses this characteristic. The most extreme (= pure) expression may be the ongoing performance of John Cage's *Organ²/Aslsp* at St. Burchardi church in Halberstadt, Germany, which is scheduled to end in the twenty-seventh century CE; to what particular and imaginable culture or people can this commitment to human music making be intended?[21]

For most composers, the expression of this style trait is mixed and complex. As Elliot Antokoletz (1984, 1) has observed about Bartók, whose music masterfully balances both tendencies, "[his] musical language may be approached from either of two points of view—one in which the concepts and terminology are derived from folk-music sources, and the other in which the concepts and analytical tools are derived from certain currents in contemporary art music." Much contemporary tonal music profits from being considered this way, especially certain works of Vaughan Williams, Gershwin, and Ginastera, to name a just few for whom situation in a world of place and people is a consistent theme in their work. For more nuanced cases, Hindemith's careful selection of German folk and historical sources bears noting, and a comparative study of Samuel Barber's and Aaron Copland's respective approaches to their geographical situation in the United States could be enlightening. The extent to which any composer, of any school, roots in native soil always makes for an interesting contrast with others who want to work internationally with generic and unmarked materials and techniques (refer to Whittall (2003, 1–72) for a sophisticated and sustained engagement touching on these and related matters).

For his first approach, Antokoletz focuses on tunes and scales Bartók used to localize his music (see Susanni and Antokoletz 2012). Since Bartók was a pioneer

---

21. For information as of this writing, consult http://www.aslsp.org/.

(with Kodály) in the collection and subsequent arrangement of Hungarian folk music, the option to characterize people and place by means of melodic material is easy to exercise. But it can also generalize to other composers, especially those who did similar fieldwork, such as Vaughan Williams, whose modal writing is such a distinctive stylistic feature (Bates 2012). And even for those without such credentials, secondhand arrangements of these materials could provide a basic template. A newfound appreciation for the distinctive sound of regionalized folk scale and macroharmony in contemporary tonal music results from these observations.

Pentatonic Places and Twelve-tone Universes

Analysis of source scales has been and continues to be an important way into individual works and compositional styles, as in the examples of Bartók, Vaughan Williams, Hovhannes, and others, not to mention (most suggestively) jazz. In cases where abstract scales are widely shared across cultures, scale alone may not be enough to localize, and meter and traditional rhetoric have to be enlisted to fix a regional dance, form, and groove.

Reviewing expressions of pentatonic-scale organization encountered so far in this book, extremely clear cases are found in rock and popular music, ("Sister Surround," chap. 2; "Cherry Cherry," chap. 3). The affinity of this music to traditional and folkish modal expressions has allowed easy passage of this material to the commercial pop market along with the subsequent integration and hybridization of many pentatonic regional styles. (Recall that "Sister Surround" also made strong allusion to South Asian modality.) In these cases, pentatonic source scales are global ones and not particularly localized. In these songs, genre and instrumentation further subdue expression of this trait and call attention to Art/Pop behaviors.

Although Debussy could allude to location and place using pentatonic scales, he also introduced a soundscape where these scales could be deployed in general, deracinated ways (refer to Day-O'Connell 2009 and 2007). The analysis of Marcel Dupré's prelude from chapter 4 is a particularly effective illustration. A review of the relevant figures and text show extensive range of application for "analytical tools ... derived from certain currents in contemporary art music," as Antokoletz put it. Like the pop-music examples, genre and instrumentation play a role in the analysis of Dupré's piece, although these trend away from pop expressions and embrace the catholicity of a generic prelude for organ, cast into a sonata form and heavily dosed with contrapuntal artifice. Thoughts of investigating folk-music sources for the piece do not spring immediately to mind.

We find more opportunity to explore a localizing use of pentatonicism in Xiaoyong Chen's "Wind, Water, and Shadows" from *Diary III* (2004).[22] The opening figuration, shown in Figure 5.14, is remarkably similar to Dupré's in the tonal centers involved, the "fourthiness" of its figuration and its organization into contour

---

22. A detailed general introduction to Chen and his works is available in Liang (2007). I am indebted to Zhang Wei of the Shanghai Conservatory of Music for introducing me to Chen's music.

Figure 5.14 Xiaoyong Chen, "Wind, Water, and Shadows," mm. 1–11 (©
MUSIKVERLAG HANS SIKORSKI GMBH & CO. KG, Hamburg)

waves (i.e., nested patterns of up/down motion). But the title and genre differences
are significant. The rubric "diary" is unusual if not unique for a suite of small-scale
piano works.[23] It promises abbreviated and unrevised first impressions about events
or thoughts of the day. These are also purportedly private, and thus making one
public is a self-revealing act. Diaries always indicate place, since they generally
report on particular locales and peoples. Perhaps for this reason, pieces in "Diary"
collections tend not to be individually titled, so that determinate objects of thought
that diaries record are left up to listener to imagine.

Chen's piece is an exception, describing a specific scenario of wind, water, and
shadows. It thus may be profitably approached as the sound trace of these events
as observed and transcribed by the diary writer. This approach helps to make sense
of the remarkably long stretches of low sonic activity in the piece. As documented
in Figure 5.15, fifteen seconds of very soft and slow music (mm. 20–24) separate
the active episode from a second. Similar spans separate the second from the third
(mm. 36–46), and the piece winds down with more of the same after m. 74 by
means of an extended *diminuendo* and written-out *ritardando* culminating in two
fermatas: one over the final note, an A_7 whole note with *pppp*; the second is at the
final double bar, a "freeze" demand on performer and audience.

---

23. Cf. Philipp Jarnach, *Das Amrumer Tagebuch*, op. 30, (1942), Roger Sessions, *From my Diary* (1937–
    39), and Max Reger, *Aus meinem Tagebuch*, op. 82 (1904–12).

Figure 5.15 Xiaoyong Chen, "Wind, Water, and Shadows," Sound energy graph

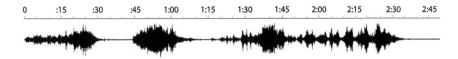

The huge variation in activity suggests that the sound trace is more under natural influence—that of variable wind speed, for example—than it is under the control of a composer interested in developing material in the way Dupré demonstrated. Signs point to something like a wind chime as the sound source. Once activated, this allusion localizes the pentatonic in East or South Asia— combining scale, timbral qualities, and the instrument's spiritual associations (*feng shui*, for example). This information locates the diary author/composer and maneuvers those interested in Chen's music toward analytic approaches that Antokoletz outlined for Bartók, proceeding along dual tracks of sourcing the musical material in a particular culture while describing abstract techniques that transform this material. For Xiaoyong Chen in particular—a Chinese pupil of Ligeti in the late 1980s who currently resides in Hamburg—this analytic tack is broad-reaching, satisfactorily explaining how vocabulary "captures both the integration and tension between contrasting cultural elements" (Liang 2007, 529).

A sketch of the formal and overtonal structure of mm. 1–9 conveys some of the technical devices at work (fig. 5.16). The cascade figuration projects pentatonic H-line polyphonic melody, tonicked with either F♯ (for all descents) or E (for ascents until m. 5). Although the layout of the figure makes it possible to trace the original course of the passage, it exposes the overtonal, white-note bedrock of the cascades as complex arpeggiations of M++ chords. The cascades are organized into ascending and descending waves—regular, at first, according to an invisible ("dotted line") 15/16 meter organizing mm. 1–3. Measure 4 shortens by three to 12/16, followed by a rebound to 18/16 in the next bar. Thereafter, cascade-length meter fluctuates inconsistently through m. 8, as Figure 5.17 illustrates. A noticeable increase in wave frequency in mm. 9–10 leads to overlapping waves in the next two bars, an effective use of metric accelerando to introduce a new idea. A surprising wave reversal (ascent from the fourth instead of the third) in m. 10 is also a piece of this rhetoric. Rectilinear movement at the lowest register is shown, and the end of the example coincides with movement in the highest, long stabilized at C♯7. The neighbor-note bump is the only deep linear content of this section. Thereafter is the closing section of this first episode, where wave energy slowly dissipates like swinging chimes losing momentum into a lull.

For a contrast to the kind of scale-based assessments undertaken in the foregoing analyses of the local/global attitude, Frank Martin's *Petite Symphonie Concertante* (1944–45) can be approached as an imposing bid to achieve a fully global neutrality. Composed by a Swiss in the closing year of the Second World War, it is an unambiguous statement of neoclassicism, reviving an antiquated *concertante* genre and even choosing a harpsichord for one of the solo instruments.

Figure 5.16 Xiaoyong Chen, "Wind, Water, and Shadows," overtonal synopsis of opening figuration, mm. 1–5

Figure 5.17 Xiayong Chen, "Wind, Water, and Shadows." Outer-voice limits of figurations in each measure, with number of sixteenth-notes in each measure of figuration shown.

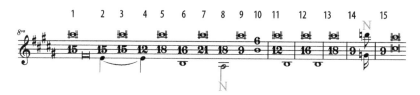

Maintaining intriguing and complex contact with overtonal hierarchies, the *Petite symphonie concertante* is a widely admired composition of a complex, bespoke technique.[24]

The leading feature of *Petite Symphonie Concertante* is its unusual orchestration: solo treatment of harp, piano, and harpsichord backed with full strings divided into two orchestras, the parts themselves richly subdivided. Most symphony orchestras find it somewhat difficult to program—split strings require an agile conductor, and the harp and certainly the harpsichord are noteworthy "specials" that (along with the piano) are bulky items to move, set up, and tune. Martin himself, worried that the arrangement as commissioned would prove too specialized for other orchestras to try—an "instrumental curiosity," in his words—made a second one "for large orchestra, without solo instruments," which, contrary to his expectations, received a unique premiere (and hasn't been heard since) while the original *concertante* arrangement endures—though the difficulties in

24. The analytical literature on this work is meager. Martin himself offers some generalities in Hines (1970, 153–57); it is regrettably missing from the useful Riemann/Hindemith approach taken in Billeter (1971); Adams (1984) provides a start, but the attempt to derive all motivic material from a particular theme is unconvincing.

programming it are well-founded enough that live performances are, in North America at least, rather rare.[25] The apparently indispensable nature of the original arrangement is an inviting analytic opening: the *Petite Symphonie Concertante* is about disparate elements: their contrasts and their combinations. A roster of these elements has: three solo instruments, two orchestras, two movements, four main themes, and five discrete small-interval cells that characterize the pitch relations in the work at multiple levels; these will be teased out of the complex surface in the analysis that follows.

The technical issues in orchestration that Martin worked with are significant and worth noting. Making space for the weak projection of the harpsichord is one; pedaling effectively for the chromatic harp is another; good ideas for interaction among the solo instruments/timbre are perquisite, of course. Ultimately, taking on the challenge of splitting the string orchestras calls for some display of antiphonal writing. Considering the range of orchestrational combinations as well as the special-effects opportunities afforded by the unusual *concertante* instruments, the first tonal impression of the work leads analytically to polychords, coloring agents, and other types of dissonance *appliqué*. These are sometimes laid on so thick that the texture crosses over into "composed heterophony."

As to overtonality in the *Petite Symphonie Concertante*, it is primarily experienced as a fluctuation technique of clarity, producing on one extreme, entire sections with a single fully-realized M++ tonic chord (reh. 66–end), and on the other, sections heavily colored with polychords, pedal points, *ostinati*, etc. (illustrated in the following sections). With valves fully open, musical flow is thickly atonal—but soon fluctuated, clarified, channeled, and modulated. Overall, the ambient glow of the *Petite symphonie concertante*, in its first movement especially, is a heavily colored overtonality on G, often episodic and sequenced according to a "schedule of ideas" as detailed below.

Figure 5.18 gives a sample of the techniques involved, at least in split-orchestra writing *without* the solo instruments, analyzing the passage between rehearsal nos. 3 and 4 (mm. 25–37). The lower section transcribes the first few measures, both detailing the division of labor between the two orchestras and bringing out the separate register couplings for the melody and its chordal accompaniment. The upper section distills these to the main concentration of chord mass in the fourth octave, with the leading line encased between supporting chord tones. Octave and superoctave doublings make the motivically derived tune emerge clearly at the top of the combined texture. Meanwhile, the accompanimental chord tones are all distinctly doubled 8vb, lightly filling the third octave, but leaving the second empty.

This conspicuous void isolates the contrabasses in the first octave, which proceed independently of the cellos above to a striking degree, in contrast with typical orchestrational practice where *vc. e bassi* is the rule. This treatment is typical in the work. On their own, the contrabasses are sovereigns of the first octave, holding court on pedal points or otherwise moving much more deliberately than parts above. Martin writes carefully for these instruments, and the

---

25. As related by Martin himself in *Philharmonia Partituren* PH 385, iii–v.

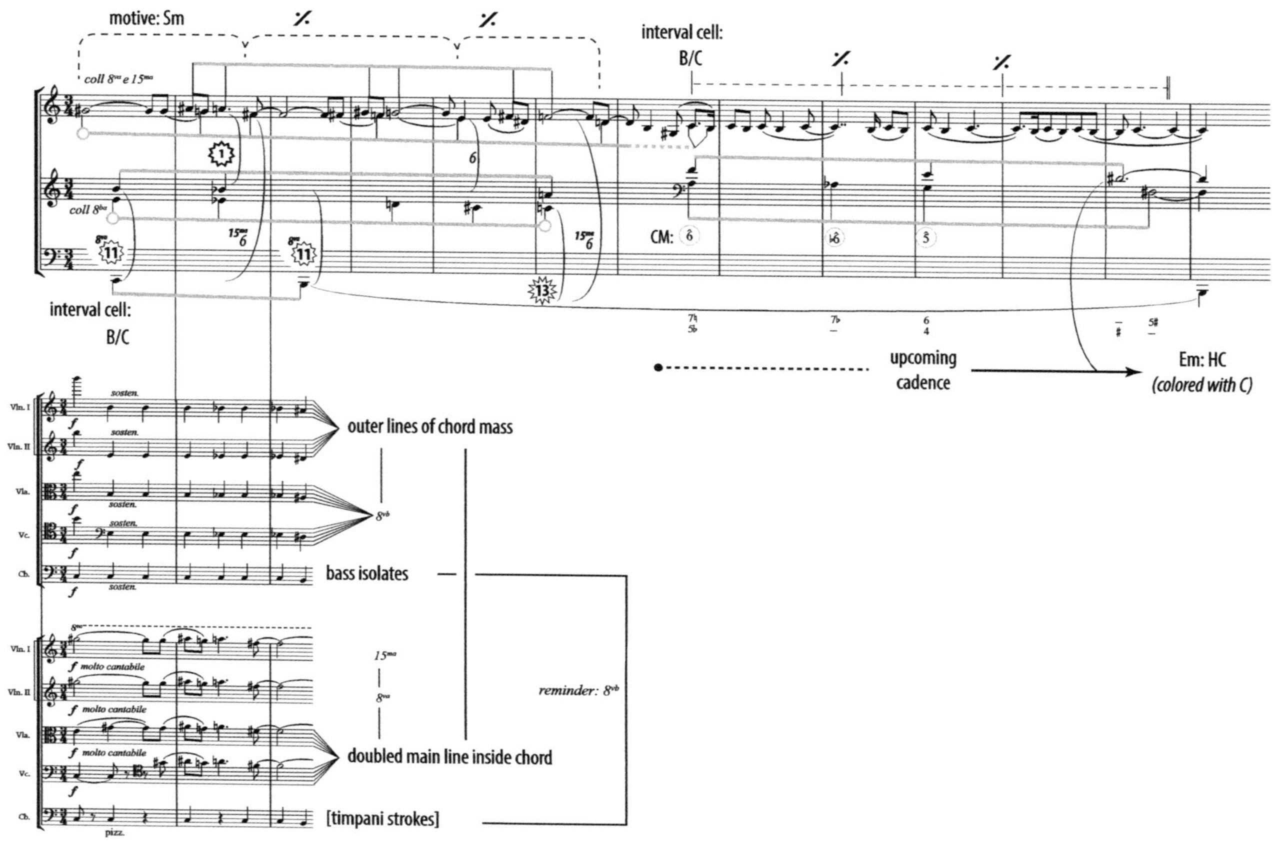

Figure 5.18 Linear analysis of Martin, *Petite Symphonie Concertante*, reh. 3 to 4

passage at hand is particularly brilliant. Note that the basses of two orchestras double each other at the unison: the first plays *sostenuto* while the second, *pizz.* Because their line is put into sharp relief by very prominent i[11] and i[13] relations in registers above, upper-harmonic resonances of the contrabass pitches are suppressed—an effect that unmistakably conjures the timpani among the strings, a perfect slow-march accompaniment to the ominous mood of sustained chromatic descent above, all directed toward a section-ending anticlimax at the end of the passage.

As Figure 5.18 shows, the *Petite Symphonie Concertante* is a piece of chromatic music, with generally high turnover rate of the twelve-pc aggregate. Pointedly, this activity is thematically registered in the work as a "twelve-tone row," which is unfolded as the characteristic melody that opens the work, transcribed in Figure 5.19. As inspection of the rest of the piece discloses, Martin treats this theme *12t* not as a set of pitch classes, but as a set of directed pitch intervals, regularly producing the compound melody of H-lines shown in the figure. In the first part of the row, these lines are similar to those analyzed in Figure 5.18— descents mostly by chromatic step. Toward the close, H-lines shorten, simplify, and generally ascend to the next row cycle, T_4 of the first, reached by a palpable discharge of a leading-tone, B to C.[26] The cycle continues into the upper octaves until the G♯$_6$ that begins the passage of Figure 5.18. At that point, *12t$_8$* is scheduled to begin again, but is declined in favor of the passage.

In the opening of the *Petite Symphonie Concertante*, the row is styled as a traditional passacaglia—a rhythmically regular bass in slow triple meter, here deliberately sounding out each note of the aggregate in equal note values. This expression is comparable to similar ostentatious aggregate-completing themes, such as the well-known examples in Liszt's *Faust Symphony* and Strauss's *Also Sprach Zarathustra*. It is even closer to the lengthy, wandering, obscure, and "almost aggregate" passacaglia themes of Reger. The connection becomes clearer once the accompaniment gets underway in m. 2 of the work. It, too, is a twelve-tone row, though different from *12t*. Most noticeably, as suggested in Figure 5.20, it moves three times as slowly as the passacaglia *12t* theme. (The accompaniment is aligned visually with the *12t* passacaglia in order to facilitate set-classes analysis.) The first hexachords of each row, taken as unordered pitch classes, are tritone transformations of the other. The second hexachords seem to analyze best as two trichords relating in the specific ways shown in the figure. None of these ways, however, complete the aggregate for the accompaniment. Even so, the potential for the first hexachord of *12t* to be extracted for "head motive" use is strongly suggested, and the thematic realization of *12t* in compound-melody descending H-lines also forms a strong association. In the accompaniment row, the effects of those aggregate-*declining* transformations identified in the second hexachord allow fully chromatic H-lines to complete through the whole gesture, without the break between a first and second part modeled in the *12t* passacaglia. The similarity of H-lines points to certain habits of interval disposition evident in

---

26. This identification of a traditional tonal function (double-flagged in the figure) is the best argument in favor of the *directed-interval* row. Completion of the row isn't on the twelfth object, but upon spanning the twelfth interval after it.

Figure 5.19 Theme 12t, mm. 1–4. Theme starts on pc 8; next iteration starts on pc 0. H-lines analyzed with beams

Figure 5.20 Martin, *Petite Symphonie Concertante*, (a) analysis of theme 12t, mm. 1–4; (b) analysis of contrabass accompaniment, mm. 2–13, to 12t

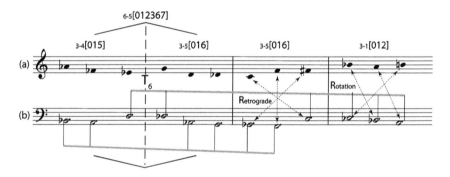

the composition: just as harmonies will normally be colored and polychorded, melodies will normally be compound and polyphonic.

At this point, it is prudent to collate observations of this sort with the main themes of the work, the incipits of which are shown in Figure 5.21. Theme *12t* (and its accompaniment) comprises the introduction to a sonata form, whose P theme commences at reh. 5 + 2 (m. 49). After a P-based TR, S₁ launches at reh. 15–1, amplifying the passacaglia topic of *12t* by more clearly articulating its triple-meter rhythm and cadence-like falling fifths in the first ending. The gesture towards antecedent/consequent construction marks a more relaxed formal treatment than previously (though the seven-bar container is a sign of contact with the prevailing tone of asymmetrical phrases in the piece). S₁ has a variant in S₂, with which it shares a head, motive *Sm*. The second movement of *Petite Symphonie Concertante*, starting at reh. 41 is based largely on a third theme, T, which is introduced over a root and fifth overtonal drone. This structure suggests some hierarchical hearing of the coloring thirds and sixths, as shown between the staves. In its final form at reh 50, T is styled *alla Marcia*, and is the site for one of Martin's masterstrokes in this work. The transformation from the doleful, droned presentation shown here into jaunty march reverses the usual effects of direct parallel-mode darkening, which signals a sad, clouded, troubled, or tragic state—as famously encapsulated in the opening of Strauss's *Also Sprach Zarathustra*. Here, it plays against this type and, accompanied by triadic chord changes of thrilling root-motion velocity, portrays something rather hopeful, supported by the determined metrical hierarchy of the march. In the aftermath of a cultural cataclysm that was the Second World War, this inversion of the topical system—minor is made hopeful, and the march pacified—is a remarkable contextual achievement in this work.

Figure 5.21 is annotated with symbols showing the limited number of directed intervals used for thematic construction. This is chiefly responsible for creating compound H-lines found in *12t* and even more clearly in P. Their shaping effects in S and T are clear enough to need no further comment. More revealing is their influence over the whole texture, which Figure 5.22 is designed to highlight. This passage shows Martin's characteristic *concertante* writing for harp, piano, and harpsichord. The P incipit is reproduced on the lowest staff and extended to the end of the phrase. In the middle staves, the piano part sustains tonic G in one hand while making a thick K-line stroke in the fourth octave. (For ease of identification, i[4] thirds are stemmed up, and i[3]s are down.) The piano's upper line moves from one plateau to another via an i[5] H-line, continuing the linear energy that the harpsichord had just left off. The harp has an increasingly irregular ostinato between i[3]-related pitches, G♭ and D♯. It, too, reconfigures in response to the end of the harpsichord lift, and proceeds underneath the piano's H-line to C. Similar writing follows in the subsequent *Fortspinnung* of these ideas, which continues for an additional five measures before another rotation begins (at reh. 7).

While this chapter cannot sustain effort to reach the final level of analysis—a comprehensive reading of its major sections—the observations made so far can point the way. The motivic pitch-interval vocabulary of the piece can be characterized according to the following schedule:

- i[1] and i[2] make K- and H-lines.
- i[3] is a thematic harmonic interval, important for compound melody constructions. It can be filled as chromatic tetrachord 4-1[0123], and characteristically so as motive S_m, and it can also be filled as characteristic trichord 3-2[013]. (See the upper beams in *12t$_8$* and theme T in Figure 5.21.)
- i[4] is a harmonic interval of generative structural importance: it separates statements of *12t* in the introduction. It is also important for compound melody constructions, and its characteristic motivic fill is 4-3[0134]. This tetrachord is a highlighted motive throughout the work. (See the curly braces at the end of theme S_2, fig. 5.21.)
- i[5] is a melodic interval of themes *12t*, P, T. Its relationship to i[7] is suggested in theme S_1 as well as in the opening of P.

Several of these pitch-interval relationships are motivicized in the work, and some become associated with individual pitch classes, establishing an event-hierarchical link to an underlying tonal structure. Figure 5.23 gives a very rough and partial account, taking its bearings from the overtonal organization of the sonata in G as well as the affirmational GM++ at end of the work. Also considered is the *12t* opening on A♭ and its composing-out of i[4]. Both of these generate

Figure 5.21 Martin, *Petite Symphonie Concertante* thematic catalog

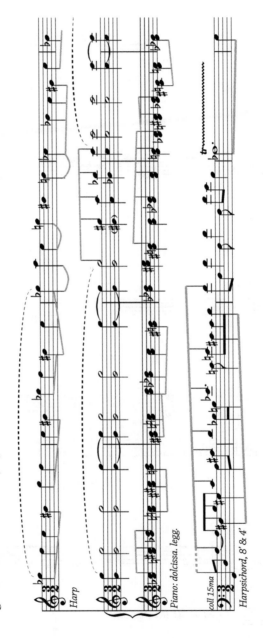

Figure 5.22 Martin, *Petite Symphonie Concertante*, transcription of reh. 5 + 2 through 6

Figure 5.23 Martin, *Petite Symphonie Concertante*, chart of motivic deployment

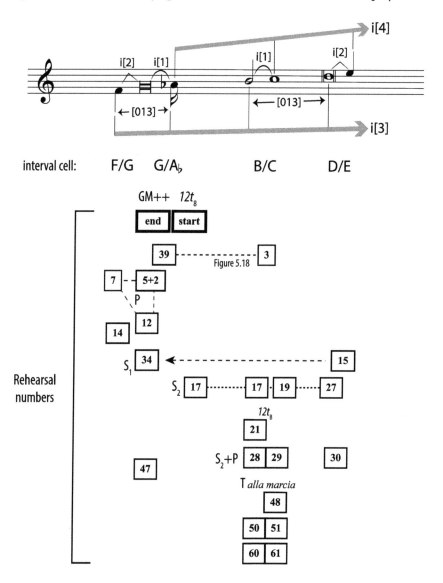

relations shown as two divergent interval cycles from A♭.[27] Rehearsal numbers mark important thematic statements throughout the work where the resulting *interval cells* are foregrounded. These may be realized as local tonics, as starting points for thematic statements, or as noticeable changes in slow contrabass lines. The definitive S-theme relationship for the sonata is shown with a dotted line

27. From reh. 21 + 2 to reh. 27, complex interactions of this sort between i[4] and i[3] cycles is thematized using various transformations of *12t*.

between rehs. 15 and 34. Resolving D into G is also part of local structure, where it sets up all thematic statements centered on G. More action, however, is found at B/C, which is especially conspicuous after reh. 48, during the T-theme march.

The schematic shown in Figure 5.23 and the pitch-interval schedule it is based on do not yet provide a comprehensive account of pitch structure in the *Petite Symphonie Concertante*. A more detailed accounting of "cycles-within-cycles" is necessary to bring more pitches into association. This would, for example, locate the first appearance of theme T (over the drone at reh. 41) as a product of the G/ A♭ interval cell, with the tonic D♭ acting as root to A♭'s fifth. The work is a master-piece of motivic cell composition, with the characteristic themes heavily regulated by a limited set of pitch intervals Attaching to specific pcs, these intervals scale up and down throughout the structure—from the beginning and ending A♭/G at the deepest level, to the realization of this very cell on successive downbeats of the opening *12t*$_8$ row. This highly abstracted technique—specific combinations of pure pitch intervals, deployed throughout—perfectly accompanies the other estranging moves Martin made in orchestration, instrumentation, and genre in order to comment meaningfully on the world situation of 1945, composed from a position of unique, neutral disinterest. Using a twelve-tone theme, especially one as overtonally impassive as *12t*, is a generous and ecumenical gesture, a bid to repair aesthetic rifts ultimately made worse by the war.

Martin's treatment of the twelve-tone "passacaglia theme" brings to mind Samuel Barber's in *Nocturne*, op. 33, about which I have written elsewhere (Harrison 2012). An outstanding common element in both aggregate-completion schemes is their construction as regular themes marked by characteristic figurations. That is, while Martin styled the unfolding like a Regerian passacaglia, Barber—trying to get out from under Chopin by dedicating this piano work to John Field—styled his row as a filigreed melodic line for the right-hand part, a seeming improvisation supported by strongly overtonal arcades of left-hand arpeggios. Figure 5.24 gives the idea. The arpeggios set up A♭M in m. 1, enriching this to A♭M+ in the following measure. A♭ stays secure as a pedal tone in outer voices while a functionally mixed and sharp B-chord is introduced in the second half of m. 2. This chord covers for the right hand's jagged ascent to goal-tone C$_6$, whereupon harmonic tension relaxes back to A♭M+ and beyond. As the row retrogrades back to C$_4$, the bass line begins a slow descent toward C$_2$, not completed until the row is retrograded again in m. 5, in a different contour and rhythm, though once again pointedly arriving on C$_4$ (via resolution from a B-chord) to complete the phrase.

Barber's employment of retrogression is a "classic" serial technique that Martin pointedly avoided. He preferred instead to experiment according to his lights, first by providing *12t* with a derived, near-aggregate accompaniment, and then by play-ing with the rhythm of the melody while maintaining its direction and contour. Martin composed an abstract theme to express the abstract rules of the tone row, while Barber composed an ornamented *cantando* melody in spite of these abstract rules. Both, however, shared a concern for ending their rows with local tonic-ity—Martin by arranging a functional discharge to mark the beginning of each row statement, and Barber by fluctuating the supporting harmony to make the row beginnings at mm. 3, 5, and 6 coincide with phrase endings. In both cases,

Figure 5.24 Barber, *Nocturne*, op. 33. Score and analysis of mm. 1–6

meter supports the tonicizing effects; Martin's triple-metering of trichords creates a traditional four-measure span, with hypermetric accent to fall on m. 5. Barber's melody is more rhythmically varied, but the arpeggios clearly mark out four-chord overlapping spans supporting the first row in m. 2 to the middle of m. 3, and another one from m. 3 to the first half of m.5. An unexpected two-chord span into m. 6 is compensated for in the melody by new regularity in motive—three sequential statements prefacing the melodic arrival in m. 6.

To see how far disciplining tone-rows with overtonality can be pursued, David Shire's soundtrack to the 1974 Joseph Sargent film, *The Taking of Pelham 123*, is an illustrative extreme case. The theme for the main title sequence is transcribed in Figure 5.25. Here, the final A♭ is well placed by the agogic accent and restoration of the original rhythm and contour motive in mm. 1–2. Unlike Barber and Martin, who arranged for discharges onto the first note of a new row form, Shire closes on

Figure 5.25 Shire, Main title theme from *The Taking of Pelham 123*

the final note, strictly sealing off the row into trichordal segments of two measures each. This removes a strong overtonal prop provided in the "thirteen-tone" realization of Barber and Martin, so that the final note of Shire's row is only weakly conclusive, with an unpredictable continuation. It suggests no overtonal frame by itself. This responsibility is offloaded to the music shown in Figure 5.26, a jazzy groove in B♭m that drones repetitively for the entire cue. (The drummer varies on the kit slightly, especially fills, and the donno drummer improvises freely; otherwise, the groove never changes.) The groovy dronality here provokes inquiries about Art/Pop style traits, reconfiguring the motivic plan in terms of an SRDC pop-song scheme.

The drone also illuminates certain aspects of the theme, which Figure 5.27 shows. The anapestic rhythm leaves the final note of each trichord exposed against the drone. The arrangement of these notes is designed with a harmonic fluctuation scheme in mind. The row begins with high harmonic tension, with passing i[11] intervals before settling into a very sharp i[13] against the overtonal root at the end of the first trichord. The second trichord passes through the dronal notes at the beginning but ends with an i[13] against the root's minor-third coloring—an easing of tension yet still quite sharp. The third trichord dispenses with sharpness and activates i[6] instead, and the final alights upon notes of a B♭m+ chord, draining out the tritone and ic1 sharpness.

More tone-row activity follows the opening presentation, also organized according to SRDC but less clear cut, as Figure 5.28 demonstrates. The opening SR modules are only loosely based on the opening row,[28] but the D and C are structured by interactions between P9 (plus its retrograde) and RI9, worked out hexachordally. Evidence of precompositional planning is found at the end of m. 5, where the soprano saxophone starts up P9 but switches over to RI9, taking advantage of the invariant trichord between the two rows. The C module makes a vamp out of the second hexachord of P9, using it to introduce the next rotation of the P9 head tune. More of the same type of precision pc-deployment is found in the rest of the work, yet all is overtonally anchored by the drone and rhythmically enlivened by a rock-steady groove. Shire's composition is styled and formed as a popular, commercial piece, yet like Barber and Martin, he uses a globalized technique of twelve-tone serialism to express higher-art impulses. These two elements together ultimately signal a delightfully ironic attitude about the techniques of serialism—a stark contrast to the sincerity and seriousness Martin's treatment of them in the *Petite symphonie concertante*, and less conflicted than Barber's experiments in the *Nocturne*.

---

28. The drone can be analyzed as supplying the first two pcs of RI9 (or P10) that is subsequently partially worked out in S module; the R module brings the chords back to the neighborhood of P9.

Figure 5.26 Shire, Main title from *The Taking of Pelham 123* dronal groove

Figure 5.27 Shire, Main Title from *The Taking of Pelham 123*, harmonic fluctuation between groove and theme

Envoi: Prokofiev, Sonata for flute, op. 94, I.

I'm grateful to a reader of this manuscript for the reminder that I had started this whole enterprise off with the first eight measures of Prokofiev's Flute Sonata, op. 94 (fig. 1.1), a passage I had offered as a way into emancipated practices of tonality characteristic of the last century. Why, wondered the reader, had I not returned at the end of the book to revisit and comment? What did I have to show that was going to do a better structural analysis of the passage than the (apparently) defective modernizations of Schenker and Riemann I cited then, or the problematic attempts of Hindemith and others to systematize these emancipated practices? After all the foregoing, Figure 1.1 and the piece it is excerpted from deserves revisiting.

Prokofiev's implementation of sonata-form in this movement attracts immediate interest. Figure 5.29 provides the schematics. We can take bearings from the

Figure 5.28 Shire, Main Title from *The Taking of Pelham 123* mm. 13–20

$$P9 \longrightarrow \quad 9 \ 0 \ B \ | \ A \ 1 \ 2 \ | \ 3 \ 6 \ 7 \ | \ 4 \ 5 \ 8 \ |$$
$$| \ A \ 1 \ 2 \ | \ B \ 0 \ 3 \ | \ 4 \ 5 \ 8 \ | \ 7 \ 6 \ 9 \ \longleftarrow \ I9$$

Figure 5.29 Prokofiev, Sonata op. 94, I. The sonata-formal scheme. Columns group contents according to the four action zones. New content heads a new column. Rows indicate rotations

P	TR	S	C	*march*
‖: 1————8	9————21	22 ——————— 38	38–41 :‖	42–51
1–4 5–8				
52–5		58–61		55–8
	62–5	65 ——————— 75		
	76——— 84			85–8
89————96	96————103	104————————114	115—122	122–24
125–29 ‖				

top row, where the action zones of the exposition are laid out neatly. No complications of any kind are in evidence. Each zone is amply marked and generically conforming. The textbook assembly of parts is only underscored by the mandatory repeat. The P module, mm. 1–8, was exemplified in Figure 1.1.

Modular construction is confirmed at the onset of the development, which introduces a new theme in a march topic. This theme's characteristic sixteenth-triplet rhythmic motive suffuses the rest of the development, though becoming less obvious over the course of the section. As to P, the figure makes clear how it is treated in the development, with its antecedent phrase, mm. 52–55, separated from the consequent, mm. 62–65, by means of intervening march and even S material, mm. 55–58 and 58–61, respectively. P returns unchanged at the recapitulation, mm. 89–96 (= mm. 1–8), and then is wistfully recalled a final time in mm. 125–26, a pianissimo rendering of the first two measures. We will return to this emblematic theme of the piece shortly.

Continuing the large-scale survey, the form can also be reconfigured as a progression of tonal centers, which Figure 5.30 enacts. The very strong tethering to DM in the exposition gives way in the development to a set of minirotations of P and S, centered on the degrees as shown. While the relations appear to be remote and characteristically modern, they are better heard as "shadows" of strongly established DM degrees—that is semitonal displacements of the kind identified in Bass (1988). The case of P in m. 52 is particularly persuasive about this, as the flute timbre of the opening is certainly recapitulated if not the actual notes. The version at (b) renotates the passage with the shadowed degrees, altered with accidentals to show the displacement.[29] We can conclude from this that the DM overtonality in this piece is largely a CP one that is subject to displacement.

Comparing the tonal plan to the degree progression in the P theme is instructive, as similar kinds of deformations can quickly be spotted. The conspicuous role of B♭ in mm. 125–29, for example, is previewed in the opening bars. The tritone, too, as an important pivot point on the way back to D, via B♮ (as seen in m. 7 of fig. 1.1). These kinds of observations lead naturally to creating a "schedule of motives" that Martin's work suggested. Instead of pursuing that familiar line, we will maintain focus on the P theme, moving more deeply into its formal construction.

Figure 5.31 analyzes the linear and harmonic structure of the opening P theme, mm. 1–8.[30] Formally, it models an antecedent/consequent construction, thanks to the 4+4 grouping and the thematic parallelisms of mm. 1 and 5. The four-squareness of this theme typical of the movement and is responsible for the exceptionally clear boundaries found in the exposition.[31] The antecedent ending on a half cadence in C, the subtonic, is deformational yet nonetheless well-predicated by replacement of F♯ with F♮, starting in m. 2, and the descending-fifth degree progression into m. 4, which supports converging H-lines. The consequent, mm. 5–8, at first carries out the moves of m. 1–2, adjusted to CM. Its modulatory pivot not only refuses another downward move, but also a return to the opening CM. Instead, it returns to opening DM by recomposing the converging H-lines so

---

29. Figure 4.17 provides another example of this notation.
30. The melodic structure of the flute line alone was displayed in Figure 3.26.
31. The importance of such traditional phrase rhetoric to Prokofiev's style is examined in Rifkin (2006).

180 ∞ *Pieces of Tradition*

Figure 5.30 Prokofiev, Sonata op. 94, I. (a) Progression of tonal centers through the work, calibrated to D. (b) Diatonic shadows projected from the surface

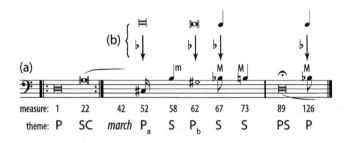

that the ascending pair is made to be specifically i[3] thick and contrived to meet up with the descending upper H-line that extends to the final F♯ of the phrase. This, too, is a well-predicated return, at least from the linear perspective.

This perspective tempts one toward considering an undisplaced version of the analytic sketch as presented here, to hammer out the dents Prokofiev has made in the diatonic structure and to get back to a normative antecedent/consequent construction in DM. Doing so doesn't commit the analyst to compose some mythical *actual* prototype, but rather to notice where the dents are knocked in a *plausible* prototype, and to notice how they are worked out in the sequel. For example, the first half of m. 1, with its broken-chord figuration, could have been written by a *galant*-period composer; a number of CP continuations of that opening can easily be imagined. The second half of the measure, however, is modern, but the sustained F♯ along with the high flute D_6 keep DM of the first half well in sight. The remaining degrees of the functionally mixed chord are minor shadings of subdominant function, tending downward and supported by a well-defined base. The chord itself is thus designed to trouble the easy DM opening while maintaining its F♯ agency in the piano figuration and pointedly keeping the flute on DM task, even into the next measure.

It is there, at m. 3, where the decisive move is made: depressing the modal third from major to minor, which is supported by another minor-shaded pitch in the bass, B♭. Thereafter, harmonic action has relaxed into a decidedly CP progression of diatonic descending fifths supporting conventional seventh chords in the key of C: VI^7–II^7–V^{4-3}. The displacement is clearly associated with events surrounding mm. 1–2. Information about harmonic fluctuation, shown at the bottom of the figure, is useful in analyzing those events. Here, the special effect of m. 1's second half is best registered: a sharpened sonority thanks to ic1, but softened as an i[11] filled as i[8,3]; it is a B-chord as well, with the tritone expressed between F♯$_4$ and C$_5$ in the piano. The increase in tension is tied to the increase in functional complexity and coordinated to discharge back to an A-chord on the downbeat of m. 2. Sharp dissonance is not fully discharged then, but softened to a minimum as an i[35] and filled with three other pitches. Thereafter, it disappears and dissonance is registered with i[10]s at various octave removes before a consonant GM triad appears in the second half of m. 4. The fluctuation scheme is appropriately represented in Hindemith-style graphics, as shown.

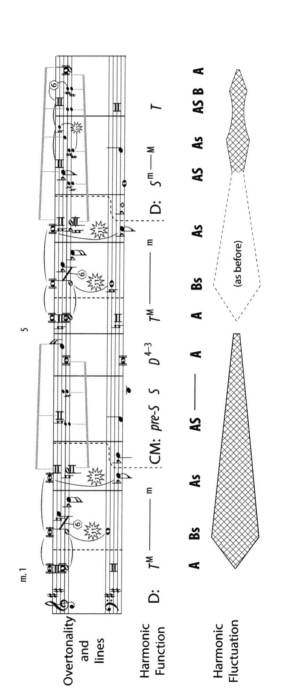

Figure 5.31 Prokofiev, Sonata op. 94, I. Analysis of mm. 1–8

The pressure point of the consequent is mm. 6–7, where the bass degree-progression, having reached a far tritone away from the initial tonic, turns to cover the return distance in a quarter of time of the outbound motion. As mentioned, the linear structure makes this return plausible, but the fluctuation effects help considerably. As the Hindemith-style graphic makes clear, some sharpness accompanies the motion, an upper-voice i[11] filled as i[3,3,5]. The consecutive i[3]s fill a tritone, and in this chord ecosystem of consonant or mildly dissonant A-chords, even potential B-chords like this attract attention. The same holds true for events in m. 8, after the bass line and flute reach DM tonic. While the lower of the two i[3]-related H-lines continues in quarter-notes, the upper peels off in eighths; yet the brief eighth-note passing through G♯ makes a tritone impression, as if it were still attached to the quarter-note line. The fluctuation diagrams, in short, appear to locate the dents in the putative diatonic antecedent/consequent structure with accuracy.

Further work along these lines can be undertaken, identifying moments where displacement pressure is registered and then tracing subsequent compensatory events. The S-theme in particular responds to this line of inquiry. A high-level sketch of just the opening portion of the S-theme gives the outlines (fig. 5.32). Like P, S is based on an antecedent/consequent prototype, though at twice the scale. In this way, it bears comparison to a sixteen-measure double period, with its nested antecedent/consequent schemes. Thus, the eight measures in the figure comprise a large tonic to dominant motion. The articulation at the fourth measure is also cadential, receiving discharge from an augmented-sixth chord. As in previous examples, deformational displacement is pretty well localized to a point early in a phrase, as the second or third event. The indentation is then allowed to relax—in this case, by means of functional discharge. It is not clear what the functional charge of the G♯M chord at m. 25 should be. The indent having been made on the AM tonic chord established in mm. 22–23, the first option is to maintain tonic function through m. 25, a hearing endorsed by the bass A♯ at the end of m. 24, which relaxes the chord's tritone content from a French to a German configuration, and also de-chromaticizes all the discharge pathways into the G♯M, making it a traditional V–I motion with a natural chordal fifth instead of a French-sixth approach with flattened fifth. Even

Figure 5.32 Prokofiev, Sonata op. 94, I. Analysis of mm. 22–29

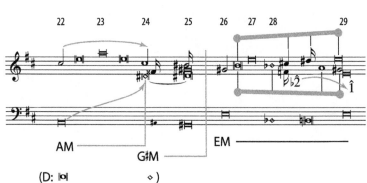

so, the schematics of the period intrude, and the possibility of hearing discharge half-cadentially onto an active dominant of C♯ cannot be dismissed. As has been done occasionally in previous graphs, two note-value symbols are hybridized in order to keep this active-dominant possibility in view—the upstemmed half note for G♯'s modal third crossed with the sixteenth-note flags belonging to the leading tone of C♯.

The consequent phrase to these events, mm. 26–29, restarts the S tune, but in dominant-key EM. Like before, it enjoys an untroubled two measures before events at m. 28 promises even more dramatic results than previously encountered. The bass tritone leap and the simultaneous darkening of the prevailing chords from major to minor registers as a strong chromatic sheer, even stronger than that encountered in m. 24, where common-tones absorbed and some of the displacement pressure. Here, no such mediation is available in the chord change from EM to B♭m, so the effect is stronger. Yet, as the figure shows, two diverging S-lines start at the pivot in m. 27, which proceed directly to the concluding EM. The upper is diatonic, while the lower supports a chromatic passing tone, B♭, which funds the strong bass note at that point and which also creates parity with the upper S-line at four-notes each. While the harmony supporting return to EM is an unrelaxed French-sixth and hence creates some ambiguity about where functionally it discharges its energies. Again, completion of the formal scheme intrudes and directs analysis along an authentic resolution to EM, as graphed.

The analysis of these Prokofiev sonata excerpts has smuggled in concepts useful for the chromatic tonal music of the early twentieth century, the kind epitomized by the leading compositional styles that the Class of 1890 would have encountered during their training and formation. This shows how close to the CP this sonata movement resides, how traditional its formal rhetoric is, and even how restricted its chord vocabulary is. One could imagine, for example, working out a thorough Schenkerian reading of the piece—subject to explanation and adjustment—which act would bring it in from the outer area into which Figure 1.1 had consigned it. But explanations and adjustments are what is at issue here: the compositional technique involved is not one that the CP could appreciate, as the overtly ironic and impious attitude toward inherited forms, genres, and structures—denting, displacing, sheering—is foreign to its sensibilities. It sounds tantalizingly close to a CP piece, which is what made it an inviting portal into this study, but traditional analytic techniques would choke on it at the displacement seams this analysis identified. So, in the end, Prokofiev's sonata is very much a piece of tradition, but it also stands out as reaching for the innovative and contemporary. Developing a critical attitude that can honor both qualities—an approach requiring a variety of tools and ideas—has been the main object of this analysis, and of this book. If problems attend to it, let them be about usefulness and application. I trust that the old problems, of uncertainty and lack of generality, have been more than adequately addressed at this point in these proceedings.

ACKNOWLEDGMENTS

The first ideas about this project were shared with and improved by undergraduates attending the University of Rocheter during the 1990s. Graduate students at the university's Eastman School of Music began to think them over with me in a 1995 seminar. Adam Ricci, Deborah Rifkin, Peter Silberman, Noel Painter, and Stefanie Dickenson were particularly influential interlocutors. More developments were undertaken in an Eastman seminar offered in 2002, where Danny Jenkins and James McGowan contributed important insights.

Valued faculty colleagues at Eastman during my years there constantly sharpened my thinking. I particularly thank the Roberts (Wason, Morris, and Gauldin) for extended conversations that never failed to include valuable suggestions for works to investigate. The disciplinary support of Eastman's large and energetic Theory Department, especially from Dave Headlam, Elizabeth West Marvin, Steven Laitz, Marie Rolf, Ciro Scotto, Matthew Brown, Deborah Stein, and David Beach, is herewith recorded with gratitude.

In Rochester's College of Arts & Sciences, this project was fortunate to have Kim Kowalke's strong interest, and although only one brief musical passage from Kurt Weill appears in these pages, Kim's energetic work on behalf of that composer's life and works was one prompt to undertake the historical and cultural analyses in chapters 1, 3, and 5.

If Kurt Weill was a landmark on one shore, so was Herbert Howells on another, though I ended up not citing a note of his work. Invaluable associations with Episcopal churches in Rochester (St. Paul's) and New Haven (St. Thomas's) have been foundational. First as organist, then as choir member, I have worked with (and studied) many vigorous strains of contemporary tonal music, and this project has benefitted from making music in houses of divine worship with many friends over the years and on the way. I have special gratitude and prayers for all.

An NEH Summer Stipend award in 1999—which committed me to see this project through—makes me grateful that the United States of America promotes the humanities and arts. I remain anxious and watchful that she continue providing for them.

At Yale University, two generations of students shaped ideas and prose. In 2008, Joseph Salem, Anna Gawboy, Andre Redwood, Christopher Brody, Christopher Wm. White, Kara Yoo Leaman, Esther Morgan-Ellis, and Danielle Ward-Griffin critiqued the first chapter drafts. And in 2010, Jonathan Guez, Elizabeth

Medina-Gray, Megan Kaes Long, John Muniz, Rebecca Perry, Noah Horn, and James Park responded helpfully to later ones.

Hugely beneficial conversations with colleagues at Yale stimulated the final refinements undertaken in last few years. Ian Quinn, James Hepokoski, Richard Cohn, and Robert Morgan were particularly helpful. Everyone else contributed to my professional happiness and productivity, and I hope that I returned the favor. Allen Forte attended an early PowerPoint presentation about chapter 4, but did not live to see the whole work completed. Characteristically supportive and encouraging, he would, I hope, have been pleased to read this dedication to him in the book's acknowledgments.

Many scholars in the field critiqued, corresponded, and provided information over the long course of this project. In my folders I see important contributions from Joseph Straus, Steven Rings, Eric Drott, Dmitri Tymoczko, Henry Martin, Scott Murphy, Carol Krumhansl, and Sue Hudd.

The entire range of the project (and then some) was first presented at a lecture during a University of Michigan Distinguished Residency in Music Theory in 2009. My thanks to the faculty and students there for the invitation and subsequent discussions. Feedback from that event informed a more extended keynote presentation at a 2010 conference at Duke University, Tonality: 1900–1950. Thanks to organizers Philip Rupprecht and Felix Wörner for a stimulating and productive conference.

And thanks to Suzanne Ryan, who encouraged me to propose this book to Oxford University Press, and to Adam Cohen, Andrew Maillet, and others at the press who were associated with its production. Bruce Salender helped immensely with copyediting at an early stage, and Mary Sutherland oversaw the final polish. My thanks to them both. (Authors: they come with my strongest recommendation!)

And to those who lived with this project from beginning to end—fitful years, patchy months, intense weeks, focused days—I owe the most profound gratitude for the patience, forbearance, love, and, understanding that supported me. To Glenn, Theo, and Charlotte, for your lifelong amusement and continuing interest; and to Anne, until death us do part.

BIBLIOGRAPHY

Adams, Byron. 1984. Part I: Concerto for Violin and Orchestra. (Original Composition). Part II: Frank Martin's "Petite Symphonie Concertante": An Analysis. DMA diss., Cornell University.

Agmon, Eytan. 1990. "Music Theory as Cognitive Science: Some Conceptual and Methodological Issues." *Music Perception* 7.3: 285–308.

Albersheim, Gerhard. 1960. "The Sense of Space in Tonal and Atonal Music." *Journal of Aesthetics and Art Criticism* 19.1: 17–30.

Aldwell, Edward, and Carl Schachter. 2003. *Harmony and Voice Leading*. 3rd ed. Boston: Cengage, Thomson/Schirmer.

Allport, Gordon W. 1937. *Personality: A Psychological Interpretation*. New York: H. Holt and Company.

Antokoletz, Elliott. 1984. *The Music of Béla Bartók: A Study of Tonality and Progression in Twentieth-Century Music*. Berkeley: University of California Press.

Babbitt, Milton. 1965 [1972]. "The Structure and Function of Music Theory." In *Perspectives on Contemporary Music Theory*, edited by B. Boretz and E. T. Cone. New York: Norton. *College Music Symposium*, 5:18.

Bach, C. P. E. 1753 [1949]. *Essay on the True Art of Playing Keyboard Instruments*. Translated by William J. Mitchell. New York: Norton.

Backus, John. 1977. *The Acoustical Foundations of Music*, 2nd ed. New York: Norton.

Bailey, Robert. 1985. *Prelude and Transfiguration from Tristan and Isolde*. New York: Norton.

Bass, Richard. 1988. "Prokofiev's Technique of Chromatic Displacement." *Music Analysis* 7.2: 197–214.

Bates, Ian. 2012. "Vaughan Williams's Five Variants of 'Dives and Lazarus': A Study of the Composer's Approach to Diatonic Organization." *Music Theory Spectrum* 34.1: 34–50.

Beaumont, Antony. 1985. *Busoni the Composer*. Bloomington: Indiana University Press.

Benjamin, Thomas, Michael Horvit, and Robert Nelson. 2003. *Techniques and Materials of Music: From the Common Practice Period through the Twentieth Century*. Belmont, CA: Thomson/Schirmer.

Bernard, Jonathan W. 1998. "Tonal Traditions in Art Music since 1960." In *Cambridge History of American Music*, edited by D. Nicholls,. Cambridge: Cambridge University Press, 535–66.

Berry, Wallace. 1976. *Structural Functions in Music*. Englewood Cliffs, NJ: Prentice Hall.

Bharucha, J. J. 1984. "Event Hierarchies, Tonal Hierarchies, and Assimilation: A Reply to Deutsch and Dowling." *Journal of Experimental Psychology: General* 113.3: 421–25.

Bharucha, Jamshed J. 1994. "Tonality and Expectation." In *Music Perceptions*, edited by R. Aiello and J. Sloboda. New York: Oxford University Press, 213–39.

Biamonte, Nicole. 2010. "Triadic Modal and Pentatonic Patterns in Rock Music." *Music Theory Spectrum* 32.2: 95–110.

Billeter, Bernhard. 1971. *Die Harmonik Bei Frank Martin: Untersuchungen Zur Analyse Neuerer Musik*. Vol. 23. Bern: P. Haupt.

Bregman, Albert S. 1990. *Auditory Scene Analysis: The Perceptual Organization of Sound*. Cambridge, MA: MIT Press.

Brown, Matthew, and Douglas Dempster. 1989. "The Scientific Image of Music Theory." *Journal of Music Theory* 33: 65–99.

Bruner, Cheryl L. 1984. "The Perception of Contemporary Pitch Structures." *Music Perception: An Interdisciplinary Journal* 2.1: 25–39.

Bullivant, Roger. 1971. *Fugue*. London: Hutchinson.

Burke, Kenneth. 1935. *Permanence and Change: An Anatomy of Purpose*. New York: New Republic.

Busoni, Ferruccio. 1907 [1962]. *"Sketch of a New Esthetic of Music."* Translated by T. Baker. In *Three Classics in the Aesthetic of Music*. New York: Dover Publications. Original edition: G. Schirmer, 1911, 73–102.

Butler, David. 1989. "Describing the Perception of Tonality in Music: A Critique of the Tonal Hierarchy Theory and a Proposal for a Theory of Intervallic Rivalry." *Music Perception* 6.3: 219–41.

Cazden, Norman. 1954. "Hindemith and Nature." *Music Review* 15.4: 288–306.

Chailley, Jacques. 1977 [1986]. *Historical Treatise of Harmonic Analysis*. Translated by S. Kleinman. Paris: Alphonse Leduc.

Chapman, Alan. 1981. "Some Intervallic Aspects of Pitch-Class Set Relations." *Journal of Music Theory* 25.2: 275–90.

Chrisman, Richard. 1977. "Describing Structural Aspects of Pitch-Sets Using Successive Interval Arrays." *Journal of Music Theory* 21.1: 1–28.

Clarke, Michael. 2005. "An Interactive Aural Approach to the Analysis of Computer Music." Proceedings of the 2005 International Computer Music Conference.

———. 2006. "Jonathan Harvey's 'Mortuos Plango, Vivos Voco.'" In *Analytical Methods of Electroacoustic Music*, edited by M. H. Simoni, London: Routledge, 111–43.

———. 2012. "Analysing Electroacoustic Music: An Interactive Aural Approach." *Music Analysis* 31.3: 347–80.

Clevenger, John Robert. 2002. The Origins of Debussy's Style. PhD diss. University of Rochester, Eastman School of Music.

Cohen, David E. 2001. "'The Imperfect Seeks Its Perfection': Harmonic Progression, Directed Motion, and Aristotelian Physics." *Music Theory Spectrum* 23.2: 139–69.

Copeland, Philip Larue. 1998. "The Role of Drama and Spirituality in the Music of Leonard Bernstein." DMA diss., Southern Baptist Theological Seminary.

Crotty, John. 1982. "Symbolist Influences in Debussy's Prelude to the Afternoon of a Faun." *In Theory Only* 6.2: 17–30.

Day-O'Connell, Jeremy. 2007. *Pentatonicism from the Eighteenth Century to Debussy*. Rochester: University of Rochester Press.

———. 2009. "Debussy, Pentatonicism, and the Tonal Tradition." *Music Theory Spectrum* 31.2: 225–61.

Debussy, Claude. 1927 [1962]. "A Talk about the *Prix de Rome* and Saint-Saëns." In *Monsieur Croches the Dilettante Hater*, 1927. Reprinted in *Three Classics in the Aesthetics of Music*. New York: Dover, 1962, 8–16.

Deutsch, Diana. 1972. "Octave Generalization and Tune Recognition." *Perception and Psychophysics* 11.6: 411–12.

Deutsch, Diana, and John Feroe. 1981. "The Internal Representation of Pitch Sequences in Tonal Music." *Psychological Review* 88.6: 503–22.

Drott, Eric. 2005. "Timbre and the Cultural Politics of French Spectralism." Proceedings of the Conference on Interdisciplinary Musicology (CIM05), March 10–12, Montreal.

Easterbrook, Gregg. 2003. *The Progress Paradox: How Life Gets Better While People Feel Worse.* 1st ed. New York: Random House.

Erpf, Hermann. 1927 [1969]. *Studien Zur Harmonie- Und Klangtechnik Der Neueren Musik.* 2. Aufl. ed. Wiesbaden: Breitkopf and Härtel.

Everett, Walter. 2004. "Making Sense of Rock's Tonal Systems." *Music Theory Online* 10.4. http://mto.societymusictheory.org/issues/mto.04.10.4/mto.04.10.4.w_everett.html.

———. 2009. *The Foundations of Rock: From "Blue Suede Shoes" to "Suite: Judy Blue Eyes".* New York: Oxford University Press.

Farrell, Dennis A. 1971. "Some Suggested Corrections in the Hindemith Chord Tables." *Canadian Association of University Schools of Music* 1.1: 71–89.

Féron, François-Xavier. 2011. "The Emergence of Spectra in Gérard Grisey's Compositional Process: From Dérives (1973–74) to Les Espaces Acoustiques (1974–85)." *Contemporary Music Review* 30.5: 343–75.

Fineberg, Joshua. 2000a. "Musical Examples." *Contemporary Music Review* 19.2: 115–34.

———. 2000b. "Spectral Music." *Contemporary Music Review* 19.2: 1.

Gjerdingen, Robert O. 2013. "The *Fugue D'école* Revisited: Beaux-Arts Finesse Builds Upon the Artisanal Traditions of Partimenti." Paper presented at the Annual Meeting of the Society for Music Theory. Charlotte, NC.

Grisey, Gérard. 1991. "Structuration Des Timbres Dans La Musique Instrumentale." In *Le Timbre, Métaphore Pour La Composition,* edited by J.-B. Barrière. Paris: Christian Bourgois, 352–85.

Groth, Renate. 1983. *Die Französische Kompositionslehre Des 19. Jahrhunderts.* Wiesbaden: F. Steiner.

Guerrero, Jeannie Ma. 2009. "The Presence of Hindemith in Nono's Sketches: A New Context for Nono's Music." *Journal of Musicology* 26.4: 481–511.

Hall, Edward Twitchell. 1976. *Beyond Culture.* 1st ed. Garden City, NY: Anchor Press.

Hamilton, Kenneth. 2010. "Busoni's Schoenberg Critique—The Strange Case of Op. 11 No. 2." Paper read at the American Musicological Society Annual Meeting, November 7, Indianapolis, IN.

Harris, Simon. 1989. *A Proposed Classification of Chords in Early Twentieth-Century Music.* New York: Garland Publishing.

Harrison, Daniel. 1992. "Review of V. Kofi Agawu, *Playing with Signs*." *Integral* 6: 136–50.

———. 1994. *Harmonic Function in Chromatic Music: A Renewed Dualist Theory and an Account of Its Precedents.* Chicago: University of Chicago Press.

———. 1995. "Supplement to the Theory of Augmented-Sixth Chords." *Music Theory Spectrum* 17.2: 170–95.

———. 1997. "Bitonality, Pentatonicism, and Diatonicism in a Work by Milhaud." In *Music Theory in Concept and Practice,* edited by J. M. Baker, D. W. Beach, and J. W. Bernard. Rochester, NY: University of Rochester Press, 393–408.

———. 1997–98. "First Thoughts About the Second Practice." *Theory and Practice* 22–23: 147–61.

———. 2004. "Max Reger Introduces Atonal Expressionism." *Musical Quarterly* 87.4: 660–80.

———. 2011. "Three Short Essays on Neo-Riemannian Theory." In *The Oxford Handbook of Neo-Riemannian Music Theories*, edited by E. Gollin and A. Rehding. New York: Oxford University Press, 548–77.

———. 2012. "Samuel Barber's *Nocturne*: An Experiment in Tonal Serialism." In *Tonality 1900–1950: Concept and Practice*, edited by F. Wörner, U. Scheideler, and P. Rupprecht. Stuttgart: Fritz Steiner, 261–76.

———. 2014. "Extending Harmony to Extended Chords." Paper read at Annual Meeting of the Society for Music Theory, November 7, Milwaukee, WI.

Harvey, Jonathan. 1981. "'Mortuos Plango, Vivos Voco': A Realization at IRCAM." *Computer Music Journal* 5.4: 22–24.

Hasegawa, Robert. 2009. "Gérard Grisey and the 'Nature' of Harmony." *Music Analysis* 28.2/3: 349–71.

Hasty, Christopher Francis. 1997. *Meter as Rhythm*. New York: Oxford University Press.

Helmholtz, Hermann von, and Alexander John Ellis. 1954. *On the Sensations of Tone as a Physiological Basis for the Theory of Music*. New York: Dover Publications.

Hibberd, Lloyd. 1961. "Tonality and Related Problems in Terminology." *Music Review* 22: 13–20.

Hindemith, Paul. 1937 [1942]. *Craft of Musical Composition*. Translated by A. Mendel. Vol. 1 (Theoretical Part). New York: Associated Music Publishers. Original edition, *Unterweisung im Tonsatz*. Mainz: Schott, 1937.

Hines, Robert Stephan. 1970. *The Orchestral Composer's Point of View: Essays on Twentieth-Century Music by Those Who Wrote It*. Norman: University of Oklahoma Press.

Horlacher, Gretchen. 1992. "The Rhythms of Reiteration: Formal Development in Stravinsky's Ostinati." *Music Theory Spectrum* 14.2: 171–87.

Hyer, Brian. 1994. "'Sighing Branches': Prosopoeia in Rameau's Pigmalion." *Music Analysis* 13.1: 7–20.

———. 2000. "Tonality." In *Cambridge History of Western Music Theory*, edited by Thomas Christensen. Cambridge: Cambridge University Press, 726–52.

Kramer, Jonathan D. 1988. *The Time of Music*. New York: Schirmer.

Krenek, Ernst. 1940. *Studies in Counterpoint*. New York: G. Schirmer.

Krumhansl, Carol L. 1983. "Perceptual Structures for Tonal Music." *Music Perception* 1.1: 28–62.

———. 1990a. *Cognitive Foundations of Musical Pitch*. New York: Oxford University Press.

———. 1990b. "Tonal Hierarchies and Rare Intervals in Music Cognition." *Music Perception* 7.3: 309–24.

Landau, Victor. 1960. "Paul Hindemith, a Case Study in Theory and Practice." *Music Review* 21.1: 38–54.

———. 1961. "Hindemith the System Builder: A Critique of His Theory of Harmony." *Music Review* 22.2: 136–51.

Lerdahl, Fred. 1988. "Cognitive Constraints on Compositional Systems." In *Generative Processes in Music: The Psychology of Performance, Improvisation, and Composition*, edited by J. A. Sloboda. Oxford: Clarendon Press, 231–59.

———. 2001. *Tonal Pitch Space*. Oxford: Oxford University Press.

Lerdahl, Fred, and Ray Jackendoff. 1983. *A Generative Theory of Tonal Music*. Cambridge, MA: MIT Press.

Lester, Joel. 1989. *Analytic Approaches to Twentieth-Century Music*. New York: Norton.

Lévi-Strauss, Claude. 1969. *The Raw and the Cooked*. Translated by J. and D. Weightman. First US ed. New York: Harper and Row.

Lewin, David. 1968. "Inversional Balance as an Organizing Force in Schoenberg's Music and Thought." *Perspectives of New Music* 6.2: 1–21.

Lewis, Christopher. 1989. "Into the Foothills: New Directions in Nineteenth-Century Analysis." *Music Theory Spectrum* 11.1: 15–23.

Liang, Lei. 2007. "Colliding Resonances: The Music of Xiaoyong Chen." Collected Work: *Contemporary Music Review*. 26/5–6 (October–December 2007): "China and the West—The Birth of a New Music," 529–45.

London, Justin. 2004. *Hearing in Time: Psychological Aspects of Musical Meter*. New York: Oxford University Press.

Martin, Henry. 2005. "From Classical Dissonance to Jazz Consonance: The Added Sixth Chord." Unpublished Manuscript.

Mathieu, W. A. 1997. *Harmonic Experience: Tonal Harmony from Its Natural Origins to Its Modern Expression*. Rochester, VT: Inner Traditions.

Mazullo, Mark. 2010. *Shostakovich's Preludes and Fugues: Contexts, Style, Performance*. New Haven: Yale University Press.

McGowan, James John. 2005. "Dynamic Consonance in Selected Piano Performances of Tonal Jazz." PhD diss., Theory, University of Rochester.

Messiaen, Olivier. 1956. "The Technique of My Musical Language." Translated by John Satterfield. Paris: Alphonse Leduc, 1956.

Meyer, Leonard B. 1989. *Style and Music: Theory, History, and Ideology*. Philadelphia: University of Pennsylvania Press.

Minturn, Neil. 1997. *The Music of Sergei Prokofiev*. New Haven: Yale University Press.

Morgan, Robert P. 1990. Review of *The Time of Music* by Jonathan D. Kramer, 1988. *Music Theory Spectrum* 12: 247–55.

———. 1991. "Communications." *Music Theory Spectrum* 13: 117–19.

Morris, Robert. 1987. *Composition with Pitch-Classes: A Theory of Compositional Design*. New Haven: Yale University Press.

———. 2001. "Variation and Process in South Indian Music: Some *Kritis* and their *Sangatis*." *Music Theory Spectrum* 23.1: 75.

Murphy, Scott. 2004 "Relations among Boundaries, Expectations, and Closure in Music." PhD. diss., University of Rochester, 2004.

Neumeyer, David. 1986. *The Music of Paul Hindemith*. New Haven: Yale University Press.

Parncutt, Richard. 1988. "Revision of Terhardt's Psychoacoustical Model of the Root(s) of a Musical Chord." *Music Perception* 6.1: 65–94.

Peles, Stephen. 1992. "Continuity, Reference, and Implication: Remarks on Schoenberg's Proverbial 'Difficulty.'" *Theory and Practice* 17: 35.

Perle, George. 1962. *Serial Composition and Atonality: An Introduction to the Music of Schoenberg, Berg, and Webern*. Berkeley: University of California Press.

Persichetti, Vincent. 1961. *Twentieth-Century Harmony: Creative Aspects and Practice*. New York: Norton.

Peters, Penelope. 1990. "French Harmonic Theory in the *Conservatoire* Tradition: Fetis, Reber, Durand, and Gevaert," PhD diss., University of Rochester.

Piekut, Benjamin. 2004. "No Common Practice: The New Common Practice and Its Historical Antecedents." *NewMusicBox* 58. http://www.newmusicbox.org/page.nmbx?id=58tp00.

Piston, Walter. 1933. *Principles of Harmonic Analysis*. Boston: E. C. Schirmer Music Co.

———. 1941. *Harmony*. New York: W. W. Norton.

Pleasants, Henry. 1969. *Serious Music, and All That Jazz: An Adventure in Music Criticism*. New York: Simon and Schuster.

Pomeroy, Boyd. 2004. "Tales of Two Tonics: Directional Tonality in Debussy's Orchestral Music." *Music Theory Spectrum* 26.1: 87–118.

Pressnitzer, Daniel, and Stephen McAdams. 2000. "Acoustics, Psychoacoustics and Spectral Music." *Contemporary Music Review* 19.2: 33.

Rameau, Jean Philippe. 1722 [1971]. *Treatise on Harmony*. Translated by P. Gossett. New York: Dover Publications.

Reck, David B. 1992. "India/South India." In *Worlds of Music: An Introduction to the Music of the World's Peoples*, edited Jeff Todd Titon,. New York: Schirmer Books.

Reynolds, William H. 1985. *Common Practice Harmony*. With Gerald Warfield. New York: Longman.

Ricci, Adam. 2003. What's Wrong with the Minor Ninth?: Chord Roots and Extensions. Paper presented at the Society for Music Theory conference, Madison, WI.

Rifkin, Deborah. 2006. "Making It Modern: Chromaticism and Phrase Structure in Twentieth-Century Tonal Music." *Theory and Practice* 31:133–58.

Rings, Steven Marshall. 2006. "Tonality and Transformation." PhD diss., Music, Yale University.

Roeder, John. 1989. "Harmonic Implications of Schoenberg's 'Observations of Atonal Voice Leading.'" *Journal of Music Theory* 33.1: 27–62.

Rothfarb, Lee Allen. 1988. *Ernst Kurth as Theorist and Analyst*. Philadelphia: University of Pennsylvania Press.

Rowell, Lewis. 1983. *Thinking About Music: An Introduction to the Philosophy of Music*. Amherst, MA: University of Massachusetts Press.

Russell, George. 1959. *The Lydian Chromatic Concept of Tonal Organization for Improvisation*. New York: Concept Pub. Co.

Salzer, Felix. 1952. *Structural Hearing: Tonal Coherence in Music*. 2 vols. New York: C. Boni.

Samplaski, Arthur G. 2000. "A Comparison of Perceived Chord Similarity and Predictions of Selected Twentieth-Century Chord-Classification Schemes, Using Multidimensional Scaling and Cluster Analysis." PhD diss., Music Theory, Indiana University.

Schoenberg, Arnold. 1912 [1978]. *Theory of Harmony*. Translated by R. E. Carter. Berkeley: University of California Press.

Schoenberg, Arnold, and Leonard Stein. 1984. *Style and Idea: Selected Writings of Arnold Schoenberg*. Berkeley: University of California Press.

Schuijer, Michiel. 2008. *Analyzing Atonal Music: Pitch-Class Set Theory and Its Contexts*. Rochester, NY: University of Rochester Press.

Schwartz, Barry. 2004. *The Paradox of Choice: Why More Is Less*. New York: Ecco.

Searle, John. 1992. *The Rediscovery of Mind*. Cambridge, MA: MIT Press.

Serly, Tibor. 1975. *Modus Lascivus (the Road to Enharmonicism): A New Concept in Composition*. Ann Arbor: Modus Associates.

Sessions, Roger. 1951. *Harmonic Practice*. New York: Harcourt Brace.

Sheppard, W. Anthony. 1996. "Bitter Rituals for a Lost Nation: Partch's Revelation in the Courthouse Park and Bernstein's Mass." *Musical Quarterly* 80.3: 461–99.

Silberman, Peter Scott. 2006. "Neighbor Spaces: A Theory of Harmonic Embellishment for Twentieth-Century Neotonal Music." PhD diss., Music Theory, University of Rochester.

———. 2008. "Analyzing Tonal Embellishment in Post-Tonal Music." In *Musical Currents from the Left Coast*, edited by J. F. Boss and B. W. Quaglia. Middlesex: Cambridge Scholars Publishing.

Stewart, Michael. 1987. "The Feel Factor: Music with Soul." *Electronic Musician* (October) 3.1: 57–65.

Straus, Joseph N. 1982. "Stravinsky's Tonal Axis." *Journal of Music Theory* 26.2: 261–90.

———. 1990. *Remaking the Past: Musical Modernism and the Influence of the Tonal Tradition*. Cambridge, MA: Harvard University Press.

———. 2009. *Twelve-Tone Music in America*. Cambridge: Cambridge University Press.

——. 2014. "Harmony and Voice Leading in the Music of Stravinsky." *Music Theory Spectrum* 36.1: 1–33.

Stuckenschmidt, H. H. 1959. *Arnold Schoenberg*. Translated by Edith Temple Roberts and Humphrey Searle. London: John Clader.

Susanni, Paolo, and Elliott Antokoletz. 2012. *Music and Twentieth-Century Tonality: Harmonic Progression Based on Modality and the Interval Cycles*. New York: Routledge.

Tagg, Philip. 2014. *Everyday Tonality II: Towards a Tonal Theory of What Most People Hear*. New York: Mass Media Music Scholar's Press.

Taruskin, Richard. 2005. *Oxford History of Western Music*. 6 vols. New York: Oxford University Press.

Tcherepnin, Alexander. 2007. *Basic Elements of My Musical Language* (2002) 1962 [cited 2007]. Available from http://www.tcherepnin.com/alex/basic_elem1.htm.

Terhardt, Ernst. 1974. "Pitch Consonance and Harmony." *Journal of the Acoustical Society of America* 55: 1061–69.

——. 1984. "The Concept of Musical Consonance: A Link between Music and Psychoacoustics." *Music Perception* 1.3: 276–95.

Thomson, William. 1991. *Schoenberg's Error*. Philadelphia: University of Pennsylvania Press.

——. 1993–94. "Music as Organic Evolution: Schoenberg's Mythic Springboard into the Future." *College Music Symposium* 33/34: 191–211.

——. 1999. *Tonality in Music: A General Theory*. San Marino, CA: Everett Books.

——. 2006. "Pitch Frames as Melodic Archetypes." *Empirical Musicology Review* 1.2: 85–102.

Tovey, Donald Francis. 1941. *A Musician Talks*. 2 vols. Vol. 1. London: Oxford University Press.

Travis, Roy. 1959. "Towards a New Concept of Tonality." *Journal of Music Theory* 3.2: 257–84.

Tymoczko, Dmitri. 1997. "The Consecutive Semitone Constraint on Scalar Structure: A Link between Impressionism and Jazz." *Integral* 11: 135–79.

——. 2004. "Scale Networks and Debussy." *Journal of Music Theory* 48.2: 219–94.

——. 2011. *A Geometry of Music: Harmony and Counterpoint in the Extended Common Practice*. New York: Oxford University Press.

Ulehla, Ludmilla. 1966. *Contemporary Harmony: Romanticism through the Twelve-Tone Row*. New York: Free Press.

Väisälä, Olli. 2002. "Prolongation of Harmonies Related to the Harmonic Series in Early Post-Tonal Music." *Journal of Music Theory* 46.1/2: 207–71.

Whitesell, Lloyd. 2004. "Twentieth-Century Tonality, or, Breaking up Is Hard to Do." In *The Pleasure of Modernist Music*, edited by A. Ashby. Rochester, NY: University of Rochester Press.

Whittall, Arnold. 2003. *Exploring Twentieth-Century Music: Tradition and Innovation*. Cambridge: Cambridge University Press.

Wile, Kip Douglas. 1995. "Collection in Neocentric Music: A Study in Theory and Analysis of the Music of Debussy, Stravinsky, Scriabin, Bartok, and Ravel." PhD diss., Music. University of Chicago.

Wingenfeld, Dirk. 1991. "Hindemiths Akkordbestimmung als Grundlage für Eine Differenziertere Akkordklassifikation." *Hindemith-Jahrbuch* 20, 110–40.

Wolpert, Franz Alfons. 1972. *Neue Harmonik Einführung: Die Lehre von den Akkordtypen und Grundakkorden*. Edited by R. Schall. Vol. 14. Wilhelmshaven: Heinrichshofen's Verlag.

Zimmerman, Daniel J. 2002. "Families without Clusters in the Early Works of Sergei Prokofiev." PhD diss.. University of Chicago.

Zuckerkandl, Victor. 1956. *Sound and Symbol: Music and the External World*. Translated by W. R. Trask. Princeton: Princeton University Press.

INDEX